Politics
and the Future of
Industrial Society

COMPARATIVE STUDIES OF POLITICAL LIFE

SERIES EDITOR: **Martin O. Heisler**

Politics and the Future of Industrial Society

Leon N. Lindberg
UNIVERSITY OF WISCONSIN

DAVID McKAY COMPANY, INC.
NEW YORK

POLITICS AND THE FUTURE OF INDUSTRIAL SOCIETY

Developmental Editor: Edward Artinian
Editorial and Design Supervisor: Nicole Benevento
Design: Pencils Portfolio, Inc.
Manufacturing and Production Supervisor: Donald W. Strauss
Composition: Automated Composition Service, Inc.
Printing and Binding: The Colonial Press, Inc.

Library of Congress Cataloging in Publication Data
Main entry under title:

Politics and the future of industrial society.

(Comparative studies of political life)
Includes bibliographical references and index.
1. Comparative government—Addresses, essays,
lectures.   2. Political sociology—Addresses, essays,
lectures.   3. Social change—Addresses, essays,
lectures.   4. Social prediction—Addresses, essays,
lectures.   I. Lindberg, Leon N.
JF51.P64   301.5'92   76-4912
ISBN 0-679-30278-6
      0-679-30309-X paper

CONTRIBUTORS

Leon N. Lindberg, the editor of this volume, is professor of political science at the University of Wisconsin in Madison and chairman of the Council for European Studies, 1974–76. His undergraduate and graduate degrees are from the University of California at Berkeley. He has written and edited several books and articles on European integration, among which are *The Political Dynamics of European Integration, Europe's Would-Be Polity* (co-authored with Stuart A. Scheingold), and *Regional Integration: Theory and Research* (co-edited with Stuart A. Scheingold). He has one forthcoming volume: *System Change and Policy Response in Advanced Capitalist Nations,* and a co-edited volume, *Energy Policy: North, South, East, West,* with John Goldthorpe, Robert Alford, and Claus Offe, which was published in 1975. He is currently working on the politics of economic policy, with special attention to inflation and unemployment.

C. J. Abrams is currently completing her Ph.D. at the University of California at Berkeley. She has spent three years working in the Institute for Governmental Studies.

Charles W. Anderson is professor of political science at the University of Wisconsin in Madison. He received his Ph.D. from the University of

Wisconsin in 1960. His work has dealt with Latin America and Spain, including *The Political Economy of Modern Spain, Political and Economic Change in Latin America,* and *The Political Economy of Mexico.* Public policy formation and content is his major concern, and he is currently writing a study on political choice and judgment as well as continuing research on the relation of the state to complex organizations in advanced industrial societies.

M. Donald Hancock is associate professor in the Department of Government at the University of Texas and director of the Center for European Studies at that institution. He has written or edited several books on contemporary Sweden, among which are *Sweden: The Politics of Post-Industrial Change,* and *Politics in the Post-Welfare State: Responses to the New Individualism.*

Ronald Inglehart is associate professor of political science at the University of Michigan. He received his Ph.D. from the University of Chicago in 1962 and has made numerous contributions to professional journals since then on ideological belief systems, political culture, political development and modernization, political socialization, mass participation and communications, European integration, and advanced industrial societies and will soon publish a book entitled *The Silent Revolution: Changing Values and Political Styles Among Western Publics* (Princeton, N.J.: Princeton University Press, 1977).

Todd La Porte is associate professor of political science at the University of California at Berkeley and associate director of the Institute of Governmental Studies. He received his Ph.D. from Stanford in 1963, and has been a visiting professor at Stanford and the University of Southern California. His present work concerns technology and its relationship to society. Among his recent publications are two articles published by the Institute of Governmental Studies: "Technology Observed: Attitudes of a Wary Public," written with Daniel Metlay, also to appear in *Science* magazine; and "They Watch and Wonder: The Public's Attitude Toward Technology: A Survey," also written with Daniel Metlay. He is editor and contributor to *Organized Social Complexity: Challenge to Politics and Policy.*

Jeffrey D. Straussman did his graduate work at the Graduate School and University Center of the City University of New York. He is currently in the Department of Political Science at the State University of New York at Fredonia. He is co-author with Bertram M. Gross of "The Social Indicators Movement," in *Social Policy* and, again with Gross, of an article in *The Annals,* "Full Employment, Growthmanship and the Expansion of Labor Supply."

Taketsugu Tsurutani is associate professor in the Department of Political Science at Washington State University. He received his Ph.D. from the University of Wisconsin in 1967. He has published a book entitled *The Politics of National Development* and articles in the *Review of Politics*, *Journal of Politics*, *Foreign Policy*, *Asian Survey*, *Journal of Political and Military Sociology*, and *Asia Quarterly*. He deals with the theoretical aspects of comparative analysis.

PREFACE

This book explores the political implications associated with the term "postindustrial society." It represents an important contribution to a literature that seeks to understand the transformations which are taking place at the present time in advanced industrial societies and the possible futures for these societies. Unfortunately, to date this literature has sorely neglected political variables, whether taken as dependent or independent, effect or cause. There are important and striking areas of convergence in these chapters, although each author adopts a somewhat different analytical strategy. The diversity of perspectives on common problems that results is one of the most valuable aspects of the collection, for it puts into relief the very difficult epistemological, methodological, and conceptual issues that must be confronted if we are to understand ongoing change processes and the emergent properties of large, complex social systems.

Another relatively novel feature of the volume is that it carries the discussion of postindustrial phenomena out of what has been a fairly parochial context. The bulk of the existing literature is based, implicitly or explicitly, on American experience or example; it has simply assumed that the United States is the most "post." The papers presented here challenge this assumption. They extend the field of comparison to include societies as diverse as California, Japan, and Western Europe, thus opening up yet another important set of methodological and theoretical issues. The authors suggest that industrial societies, although they experience similar changes and encounter many of the same policy or political system crises, are likely to respond in very different ways. One of the most interesting questions to ask about the future is whether a range of different types of "postindustrial" societies will emerge in response to different historical-cultural heritages, political structures, timing and patterning of change, and public and elite responses.

Taken as a whole, the collection offers not only stimulating and fascinating glimpses into the possible futures of advanced industrial societies, but also makes an important contribution to the effort to design coherent and reliable strategies for research on ongoing change and its political consequences.

Each paper printed here represents "work in progress." Each raises more questions than it can answer. The cumulative result is perforce somewhat contradictory and indecisive, as the last chapter will suggest, for each author looks at the changing industrial or capitalist system through a different lens. Our purpose has been to encourage more systematic research into these questions and to suggest some fruitful lines such research might take. The success of our venture will be judged by the rapidity with which our formulations are superseded and improved upon.

CONTENTS

Politics
and the Future of
Industrial Society

INTRODUCTION: POLITICS AND THE FUTURE OF INDUSTRIAL SOCIETY

LEON N. LINDBERG

The articles gathered together in this volume address themselves to the problems of conceptualizing, understanding, evaluating, and explaining change at the level of whole societies, and as if these tasks were not sufficiently daunting, they seek to understand ongoing, contemporary, in some cases barely emergent changes, and to draw inferences about their future implications for the political systems of advanced industrial societies.

Whatever the difficulties and pitfalls of macro-analysis and of the study of past or historical change, efforts to analyze contemporary change rigorously and to conjecture systematically about the future are fraught with formidable epistemological and normative problems, as the authors of these articles well recognize. Most of our more prudent colleagues in the social sciences would eschew such an enterprise. Yet it has seemed to us that the risks and pitfalls of such analyses are well worth daring, for the stakes are very high indeed. Bertrand de Jouvenel, one of the first to argue for a serious attention to political futurism, notes that

> forecasting would be an absurd enterprise were it not inevitable. We have to make wagers about the future; we have no choice in the matter. . . .[1] The

1

proof of improvidence lies in falling under the empire of necessity. The means of avoiding this lies in acquainting oneself with emerging situations . . . before they have become imperatively compelling.[2]

Or, to put the matter in another way, "We need to know where we may be going in order to understand where we are."[3]

The authors have all been intrigued and stimulated by the burgeoning futurist movement and its attendant literature,[4] and by the notion of social forecasting and the discussions and debates set off in the 1960s by Herman Kahn, Daniel Bell, and others about "the shape of things to come."[5] Our notes at the end of our articles will indicate the extent of our intellectual debts. Yet in an important sense, the work illustrated here also represents a critical response to futurism and to some of the central thrusts of the analysis of so-called postindustrialism. The authors are all political scientists, and although they come out of several of the distinctive analytical traditions that coexist, more or less uneasily, within the most eclectic of social science disciplines, they are united in their conviction that the literature on contemporary change and its future implications gives insufficient attention to the political dimensions of society; that it tends toward a technological, an economic, or a sociological determinism; and that it seems to be overly preoccupied with the United States as an implicit or explicit "model" of the future of industrialism.[6]

We are all, then, in our various ways, preoccupied by what remains the central problem of political science, the analysis of political choice, its attendant processes and institutions, its determinants and constraints, its cross-system variations and their correlates, its rational and non-rational elements, its duality as steering, guidance, or "goal-seeking," at the same time as domination and the maintenance of hierarchy and hegemony. In the words of William Mitchell, we are broadly concerned with how polities

> provide solutions or make decisions and choices through time and are con-
> strained by uncertainty in response to the universal necessities of employ-
> ing scarce resources among competing goals.[7]

We ask how political systems via "the intended and unintended efforts of their leaders and others . . . attempt to adapt themselves to the situational givens and to stabilize those elements within their control from disturbances."[8]

It seems to us that the literature on the possible futures of advanced industrial society, to the extent that it deals with political choice at all, relegates it to the status of a residual variable by means of what Sir Geoffrey Vickers would call an imagery of "passive adaptation to change."[9] These essays seek to shift the balance to a consideration of the political process as an active catalyst of change, to an emphasis on what Henry Kariel calls "the normative potentialities of politics." They would echo Vickers' injunction that we must go beyond an identification of trends or "threats" and the projection of alternative future scenarios.

> We have to ask not only what these threats are and what they will do to people but also what they will mean to people—and to which people. We have to ask not only what the threatened will want to do about them but also what, given their institutions and their culture, they will be able to do about them and how quickly and in what directions their institutions and their values can be expected to change.[10]

Though this joint concern for a comparative *politics* of the future of industrial society makes for an important coherence in this volume, the reader should also attend to the important differences of approach and emphasis among the authors. Indeed, given the nature of the enterprise, the stage of the art, the fact that in all cases the work described is in its formative stages, such differences are only to be expected. We only hope that this juxtaposition of divergent approaches will produce a creative dissonance and will thus constitute a stimulus to further research. A detailed comparison of the papers with one another and an extended discussion of strategies for future research are reserved for the last chapter. Nevertheless, it would seem important to locate the articles preliminarily in terms of two broad dimensions: first, the authors' approach to the analysis of macro-change and the role therein of political choice processes; and second, how the epistemological issues involved in making statements about the future are handled.

MACRO-CHANGE AND POLITICAL CHOICE

It seems to be widely agreed by economists, sociologists, and political scientists alike that their respective disciplines have either neglected the study of change or have not dealt with it very satisfactorily. Samuel P. Huntington[11] notes how sociologists "have regularly bemoaned their lack of knowledge concerning social change," but argues that they are relatively well off compared to political science, which did not really attempt to deal with problems of change until the mid-1950s' renaissance in the study of comparative politics and the concern for modernization and development. Economics has similarly been criticized for an obsession "with *marginal changes* within a given economic system . . . rather than . . . qualitative changes in the economic system,"[12] a charge echoed by Charles E. Lindblom's argument that economics is inherently conservative and superficial and hence should not serve as a model for the other social sciences. What is most needed in social science generally, says Lindblom, is the development of a "capacity to say something about sequences of social behavior and institutional organization, in addition to describing correctly a series of cross-sections." This is the case because

> societies learn. They change their ways. A society's experience with forms of economic behavior and economic organization teaches it to change these forms, as also for parties, interest groups, and other political institutions.[13]

Huntington carefully and incisively reviews the progress made in the 1950s and 1960s in the comparative study of modernization, development, and politics. In spite of very real accomplishment, he finds the literature wanting, still rife with "static assumptions," "teleological concerns," and "an evolutionary optimism reminiscent of the 19th Century." And it was these characteristics that rendered modernization theory particularly impotent in the face of the instabilities, crises, and dislocations experienced by the most advanced modern societies in the late 1960s and 1970s.

> The modernization theory of the 1950s and 1960s had little or nothing to say about the future of modern societies; the advanced countries of the West, it was assumed, had "arrived"; their past was of interest not for what it would show about their future but for what it showed about the future of those other societies which still struggled through the transition between tradition and modernity. . . . The theory of modernization thus rationalized change abroad and the status quo at home. It left blank the future of modernity. Modernization theory combined an extraordinary faith in the efficacy of modernity's past with no image of the potentialities of modernity's future.[14]

Today this optimism is, of course, gone, to be replaced by what some have termed a "millennial mood," or a "doomsday syndrome," reminiscent of the secular pessimism of the 1920s and 1930s. Far from taking the future of modernity for granted, we have become increasingly obsessed with it and troubled by what we see or think we see ahead. It is surely time to draw the lessons of our past mistakes and to correct development theory's neglect of the "future of modernity," and this is a task to which all the authors of the present volume have addressed themselves. This effort (which is only begun) can be traced on at least four distinct but linked levels: the nature of the *concepts* we use to comprehend how a society can be said to change over time; how one can depict *process* as more than "comparative statics"; the elimination of teleological or *historicist assumptions*; and the development of more complex and general *theories of change* focused upon the dynamic interactions of choice and constraint, of loads and capabilities.

1. Conceptualizing societal change. Although none of the authors has undertaken to provide a full critical evaluation of the concept of postindustrialism, or the thirty-odd other "posts" used by one author or another[15] to describe the society that presumably lies ahead, all seem to me to have taken cognizance of the pitfalls involved in such conceptualizations. Concepts such as "postindustrial," "postliberal," "postwelfare" have been *residually defined* in relation to industrialism, and so on, much as was "tradition" relative to "modernity." Huntington has pointed out how such asymmetrical dichotomizations encouraged

> the tendency to assume that the residual concept has all the coherence and precision of the positively defined concept. They obfuscate the diversity which may exist in the residual phenomenon and the fact that the differences between one manifestation of the residual concept and another manifestation of the same concept may be as great as or greater than the differences between either the residual manifestations and the more positively defined other pole of the polarity.[16]

Similarly, our authors would avoid identifying postindustrial society (or whatever) with American, or Western, or capitalist society to the degree that modern society came to be equated with "Western society writ abstractly and polysyllabically."[17] They would also argue for distinguishing between attributes of a process of change (postindustrialization?) and attributes of a societal type (postindustrial?), echoing Bendix' argument that the concept of "modernization" should have been kept distinct from that of "modernity" because

> many attributes of modernization... have appeared, or been adopted, in isolation from other attributes of modern society. Hence modernization in some sphere of life may occur without resulting in "modernity."[18]

Our authors are thus wary of the ways in which concepts like "postindustrialism" (and other metaphors of future society) can prematurely constrain and misdirect inquiry; some eschew them altogether, others use them while trying to enrich and diversify their political meanings by explicit consideration of different societies, by considering alternative postindustrial paths and models, or by disaggregating the concepts.

2. Comparative statics vs. dynamic analysis. A comparative politics of the emerging future of modernity must also beware of yet another shoal upon which many modernization theories foundered, *depicting process.* We must seek to define units of analysis in ways that comprehend their transformation over time, but that do not at the same time reify processes of internal change using the same word. Huntington points out that the writings on modernization were much more successful in delineating the characteristics of modern and traditional societies than they were in depicting the process by which movement occurs from one state to the other. They focused more on the direction of change, from "this" to "that," than on the scope, timing, methods, and rate of change. For this reason, they were more theories of "comparative statics" than they were theories of change.[19]

The danger derives in part from ambiguities about whether concepts like industrialism or postindustrialism are taken to be ideal types or historical stages, and in part, from an underconceptualization of transitional phases between types or stages. In any case we are brought back again to the perils of dichotomous conceptualizations of change.

These dangers and difficulties were certainly recognized by development theories, and numerous efforts were made to develop an analysis based on contingent sequences in development, political mobilization followed by political institutionalization, or stages in institution building, or sequential "crises of development" (identity, penetration, participation, legitimacy, and distribution). But as Hugh Heclo has pointed out, the conceptual underpinnings of these sequences or stages are quite uncertain.

> Whether there are one or many time paths to one or many, or any, end states is unknown. There is as much difficulty substantiating a probability that one state follows another as a probability that one stage needs to be preceded by another. Even assuming distinctive sequences can be identified, the most important issue in understanding dynamics is understanding the factors generating particular sequences.[20]

Thus, to the extent that we leave implicit the manner whereby "dynamic processes create adjustments" sequence analysis "reverts to the strategy of comparative statics."[21]

The chapters that follow do generally recognize the problem and seek to develop various strategies for conceptualizing transitional phases in development in terms of processes that create disturbance or disequilibrium and of processes that create or seek to create adjustments. The explicit attention to policy change, its cognitive and physical correlates, and to the relation between policy change and system change in the work of La Porte and Abrams, Anderson, and in my concluding chapter are cases in point.

3. Eliminating teleology and historicism. John Goldthorpe, in an assessment of theories of industrial society and especially of "future studies," sees a "recrudescence of historicism" in the sense that a rough historical prediction is implicitly or explicitly their principal aim, and that the postulated pattern or line of development "becomes the basis for critical evaluations of the present state of society and for present forms of socio-political action."[22] Huntington makes much the same charge of a teleological fallacy against theorists of political development, pointing out that this was perhaps inevitable if a process is defined as movement toward a particular goal or stage, rather than in terms of its inherent characteristics as a process.[23]

Among the principal dangers of creeping historicism as expressed in development theories and in the futurist literature, Goldthorpe emphasizes their general failure to provide explicit analysis of *causal mechanisms* linking historical events and future events, of

> why the social actors through whose agency the change occurs *should* act in such ways and with such outcomes, that the functional exigencies in question are in fact met. We are, for instance, left usually uninformed about how, if at all, these exigencies come to be represented in the actors' own definitions of the situation; or about the extent to which, and by whom, "solutions" are purposively sought. In other words, we are given no clear indication of the nature of the *connection* between the immediate historical world, in which individuals and groups pursue their interests, uphold their beliefs, exercise their power, etc., and the emergence of the theoretically intelligible regularities that are postulated.[24]

Goldthorpe also sees the dangers of "ethnocentrism," of "blandness and optimism," and of the tendency "to rule out of court ideals and ideas which could point to genuine sociological and historical alternatives, and which if more widely propagated and recognised, could significantly extend the range of effective socio-political choice."[25]

He argues further that future oriented studies were peculiarly prone to overemphasize technological or economic trends, which led their practitioners to a predominant concern for the "extrapolation of processes" rather than the analysis of "social actions that can impinge on processes,"[26] and to a general neglect of values and the potentialities of value change. Furthermore, they led to a technocratic bias in which the social scientist took the role of the "benevolent, skilled, and responsive administrator whose task it is to keep modern industrial societies free from major disruption."[27]

Once again, the concern of the authors of this volume with alternative models and national experiences, with choice processes, with how actors define their situation, with the intellectual tools they employ to make sense of it and to generate policy "solutions," with the pattern and potential significance of value change, should help guard against historicist thinking. It should be noted, however, that each author emphasizes a different aspect and each draws a different balance between choice and the mechanisms of constraint, although all seek to place "social actions that can impinge on processes" at the center of analysis, rather than the "extrapolation of processes."

4. More complex and general theories of political change. Some of the elements that would comprise a general theory of change have been touched upon above. A fully elaborated theory—which nobody here has really attempted—would need to include at least, on the one hand, some explicit causal statements about how and why environmental "changes," i.e., changes in economic, technological, social and demographic systems, as well as feedbacks from the political system itself, are particularly salient, and how they impinge upon the various aspects of the political system; and on the other hand, how these various changes interact spatially and temporally with each other to produce particular policy and structural changes. The authors display a good deal of variety on all these dimensions, although I detect a certain convergence of which they are perhaps not aware, and on which they may not agree. Rather than looking for the characteristics of a future society via the examination of trends (by deduction, extrapolation, or analogy), our authors would seem to recognize that opposite and contradictory trends may be "mutually entailed through time."[28] This would suggest two kinds of analytical search: on the one hand, for an understanding of the dynamic processes that throw up apparently contradictory forces or trends at particular historical junctures; and on the other hand, for an explication of how such contradictory forces and trends actually affect human choice and structural constraint, how they differentially affect decision loads and decision capabilities of the elites and institutions of advanced industrial societies.

We will return to these matters in the final chapter, but a few generalizations can be kept in mind. To repeat, none of our authors has attempted a fully worked out theory of change. By and large they have not developed their own appreciations of what the basic societal trends might be, but rather accept the formulations of others, confining themselves to exploring their alternative political implications. Nor do they go very far in the direction of an analysis of the sources of dynamic contradictions in contemporary society. Suggestive fragments there are, but not more. On the other hand, they do offer a range of varying and provocative analyses of how postulated trends might interact with the political choice behavior of elites and institutions.

"KNOWING" THE FUTURE: PREDICTIONS, FORECASTS, AND CONJECTURES

In what sense is it possible to "know" anything about the future? Heinz Eulau, in his 1972 presidential address to the American Political Science Association, reminded us that "the future is not known, hasn't happened and can't be predicted and the laws of social development are also unknown."[29] In view of this admonition, it seems only prudent to clarify the epistemological nature of the statements about "politics and the future of industrial society" which are to follow.

Otis Dudley Duncan has distinguished between two kinds of futures statements: predictions and forecasts. A *prediction* is "a conditional statement about what will happen, assuming the validity of a relevant set of scientific laws and given observations which define the initial or exogenous conditions under which these laws are expected to operate in a given instance."[30] *Forecasts*, on the other hand, are "unconditional statements," not necessarily based on any specific notion of causal structure, but rather rooted in projection or extrapolation of past series or sequences.[31] Projections of trends have been the most common tools in futures study, but they suffer from a number of obvious and serious defects. They are statements of faith that the future will be like the past, that the causal structure underlying the trend will be stationary, whereas it is changes in causal structure that should be the object of concern. Furthermore, projections are generally incapable of handling the threshold changes which can be expected to be of special importance in human systems. Finally, projections of human behavior are especially difficult since such behavior is purposive. Human systems are not simply pushed by events in the past but, because they act on the basis of intentions and anticipations, such systems also tend to be pulled by events in the future.

Strictly speaking, predictions are more "acceptable" futures statements than forecasts, because they are based on an explicit causal structure which could in principle handle discontinuities and threshold effects, and because this presumed causal structure is capable of being confirmed or disconfirmed by a correct or an incorrect prediction. An incorrect forecast, on the other hand, means only "that something happened that was not anticipated," and a correct forecast does not give much confidence that the next one will be correct.[32] But, as Eulau has argued, and as our earlier review of change and development theory would affirm, we have few, if any, scientific laws or even good theories in the realm of societal dynamics. Indeed, one may even share Vickers' skepticism about the prospects of developing such laws at all. Vickers worries in particular about the balance between science as "discovered" order and "invented" order when it comes to the social sciences. For

the processes which engage the social scientist, the political scientist, and the historian ... are learned of through and affected by human communication ... pursue an irreversible and non-repeatable course ... and ... the regularities observed owe something to the efforts of human constituents to impose on it mutually inconsistent "orders," which themselves change with time; whilst others, imposed by the ordering mind of the human observer (however scientific) are refuted or confirmed, if at all, by events to which they themselves contribute.[33]

If forecasts are inherently incapable of comprehending dynamic situations and predictions impossible to achieve in the present state of knowledge, what do our authors take to be appropriate forms of futures statements? It seems to me that, to the extent that they aspire to futures statements at all, they converge for the most part upon what Bertrand de Jouvenel has called the "art of conjecture," that is, "the intellectual construction of a likely future."

> In this composition of the mind, we should make use of all the relevant causal relations that we can find; their respective roles and their connections with one another will depend on a hypothetical model, and their triggering will depend on intervening facts, which also have to be presupposed. The conjecture will be more or less well-reasoned. What is of vital importance for the progress of this art of conjecture is that an assertion about the future should be accompanied by the intellectual scaffolding which supports it: this "construct" must be transparent and articulated, and subjected to criticism.[34]

The purpose of conjecture is to develop "futuribles"—possible futures— "what seems to be the object of thought when the mind is directed toward the future," "those descendants from the present state that now seem possible," the "mode of production from the present state of affairs [that seems] plausible and imaginable." "A futurible is a descendant of the present, a descendant to which we attach a genealogy."[35]

The utility for the social scientist or the policy maker of a systematic conjecture or *futurible*—what Eulau would, I think, call a "developmental construct," is not measured by its predictive power, but rather by its ability to stimulate research that might be relevant to the future. In order to do this, argues Eulau, these constructs must be developed in terms "that can be observed at the micro-level of individual... behavior."[36] He echoes Goldthorpe in noting that "the weakness of futuristic extrapolation of trends is its neglect of the puzzling problem of how past, present, and future are connected in human action."[37] "One-sided trend extrapolation" are also incapable of handling what Eulau, citing Morris R. Cohen, calls the "polarity principle." The polarity principle "assumes that there is no action without reaction, no force without resistance, no unity without plurality, no identity without difference, no growth without decay."[38] It was postulated by Cohen as a "supplement to the principle of causality." "Not only must every natural event have a cause which determines that it should happen, but the cause must be opposed by some factor which prevents it from producing any greater effect than it actually does."[39]

The imperatives of focusing on observable individual behavior and on the contradictory social forces that are implicit in any given time or situation bring us back to one of the principal common preoccupations of the authors of this volume, namely, political perception and political choice, and the often competing and contradictory efforts of elites or counterelites to interpret experience and to impose order and stability by means of public policies.

THE PLAN OF THE BOOK

Having identified the basic lines along which these articles converge and diverge, and how they can as a group be related to futures study, on the one hand, and to macro-change theory, on the other, let me now briefly summarize the papers to indicate more specifically their preoccupations and how they relate one to another.

Todd La Porte and C. J. Abrams in "Alternative Patterns of Postindustria: The Californian Experience," set out to demonstrate that California has displayed the basic characteristics attributed to "postindustrial" society (technology-induced sectoral shifts in employment, growth of knowledge-intensive industries, increasing affluence and leisure, a multiplicity of value patterns) longer than any other society, indeed since well before World War II, and possesses them now to a higher degree than the United States as a whole. They argue that the state thus offers a useful "testing ground for illuminating the politics of advanced industrial societies." They construct a model of "Stable Postindustria," inferring its social dynamics from the available literature, and seeking to make the variables operational. In this model technology is treated as a crucial "stimulus variable." The model describes the sequential cycles of increasing social and organizational capacity created by technological advances and the increased organizational differentiation and interdependence that is the overall result. The "new society" that emerges from this process is characterized by an increasing "apparent" organizational capacity to deal with social problems and by increased importance attributed to knowledge producing and using classes in dominant institutions. But politics in this society "is likely to take on an odd cast of promise and reassurance" because of "a contradictory undertone of latent confusion associated with complexity."

If planners and leaders are able to understand what the public wants and have adequate causal knowledge about the dynamics of the system, the system can remain stable in its development and such presumed characteristics of "postindustrial society" as continued affluence, ascendency of a knowledge elite, new value orientations, etc., will predominate. But La Porte and Abrams are not optimistic in this regard, holding it more likely that leaders "and their knowledgeable assistants" will have great difficulty in determining what the public wants and in managing the system. They thus see "Unstable Postindustria" as the second stage of postindustrial development. This model stresses the discontinuities and rising levels of political and personal insecurity that are produced by ever more frequent policy failure in the midst of high expectations and interorganizational complexity. Recent California experiences of political tumult and the emergence of extremism of the Left and Right are cited as testimony to these discontents and uncertainties.

Ronald Inglehart focuses directly on "The Nature of Value Change in Postindustrial Societies." He, too, concludes that "the future looks difficult for Western governments," citing some of the same factors as La Porte and Abrams, i.e., the salience of new issues (social equality, belonging, self-expression, dissatisfaction with hierarchically structured organizations) that the governments of advanced industrial societies are not well equipped to handle, a realignment of voting patterns, a decline in public confidence in government. But Inglehart traces these phenomena to *secular processes of value change* that are the consequence of childhood socialization experiences of certain age cohorts with economic and physical security. On the basis of extensive survey research data from the United States and Western Europe, he argues that a gradual but deeply rooted and pervasive process of value change is taking place among the populations of Western societies—a shift from Materialist to Postmaterialist orientations. He argues that the politics of the future will be "quite different" from that of the past because "the cohorts now entering the electorate (and eventually the decision-making posts) seem to want very different things than those who are already there."

The article is especially rich in its methodological treatment of the problems of conceptualizing and measuring value change in mass publics, in its substantive detail on the patterns of value priorities the author sees emerging, and on their relationship to attitudes toward the economy, the environment, occupational choices, parochialism or cosmopolitanism, attitudes toward innovation and change, and party preferences. He concludes by showing how these value changes *and the expectations to which they give rise* have been associated with rapid economic growth, and by asking what would be the political consequences of a failure of Western governments to sustain these growth rates in the face of the mounting economic problems of the 1970s.

Taketsugu Tsurutani considers "Japan as a Postindustrial Society." He argues that certain industrial and technological dynamics are producing a variety of important political transformations in Japan. These dynamic forces seem similar to those affecting other advanced industrial societies, but Japan offers some distinct advantages as a site in which to observe their political implications because Japan is not handicapped by overinstitutionalization of the mode of thought and pattern of behavior long regarded as characteristic of modern industrial open societies, and thus may more readily manifest certain symptoms and phenomena associated with postindustrial society.

Tsurutani singles out four interrelated aspects of political change and documents their appearance in recent Japanese politics. The first is *the rise in salience of cross-stratal issues.* Direct experience by citizens with the effects of pollution, inflation, urban congestion, housing and transportation crises; their realization of the extent to which these are the consequences of the policies of the dominant elites in the ruling Liberal Democratic party, the bureaucracy, and industry; and the continued unresponsiveness of these elites to demands produced by these negative side effects of exclusive dedication to economic growth have all led to a politicization of the costs of industrial society and thus to the rise of issues that cut across existing lines of political cleavage. This has given rise to *new patterns of political participation*—a decline in the salience of voting in national elections, a striking disengagement from traditional parties, and an amazing rise of local action groups of all kinds. As a consequence of these phenomena, the author sees *an emerging elite-mass strain*, a growing vertical value incongruence in Japanese society, a declining consensus on central values considered desirable as a source of status or power, and a *demand for a new legitimacy* as existing parties and national political leaders are shown to be at best irrelevant and at worst structurally responsible for the deepest problems of the society.

Jeffrey D. Straussman's "Technocratic Counsel and Societal Guidance" signals a shift in emphasis from the input to the output side of the political process. Straussman is interested in "societal guidance"—the coordination and utilization of information by policy makers, and in "technological counsel"—the roles and influences of experts in policymaking. As such his paper parallels La Porte and Abrams' identification of the apparent capacity for control and planning, the increased societal investment therein, and the subsequent rise of expert and knowledge elites as the primary characteristics of the emerging society. His analysis bears directly on one of the crucial variables they argue will mediate the shift from Stable to Unstable Postindustria, namely, the ability (or willingness) of leaders to make use of adequate knowledge about societal dynamics as a response to policy problems.

Straussman calls our attention to how little we actually know about the dynamic and expanding power structure of advanced industrial capitalist states. He rejects both the classical technocracy position that there has been a shift in power from politicians and entrepreneurs to a new class of specialists, and the classical Marxist position that technocratic elites merely serve those who have always been in control. Both are plagued by "obscurant deductivism"; further conceptual and empirical clarification is clearly required. Straussman offers an empirical analysis of the role of experts in four guidance areas that have become preeminent in the United States since 1960: the political economy of "new economics" growthmanship, program budgeting, social indicators, and futures research. He argues that there are three reasons to doubt that experience in these areas warrants the conclusion that there has been a significant increase in societal guidance capacities: a persistent imbalance of commitment or real resources to social goals as against those preferred by existing military and industrial elites; the political vulnerability of experts because of gaps in their knowledge; and the fact that technological counsel always accepts the strategic prescriptions of policy makers as given, thus limiting itself to tactics. There have been some interesting structural changes in the incidence of *technocratic counsel* in the structure and process of public policy (for which the author offers some tentative measures), but these have too often involved legitimation of what dominant elites want to do, and express the values of a "perfumed technocracy" rather than constituting what the author considers the ingredients of a real capacity for societal guidance. This latter would presume "system transforming reforms emanating from rejuvenated guidance areas with experts that recognize both the valuations of guidance and the social obligations of the expert."

In "Elite Images and System Change in Sweden," M. Donald Hancock argues that the present disparity in conceptions of change and views of the future of postindustrial society—the proliferate literature on energy, pollution, population crises, on the one hand, and various deterministic theories of mono-causal change processes on the other—can be clarified by recognizing "the quality of elite choice as a determinant of both physical and sociopolitical change." Elite attitudes toward system change are then a "crucial predictive index," for "elite conceptions of policy choice," encompassing the leaders' images of both the present and the future will determine that choice and hence the direction, scope, and quality of system change.

He explores this research strategy by means of extended elite interviews in Sweden, one of the world's most industrialized, affluent, and politically modernized nations. His procedure is to posit five patterns of system change that appear conceivable for Sweden in the next decades in the light of present dominant economic and sociological trends: regressive change caused by a decline in economic productivity, regressive change caused by intensified sociopolitical antagonism, transforming collectivist change, transforming libertarian change, and ad hoc maintaining change. He then puts questions to his sample of elite relating to such trends and tries to determine from their responses which outcome patterns seem most likely. He finds that there is a "greater probability of a synthesized pattern of collectivist-libertarian transformation than the theoretical alternatives of regression and system maintenance" and speculates about the characteristics of Swedish society that might conduce to this result, and which may not be present in other advanced industrial societies.

Charles Anderson in "Public Policy and the Complex Organization: The Problem of Governance and the Further Evolution of Advanced Industrial Society" sets out to deal with "the governance of complexity" as a policy problem in policy analysis. He sees (as do La Porte and Abrams) the exponential growth in the number, incidence, and scale of complex organizations as the most distinctive social artifact of advanced industrial societies. "Modern man is more intimately governed in those matters that affect his day-to-day life by private governments than by the state." And he argues that this trend is producing, or will soon produce, a decline in trust and faith in the workability and equity of the pluralist order, unless certain changes are made in "the system of private government that is the distinguishing feature of this order." Complex organizations (corporations, trade unions, associations, universities) must be made "more responsive to individually and socially defined wants and needs"; more sophisticated conflict-resolving mechanisms must be developed to handle the diverse and intensified conflicts over their role and performance; and institutions must be developed to make the tacit rule-making authority of the organizations legitimate in our eyes.

Anderson's approach is to ask how public policy makers in any given society are apt to perceive these issues in the process of public debate and decision, and what patterns of response seem most likely. He argues that this will differ from one society to another, for each society has a characteristic "dominant policy paradigm" which is remarkably stable in time and which thus offers the most reliable basis of conjecture. These "paradigms" consist of persistent and shared bodies of political principles which specify the grounds that are appropriate for making claims within any given political order, the kinds of arguments that will be acceptable, the boundaries of the plausible, and the "range of reasons that will be taken as legitimate."

He argues that such a paradigm exists in "the Anglo-American world," that it consists of the apparatus of common law, democratic theory, and a market-based political economy, and he explores each of these elements for their potential in dealing with each of two problems posed by the growth and power of complex private organizations. He looks first at the internal governance of these organizations and at how one might innovate by the democratization of internal procedures, the creation of market effects, and the reintroduction of notions of individual rights, statuses, and obligations vis-à-vis their power. Then he examines the problems of the public regulation of the external impact of organizations on society, evaluating the contemporary adequacy of the three most characteristic "liberal" approaches, namely, neo-Keynsian economic management, indicative planning, and regulatory law. Finally, he tries to clarify the normative implications of choices among various strategies of internal and external control, pointing out not only the different values and principles associated with each, but also the ways in which they are likely to create different public expectations about performance.

In the final chapter, "Strategies and Priorities for Comparative Research," I explicitly raise questions about the implications of these papers for future research, comparing and critically evaluating their arguments, findings, and hypotheses, and relating them to other relevant work, especially that of neo-Marxist theorists (an approach not represented directly by any of the authors). In so doing I also present the outlines of my own ongoing work on system change and policy response in advanced capitalist nations, wherein I try systematically to relate what I call the "bourgeois-democratic" paradigm to aggregate trends that call its constituent elements into question by undermining their adequacy or legitimacy, and to a broad typology of alternative patterns of policy response that correspond to each element and each source of instability. It is argued that this typology can serve both as a device for classifying and illuminating the structural implications of the ongoing policy debates in advanced capitalist societies, and as the basis of a tentative theory of what pattern of policies will constitute a desirable and "truly adaptive" response, and what patterns are likely to intensify system instability or to lead to illiberal, authoritarian, and socially unjust futures.

NOTES

1. Bertrand de Jouvenel, *The Art of Conjecture* (New York: Basic Books, 1967) p. 277.

2. Ibid., p. 276.

3. Otis Dudley Duncan, "Social Forecasting—The State of the Art," *Public Interest*, no. 17 (Fall 1969): 105.

4. On futurism and futurology see the following, both of which have extensive analytical bibliographies: Charles de Hoghton, William Page and Guy Streatfield, ... *and now the future* (London: Political and Economic Planning, August 1971); and Wendell Bell and James A. Mau, eds., *The Sociology of the Future* (New York: Russell Sage Foundation, 1971). See also Albert Somit, ed., *Political Science and the Study of the Future* (Hinsdale, Ill.: Dryden Press, 1974); and Franklin Tugwell, *Search for Alternatives: Public Policy and the Study of the Future* (Cambridge, Mass.: Winthrop Publishers, 1973).

5. See Herman Kahn and Anthony J. Weiner, *The Year 2000: A Framework for Speculation on the Next Thirty-Three Years* (New York: Macmillan, 1967);

Herman Kahn and B. Bruce Briggs, *Things to Come: Thinking About the '70's and '80's* (New York: Macmillan, 1972); Daniel Bell, *The Coming of Post-Industrial Society: A Venture in Social Forecasting* (New York: Basic Books, 1973); "Post-Industrial Society—A Symposium," *Survey* 17, no. 1 (Winter 1971); Zbigniew Brzezinski, *Between Two Ages: America's Role in the Technetronic Era* (New York: Viking Press, 1971); M. Donald Hancock and Gideon Sjoberg, *Politics in the Post-Welfare State: Responses to the New Individualism* (New York: Columbia University Press, 1972); Theodore Roszak, *Where the Waste-Land Ends: Politics and Transcendence in Postindustrial Society* (Garden City, N.Y.: Doubleday, 1972); Roger Williams, *Politics and Technology* (London: Macmillan, 1971); Peter F. Drucker, *The Age of Discontinuity: Guidelines to Our Changing Society* (New York: Harper & Row, 1968); Herbert J. Muller, *The Children of Frankenstein: A Primer on Modern Technology and Human Values* (Bloomington: Indiana University Press, 1970); Dennis Gabor, *The Mature Society* (London: Secker & Warburg, 1972); Donald Schon, *Beyond the Stable State* (London: Temple Smith, 1971), F. E. Emery and E. L. Trist, *Towards a Social Ecology: Contextual Appreciations of the Future in the Present* (London: Plenum Press, 1972); Norman Birnbaum, *Towards a Critical Sociology* (New York: Oxford University Press, 1971); Alain Touraine, *The Post-Industrial Society*, (New York: Random House, 1972); Bertram M. Gross, "Planning in an Era of Social Revolution," *Public Administration Review*, May/June 1971, pp. 259–96.

6. For another statement of many of these points see Samuel P. Huntington, "Postindustrial Politics—How Benign Will It Be?" *Comparative Politics* 6, no. 2 (January 1974): 163–91.

7. William C. Mitchell, "The Shape of Political Theory to Come: From Political Sociology to Political Economy," in *Politics and the Social Sciences*, ed. S. M. Lipset (New York: Oxford University Press, 1969) p. 104.

8. Ibid., p. 124.

9. Sir Geoffrey Vickers, *Freedom in a Rocking Boat* (Harmondsworth, Middlesex: Penguin Books, 1972), p. 121.

10. Ibid., pp. 27–28.

11. Samuel P. Huntington, "The Change to Change," *Comparative Politics* 3, no. 3 (April 1971): 283.

12. Assar Lindbeck, *The Political Economy of the New Left: An Outsider's View* (New York: Harper & Row, 1971), p. 15.

13. Charles E. Lindblom, "Integration of Economics and the Other Social Sciences through Policy Analysis," in James C. Charlesworth, *Integration of the Social Sciences through Policy Analysis*, American Academy of Political and Social Science Monograph 14 (Philadelphia, October 1972), p. 12.

14. Huntington, "Change to Change," p. 294.

15. Technetronic, postindustrial, postwelfare, postbourgeois, postcapitalist, post-Christian, postcivilized, posteconomic, posthistoric, superindustrial, post-market, consultative commonwealth, humanistic capitalism, temporary society, postmodern, postorganization, post-Protestant, post-Puritan, postscarcity, posttraditional, posttribal, postliterature, postmaterialist, promethean, friendly fascism, mature society, corporate state, garrison state, postliberal, service society.

16. Huntington, "Change to Change," p. 294.

17. Ibid., p. 295.

18. Cited at ibid., p. 297.

19. Huntington, "Change to Change," p. 296.

20. Hugh Heclo, "Conclusion: Policy Dynamics." To appear in Richard Rose, ed., *Dynamics of Public Policy* (Beverly Hills and London: Sage Publications, 1976).

21. Ibid.

22. John H. Goldthorpe, "Theories of Industrial Society: Reflections on the Recrudescence of Historicism and the Future of Futurology," *Archives Européenne de Sociologie* 12, no. 2 (1971): 264.

23. Huntington, "Change to Change," p. 303.

24. Goldthorpe, "Theories of Industrial Society," p. 277.

25. Ibid., p. 278.

26. Ibid., p. 280.

27. Ibid., p. 283.

28. Heinz Eulau, "Skill Revolution and Consultative Commonwealth," *American Political Science Review* 67, no. 1 (March 1973): 172.

29. Ibid.

30. Duncan, "Social Forecasting," pp. 107–8.

31. Ibid., p. 108.

32. Ibid.

33. Vickers, *Freedom in a Rocking Boat*, p. 108.

34. De Jouvenel, *The Art of Conjecture*, pp. 17–18.

35. Ibid., p. 18.

36. Eulau, "Skill Revolution and Consultative Commonwealth," p. 172.

37. Ibid.

38. Ibid.

39. Morris R. Cohen, *Studies in Philosophy and Science* (New York: Henry Holt, 1949), pp. 11–13, as cited in ibid.

ALTERNATIVE PATTERNS OF POSTINDUSTRIA: THE CALIFORNIAN EXPERIENCE*

TODD LA PORTE / C. J. ABRAMS

California's rapid growth and change over the past century and a quarter have drawn considerable comment.[1] Many of these changes, visible since 1900, reflect features said to typify a society well beyond ordinary industrialization. Social scientists, save for a growing number of historians, do not usually view regions such as the American West as "societies" per se, but insights from the perspective of comparative politics invite this broader view of contemporary California.[2] In adopting it here, we find that the culture west of the Sierra Nevada Mountains takes on an unusual cast.

As a society, California has been subjected to enormous "pressures from the East." In the state's early days, this influence from the more highly industrialized East amounted to a kind of "foreign assistance," accompanying the expansion of the railroads and at their behest. More recently this "assistance" has been part of the direct extension of the

*Discussions with imaginative colleagues are often catalytic, and we are grateful for a conversation with Warren Ilchman which began the train of notions prompting this paper. We are indebted to Andrew McFarland, Kai N. Lee, Serge Taylor, and Stephen Zwerling for thoughtful critiques of earlier drafts. Thanks to them there is greater clarity in our effort and fewer confusions, though some have persisted in spite of their admonitions. We are also most grateful for the most able editorial assistance of Mary Fenneman, statistical assistance from Karen Chase and Roslyn Tuttle, and the typing skill of Linda Harris, all of the Institute of Governmental Studies, University of California, Berkeley.

interests of the federal government. Since the 1930s California has been the object of several successive waves of technical, military-related, and economic assistance occasioned by the Great Depression, World War II, the Korean war, the cold war, particularly its development into the space race, and finally the war in Vietnam. In all five cases, this "foreign assistance" has involved the most sophisticated technology of the particular period and has effected significant concentrations of financial resources, professional capabilities, and technical expertise. The technologies developed in this process span innovations in petrochemicals, agriculture, the transport and aerospace industries, electronics, nuclear energy, medicine and other biological fields, and important innovations in research and development and education. These developments were accompanied by the massive population shifts associated with large-scale techno-industrial growth—mainly immigration into the state. Concurrently, swift social changes have occurred within California, sometimes triggering violence.[3] Many of these disruptions accompanying social changes can be associated with lags of political and social institutions in coping with the problems of rapid growth—lags commonly associated with "future shock." In a sense, Californian culture can be seen as the product of massively induced social change. It is a culture split into two significantly different subcultures, one in the south and one in the north. One could say that these two subcultures represent two versions of the future, each with its distinctive character, each with a distinctive response to technologically induced social change.

Insofar as changes in California share certain characteristics with those advanced industrial societies which have served as prototypes of "Postindustria," we believe that the study of contemporary California can yield a twofold benefit. California may prove an excellent testing ground for present theories of "postindustrialism," while at the same time affording us the opportunity of developing alternative conceptions of "postindustrial" development. Indeed it is intriguing to view California as one of the first genuinely "postindustrial societies," its development stimulated by many of the factors intrinsic to postindustrialism, factors productive of many political and cultural phenomena included in that vaguely described set of conditions so strikingly different from those of industrial societies. With our dual aim in mind, our version of postindustrialism has been fashioned in the attempt to make that notion more operational. In so doing, we have begun with indicators derived from those characteristics so often used in the literature to describe postindustrial societies. Since the United States is the closest of those societies that have served as the touchstones for the concept of postindustrialism, we compare California with the United States on the leading indicators of postindustrialism: the dramatic increase in employment in the service sector of the economy, the tipping of the scales in the labor force on the side of the white-collar workers over blue-collar laborers, the rising affluence of the population over the past thirty years, and other manifestations of postindustrial change. We do not have great confidence that these "postindustrial indicators" will directly reveal the phenomena we seek to describe and understand. Data related to these indicators have all the limits of data collected for other purposes, but they are the only ones at present available.

In this enterprise we do not seek to engage in a definition of the postindustrial society, we are not explicitly taking up any particular version of the postindustrial notion, nor are we intent upon critically evaluating this notion, though there is sore need for this kind of rigorous analytic work.[4] Rather we are engaged in a speculative venture, initially taking the notions of others about important characteristics of advanced industrial societies and seeing what might be revealed about the particular qualities of California by viewing it *as* a postindustrial society. Our intent is to begin to explore a way of thinking about the highly advanced industrial society that is California. In the process of this effort, we have formed some alternative conceptions of potential development beyond industrialism; perhaps it is more accurate to say that these conceptions are emerging in a developmental pattern, one stage following another. Their validity must await empirical corroboration.

THE POSTINDUSTRIAL NOTION

There is an emerging body of literature which attempts to describe social developments arising out of growth beyond the industrial state.[5] It seems certain to be prompted in part by our penchant to understand events not neatly explained by the conventional wisdom. The clearest message from this literature is that important elements in industrial society no longer dominate economic, social, or political behavior. Social and economic organization is alleged to be undergoing a radical transformation from the industrial to the postindustrial. Something akin to the transformation from an agrarian to an industrial society which marked the industrial revolution is said to be occurring within today's advanced industrial states. This transformation, it is asserted, will so alter the face of industrial societies as to render contemporary understanding of their organization obsolete.

In our discussion, we are assuming that something out there has genuinely changed for which there is not yet an adequate language of analysis. We assert, without elaboration, that in past industrial societies the norms and values of industrial and commercial life came to be held as important criteria for the evaluations and operations of nonindustrial institutions. This is to say that efficiency, economies of scale, bureaucratic organization, and concerns for productivity, if not those for profits, came to be held as important criteria for the evaluations and operations of nonindustrial institutions. This was the case for governmental, military, medical, and welfare organizations and for religious or other voluntary organizations and educational institutions alike. The values of industrial organizations came to be legitimate guides to the nature of social life and to the activities of nonindustrial institutions. What seems most characteristic of the attempts to describe the *post*industrial phenomenon is the argument that this homogeneity of values and beliefs spanning most social institutions no longer exists.[6]

Much of the discussion about postindustrialism has been based on the analysis of and extrapolation from recent trends in advanced industrial societies, particularly the contemporary United States. New trends in the economic order which appear to have significance for the organization of the rest of society have been assumed to predict something about contours of the near future and to suggest a broad outline of postindustrial society. Accordingly, the term postindustrialism has been used to identify both the characteristics that distinguish the most advanced Western societies from their industrial predecessors and the process of change underlying contemporary social dynamics.

The literature indicates that the shift which marks the transition from industrial to postindustrial societies has been signaled by a change in the kind of work in which people engage to earn their livelihoods. Thus, a change in the proportional distribution of employment among various sectors from goods production to service production and the change of employees' collar colors signifies a change in the *kind* of on-the-job work performed. This change has been postulated both as evidence of a change in the relative importance of the factors of production as well as evidence of the obsolescence of existing forms of economic and social regulation. Such evidence, it is claimed, portends a new society. This new work milieu, in combination with the increasing affluence available to the society, is commonly regarded as the factor promoting value change.[7]

This change in the distribution of employment among sectors underlies the rise of the "tertiary" or "service" sector, which is commonly construed to be the distinctive economic characteristic of a postindustrial society. For analytic purposes, economies have been divided into three sectors analogous to the stages of economic development: the primary, the secondary, and the tertiary sectors. This trichotomy is intended to indicate an historic process of technological development as well as to separate kinds of economic activities. The primary sector includes those activities that provide the basic raw materials needed for living, those carried on in *agriculture, forestry, fishing,* and *mining*; it was the supporting system of preindustrial society. The secondary sector, comprised mostly of *manufacturing,* but including construction,[8] is taken as the stamp of industrial society. It emerged out of the industrial revolution's technological advances which stimulated the development of new goods and enabled increased productivity in the primary sector, thereby freeing labor to move to employment in manufacturing. The tertiary sector, comprised of services, wholesale and retail trade, transportation, communication, utilities, finance, insurance and real estate, public services or government work, is considered the supporting system of a postindustrial society. It has allegedly emerged out of the "postindustrial revolution's" technological advances which enable increased productivity in both the primary and secondary sectors, freeing the labor force formerly tied to those sectors to move to still other areas of employment. Just as the description of a society as industrial is not intended to convey an absence of preindustrial economic activities, but rather the diminished use of human labor by agriculture and mining, so the description of a society as postindustrial should not be taken to imply the absence of industrial economic activities, but simply the reduced use of physical labor in this sector. Thus, postindustrialism signifies a shift to the tertiary sector of the bulk of the labor force.[9] This is the first criterion to be examined with California data in the next section. The other indicator, increase in productivity, is also examined briefly.

Two notions attendant on the assumption of increased productivity further characterize a postindustrial society: affluence and leisure.[10] Increases in productivity per man-hour in the manufacture of goods are purportedly manifested in a greater abundance of goods as well as in wage and salary increases. Theoretically, substantial increases in productivity per man-hour allow a shorter work week to occur simultaneously with increased production of goods and increased wages and salaries. To the extent that California is a proving ground for such postindustrial notions, some demonstration of its increased income or shortened work week for some employees may be in order.

The literature suggests that postindustrialism has not only to do with a change in the mode of production but also with a change in the relative importance of the factors of production, altering therefore the relative importance of various factors in the production process. The labor-intensive industry necessary to increased production in the preindustrial era and the capital-intensive industry of the industrial era are purportedly followed by the knowledge-intensive industry of the postindustrial era. In the knowledge-intensive industry, technology as the concrete application of knowledge and professionals as its human transmitters apparently become requisite to increased productivity. The increased importance of knowledge as a factor of production leads to the increased importance of the knowledgeable—of the professional technical expert—with a consequent decrease in importance of the capitalist entrepreneur in the production process. An enhanced capacity for planning and regulating economic growth, generated by the development of increasingly sophisticated intellectual technologies, elevates the importance of the planner as the embodiment of technical skill. The investment in planning required to implement technology in industry further enhances the importance of the planner. The predominance of planning is likely to reduce the emphasis on immediate maximization of profit as a decision rule in industry and to increase attention to long-term trends which may interfere with the market's regulation of the economy. In combination with the perceived need to mitigate the stresses and strains of rapid growth (such as resource depletion, intolerable population densities, etc.) this emphasis gives planning and planners a preeminent position in the policy circles of a postindustrial society.

(It has been suggested that the emphasis on planning changes the capitalistic ethos and replaces it with something else. We shall be concerned, since a change in ethos cannot be demonstrated, at least to find evidence in California of the increase in the number of professionals and planners said to distinguish the postindustrial society.)

Whatever else the concept of postindustrialism is meant to signify, it suggests a decline in the strength of industrial norms and a rise of other norms and values characterizing distinctive features of social institutions. Advanced industrial society appears to have achieved a level of economic development that frees increasing numbers of people from *direct* involvement with agricultural and industrial production organizations, thus reducing the overwhelming effects of industrial values on other social institutions. With increasing numbers of people able to devote full-time energies to educational, governmental, religious, and service-sector activities, we can expect a multiplicity of value orientations to mingle in society.

In the discussion that follows, we use the term postindustrial society advisedly, with no suggestion that one sector's values necessarily dominate those of other sectors. Rather, we mean to suggest a much more *differentiated and interdependent situation in which multiple value systems operate within sectors, sectors that have become increasingly dependent upon one another in reciprocal ways.* Our understanding of the causal and sequential relations among the variables of postindustrialism suggested by the literature is sketched out, and data are cited that we find relevant to describing California in these terms.

THE DYNAMICS OF POSTINDUSTRIAL SOCIETY

We begin with a caveat: What follows is both tentative and presumptuous, for it presents a scheme for thinking about most of the relationships between technological growth and recent sociopolitical developments. In so doing, it takes into account many factors generally associated with the concept of postindustrialism. We suggest that our scheme is a sensible basis for further research into the structure and dynamics of highly advanced industrial societies. Finally, our view diverges significantly from other speculations about postindustrial societies. Others have been optimistic about progress; we are not.

Stable Postindustria

The theories of postindustrial societal dynamics implicit in the literature suggest a society in progress toward an extrapolated future: certain tendencies undergo constant amplification, becoming ever more dominant, shaping events rather than simply following them. The trends emerging from development of sophisticated technologies have been given particular prominence in the literature; hence technology is treated as a crucial "stimulus" variable for subsequent social processes. Our perspective, too, begins with technological possibilities as the impetus to change. Other factors as well result in social changes, but for the moment we shall assume that modern technology is a major source of change in our culture. The strong consensus among writers in the field concerning the consequences of technological change for economic and social change suggests a paradigm similar to Kuhn's "normal science" paradigm.[11] By analogy, we might call what follows "normal postindustrialism." Since this paradigm implies a kind of movement toward an evolving society never far out of equilibrium, we shall term it "Stable Postindustria."

Figure 2.1 represents our attempt to draw together the main structure of arguments relating technological development to changes in basic social patterns. In effect, it is a description of social dynamics as inferred from many of the writers on postindustrialism. The schema asserts that industrial or governmental groups, recognizing that a technological possibility is potentially useful, go on to establish organizations of *production, distribution,* and *service* which make the possibility an actuality. The literature on technical innovation gives testimony to this process as does that dealing with economic development. Large industrial firms, factories, transport and wholesaling organizations, governmental agencies, and medical and educational institutions adopt new technological devices and systems in order to improve their own capacity to alter the world around them or augment their role in it through their services.[12] When this tendency is widespread throughout a society, such adoption of innovation appears to be necessary simply to maintain a position of competition with other organizations.

One indication that technological innovation stimulates an increase in organizations of production, distribution, and service, albeit an indirect one, is increased productivity per person.[13] As technology is introduced to improve efficiency and to multiply human effort many times,

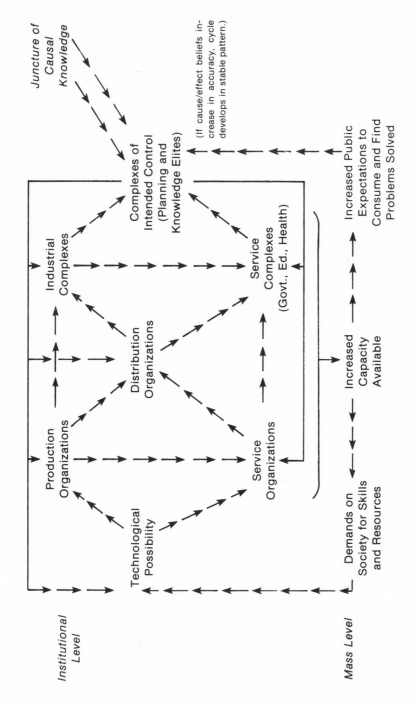

Figure 2.1. Dynamics of Stable Postindustria.

productivity per person increases. This increase is well documented for the United States as a whole, and California compares favorably with the overall trend, as figure 2.2 depicts. These data are doubly significant for increased production per person is also linked, as we shall see, to consequent shifts in employment among the various economic sectors.

As new technological possibilities emerge, either from within large organizations or from without them, new cycles of adaptation and growth take place; in each phase of this "advance," society's overall capacity for coping with its problems of sustenance and development is augmented. Technological advances with consequent widespread organizational implementation have released people from the confining necessity for physical labor, especially on farms, and have multiplied the variety of goods available to consumers. This release from agriculture has spurred massive shifts in employment patterns, with significant proportions of the work force leaving the farms to enter manufacturing and/or service employment. Thus, it is argued that there has been a decline in the proportion of people attached to the land and engaged in primary production and a consequent growth in both secondary production organizations and tertiary service activities. Figure 2.3 presents data indicating these shifts in employment.[14] As the data showing California's increasing share of America's employment might suggest, an overall increase in social and organizational capacity occurs. Such growth in scale is accompanied by increases in the overall demand for natural resources and human skills in order that the growth process be sustained. As cycles of innovation and growth continue, organized complexes of industrial production organizations result, with parallel developments of distribution and service complexes.[15] At the same time, the redistribution of employment for California over time and compared to the United States is interesting.

Data in figure 2.3 can be interpreted as evidence that implementation of technological innovation in the primary- and secondary-goods-producing industries was responsible for the shift in employment associated with postindustrialism. When dated, postindustrialism is usually considered to be a post-World War II phenomenon and to have emerged sometime prior to 1956, when for the first time in the United States the percentage employed in white-collar occupations exceeded that in blue-collar occupations.

In 1920, employment in the United States was not equally distributed among the three sectors (primary, secondary, and tertiary or service). Yet their correspondence at that time (28.9 percent; 30.8 percent; and 40.3 percent, respectively) was the closest it was ever to be, for by 1970 the distribution was to become 4.5 percent, 31.9 percent, and 63.6 percent, respectively. But by 1920 in California there was not even this rough parity. Already in this state primary industry was employing only slightly less than a fifth of the labor force (19.7 percent), secondary industry less than

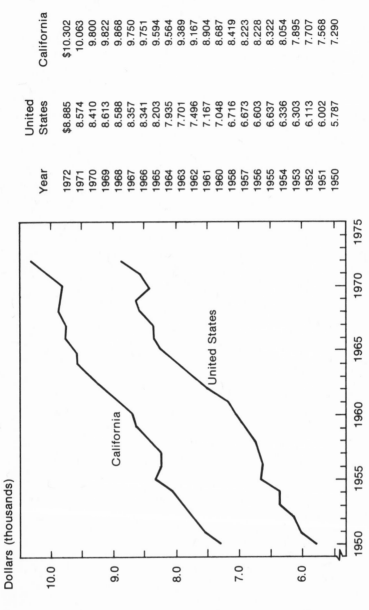

Year	United States	California
1972	$8.885	$10.302
1971	8.574	10.063
1970	8.410	9.800
1969	8.613	9.822
1968	8.588	9.868
1967	8.357	9.750
1966	8.341	9.751
1965	8.203	9.594
1964	7.935	9.564
1963	7.701	9.389
1962	7.496	9.167
1961	7.167	8.904
1960	7.048	8.687
1958	6.716	8.419
1957	6.673	8.223
1956	6.603	8.228
1955	6.637	8.322
1954	6.336	8.054
1953	6.303	7.895
1952	6.113	7.707
1951	6.002	7.568
1950	5.787	7.290

Dollars (thousands)

Figure 2.2 Output per Man-year in the United States and California, 1950–72 (in thousands of 1958 dollars). Data on the United States 1950–65 from U.S. Department of Commerce, Bureau of the Census, *Long Term Economic Growth*, pp. 188–89. Data on California for the above table and graph courtesy of the University of California, Los Angeles, Business Forecasting Project. See Appendix for further information.

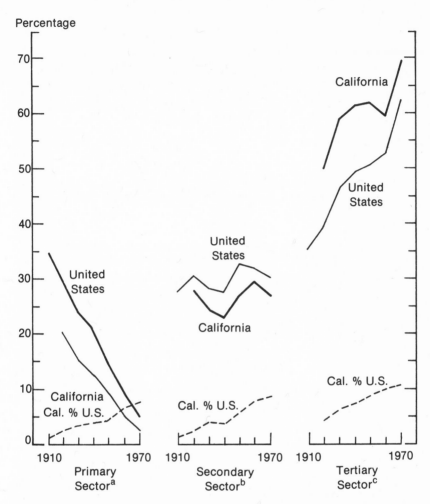

Percentage

Primary Sector[a] Secondary Sector[b] Tertiary Sector[c]

[a] Includes agriculture, forestry, and fishing industries since 1920, and mineral extraction as always under 3% of the total.

[b] Includes manufacturing and construction industries (with construction always under 8% since 1940).

[c] Includes trade, finance, insurance and real estate, transportation, communication, utilities, public administration, and the service industries.

Figure 2.3. Percent Distribution of Employment in Industry by Sector in the United States and California, 1910–70. See tables A and B in the Appendix for the percentages and raw figures from which these graphs were derived.

a third (28.6 percent), and *tertiary or service industry over one-half (51.9 percent)* of all employees in the state. By 1970, California's tertiary sector, with 69.4 percent of the employed, far outdistanced both the primary sector, whose employed had fallen to a miniscule 3.6 percent, and the secondary sector, which claimed 27.0 percent. This apportionment, on its face, appears to be quite *consistent* with the industrial/postindustrial thesis, i.e., with a rapid decline in agriculture during the heyday of industrialism, followed by an even more rapid decline, heralding the onset of an entirely new era. Yet there also appears to be a *contradiction* to what is implied in that thesis, namely, the release of labor from agriculture to manufacturing in the industrial period and the release of labor from manufacturing to the service sector during the postindustrial period: Between 1920 and 1940, the labor released from agriculture showed up in the *service* industries; while between 1940 and 1960, *manufacturing* realized this increment. This reshuffling was even more pronounced in California, where between 1940 and 1960 nearly all the labor percentage released from agriculture was regained in manufacturing. This apparent contradiction is somewhat resolved, however, when we note that California's service sector already claimed the lion's share of the employed, and especially when we also note that between 1960 and 1970 the shift in employment in both areas followed the predicted pattern. Indeed, if a high percentage of a labor force employed in the service sector is meaningful as a crucial indicator of postindustrialism, and if we take the percentage employed therein in the United States in 1960 as a standard by which to judge, *California has been postindustrial at least since the 1920s* and since then has continued to become ever more so.

Just as these data indicate a shift in employment among *industries*, a similar pattern is also apparent for *occupations*. Table 2.1 indicates that not only does California follow the trend in the increase of white-collar workers and the corresponding decrease of blue-collar and farm workers, but it *leads* that trend. Already by 1950 California white-collar workers outnumbered their blue-collar neighbors. For the United States as a whole this did not happen until sometime between 1950 and 1960, probably about 1956. By 1970, over half of those employed in California were in white-collar occupations, a figure that was ahead of the distribution for the United States generally.

Like other indicators we have used in our discussion, these two indicators of employment shifts within California suggest indirect evidence that the attitude profiles of the working population may be changing. We argued above that a shift of overall emphasis from *direct* engagement in rural or industrial production to a preponderance of workers in service and/or white-collar work was likely to decrease the application of industrial values to other institutions in a society. That is, since more employees become engaged in work related to servic-

Table 2.1 Distribution of Employment Among Major Occupational Divisions in the United States and California, 1950, 1960, and 1970 (in percent)

	1950	1960	1970
All Occupations[a]	100	100	100
White Collar			
United States	36.9	41.4	48.2
California	45.0	47.3	54.4
Blue Collar			
United States	39.8	36.7	35.9
California	36.3	33.1	30.8
Farm Workers			
United States	11.9	6.1	3.1
California	6.8	3.9	2.2
Service Workers			
United States	10.1	11.1	12.8
California	11.0	10.4	12.6

[a]1950, 1960 percentages total less than 100% because of unreported occupations, approximately 1% and 5% respectively.
SOURCE: Data compiled from U.S. Department of Commerce, Bureau of the Census, *Census of Populations* (Washington, D.C.: Government Printing Office, selected years).

ing people rather than related to producing things and products exclusively, the probability emerges that a number of values will be mixed in the culture, represented by groups deriving economic sustenance from pursuing them. We would expect these values to be played out in the appearance of social and political issues reflecting such a diversity. To be sure, many other conditions contribute to such a differentiation of value expressions. We suggest that such a development is massively enabled by the kinds of shifts characterized by the data in figure 2.3 and table 2.1.

Perhaps the most important feature of Stable Postindustria is the cycles of increasing social and organizational capacity that occur as the various organizational complexes become more differentiated and interdependent.[16] Regular bodies of statistics available for the period do not yield a direct indication of this characteristic, so we must rely on rough surrogates. When technical organizations are astutely arranged and coordinated, they find great mutual advantage in the business of production and distribution of goods and services; the advantage spills over to consumers and the public at large. Such arrangements require joint efforts for continued operations; thus we could expect increases in transportation capabilities, financial organizations, and trade activities implemented for the sake of improving communication and interaction among production, distribution, and service activities. This is to say that *indirect* indications of interdependence may be seen in variations in the relative employment figures related to transport, finance, and so on.

These activities, normally assigned to service-sector employment, are presented in figure 2.4. The data are a bit ambiguous in terms of our argument. In California there has been a dramatic increase in trading activities. But transportation employment fluctuates in such a way that it is not clear how it might relate to our reasoning. One possible interpretation is that there has been a lag, at least as reflected in percentages of employees relative to other sectors, in the development of adequate transportation capabilities. Were this interpretation actually valid, it would point to a failure of policy and programs in keeping up with the needs of an increasingly interdependent system. We could then expect public outcry and complaints to be much in evidence throughout urban California.

With the development of increasingly capable and interdependent organizational complexes, we can expect the public to come to think of society as *actually having* the resources and the technical skill to solve the problems confronting it. At the same time, managers and policy makers respond to the increased organized complexity with a greatly heightened sense of the need to plan and to coordinate in order to assure that the flow of reciprocally needed resources will be maintained.[17] They fear that if coordination breaks down, the materials, funds, and human resources needed to keep the complexes functioning may be interrupted and services halted; that many people will be put out of work and that social disruption will increase intolerably. Thus, increasing organized complexity brings with it a growing insistence that the uncertainties endemic to any complex system be reduced. To the degree this occurs, we expect greater proportional investment in coordination skill and information management. Planning units would be developed to provide the intellectual resources necessary for effective action and for reducing uncertainties risked by misdirected actions undertaken in the face of changing environmental, industrial, and political conditions.[18]

As yet there are no easy ways of measuring the degree to which planning has become expected and sought in local, state, and federal agencies or in industry and other large organizations. That there has been a remarkable growth in the perceived need for increased competence in planning is the impression conveyed by the number of new schools and programs in planning, business administration, and public policy where training and curriculum emphasize planning skills. More systematic measurement of the social investment in coordinative skills is difficult, but some indication of the managerial or coordinative capacities of a society may be obtained from the percentages of people employed as

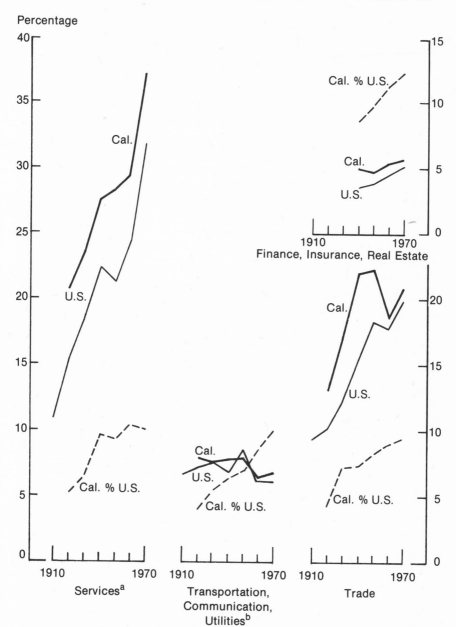

a Includes professional service, domestic and personal services, business and repair services, entertainment and recreational services, and public service industries.

b Includes utilities only since 1940.

Figure 2.4. Percent Distribution of Employment Among Industry Groups in the Service Sector in the United States and California, 1910–70. For the percentages and actual raw numbers from which these graphs were derived, see Appendix, tables A and B.

professional administrators, lawyers, industrial engineers, planners, public officials, bankers, and the like. Our assumption is that as the complexity of economic, political, and social life increases, more attention will be paid to its coordination. To the degree this is the case, we expect a slow rise in the percentages of administrative positions within the labor force. As population and organizational infrastructure grow, so grows the proportion of those charged with coordinating it.

Figure 2.5 shows the changes in the overall proportions of administrative skills in the employment pool for California and the United States. Clearly California, until the last decade, led the rest of the nation in its engagement with staffing coordinative roles. Notably there was a huge absolute increase in these positions, though it was not quite as great as the enormous absolute growth of the total labor pool. Somewhat unaccountably, the 1960s witnessed an overall relative decline in the proportions of Californians occupying such positions. The last half of that decade also included the onset of social upheaval and an increase in a sense of lost control over social institutions.

Other data add detail to this picture. As a society grows and becomes complex, especially in its services to citizens, resources for public governance, on the one hand, and resources for knowledge-based services, on the other, could be expected to increase as well. In a sense, these capacities are benchmarks of societies beyond industrialism. Figure 2.6 shows a very substantial and sustained investment in both. The curves of increased employment in the public-services and public-administration industries speak for themselves. They support the more intuitive sense of growth felt by many. But the increases in proportion of those professionally employed are the most dramatic of all our data. Since 1950 there has been a truly phenomenal increase in the absolute and the proportional employment in the knowledge-based industries. California has led the nation, and as is the case for other indicators we have used, the rest of the country is coming to be more and more like California in this respect. But the data in figures 2.5 and 2.6 also report an apparent anomaly. While there has been a sharp and *continuous* increase in the proportion of all those employed in public administration in California, there has been a relative decline in all coordinative roles within public and private organizations, suggesting perhaps that the managerial capacities of the private sector may have suffered a relative decline. To the degree that this is the case and it results in a general decline in the capacity for the private sector to anticipate and deal with greater inter- as well as intrasector interdependence, it is likely that the public sector would be turned to with demands for service and coordination. It would also be likely that the large population influx would make it difficult or impossible for California government to deal effectively with such demands.

Figure 2.5. Proportion of Employed with Coordinative Skills to Total Employed in the United States and California, 1940-70. See Appendix for source citations and explication.

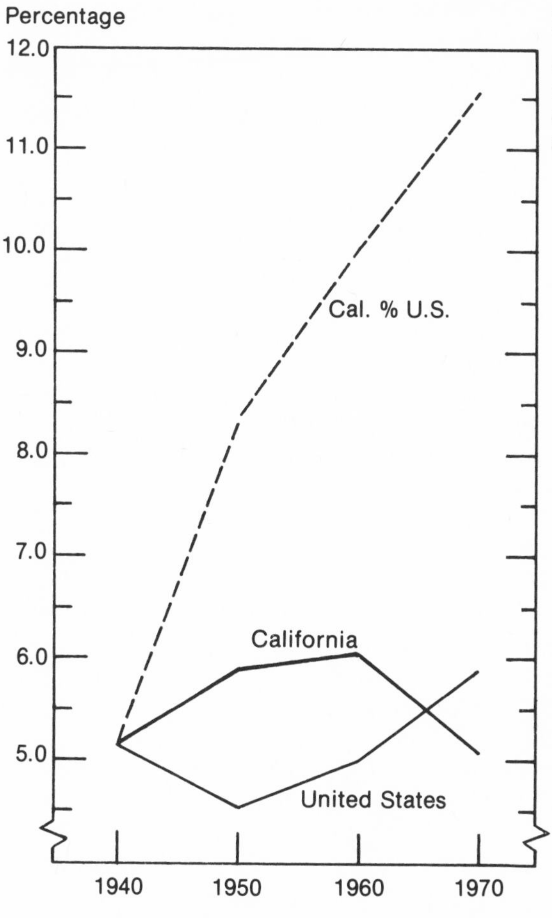

	United States		California		Calif. % U.S.
1970	$\frac{4527^a}{76,554}$	5.91%	$\frac{528}{10,319}$	5.12%	11.66
1960	$\frac{3416}{67,990}$	5.02%	$\frac{353}{5761}$	6.13%	10.33
1950	$\frac{2695}{59,230}$	4.55%	$\frac{230}{3902}$	5.89%	8.43
1940	$\frac{2431}{45,166}$	5.38%	$\frac{132}{2476}$	5.33%	5.43

[a]Numerator = employed with coordinative skills; denominator = total employed.

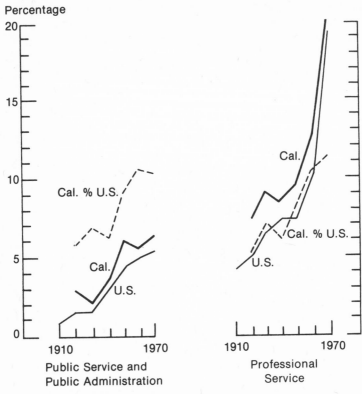

Figure 2.6. Percent Distribution of Employment Among Service Industries in the United States and California, 1910-70. For the percentages and actual raw numbers from which these graphs were derived, see Appendix, tables A and B.

We have experienced a time in which large organizations in industry and government have, indeed, altered the face of the physical and social landscape. In a sense the 1960s was the highwater mark of confidence in large-scale efforts to do the impossible. Much has been invested in hopes and expectations that large organizations can and will solve whatever problems are thrust upon them. At the same time, the unanticipated results of using this high capacity for problem solving have occasioned an increasing number of social and environmental surprises, which in turn have stimulated an even greater penchant for planning and policy studies.[19] Time and again, the emphasis upon the gathering of knowledge as a support for decision making is underscored, auguring the ascendency of a new elite composed of those who have access to and control of specialized information. New complexes of techno-political direction have arisen; groups of educated men and women have been brought together as planning units, advisory commissions, study and policy groups, and regulatory agencies, whose manifest mission is to provide knowledge and political acumen for control over the many related industrial, distribution, and service complexes that have evolved.

In this milieu of increased capacity, investment in planning, and production, the public's expectations have risen in accordance with the increase in perceived capacity to solve social problems. Accomplishments once thought of as unlikely or physically impossible have now become commonplace. In fact, for many the meaning of "impossible" seems to have changed significantly. What was once "impossible" no longer is; what is meant by "impossible" now is likely to be "politically difficult." Such confidence in attitude seems to mark private, governmental, and individual expectation equally. We have argued already concerning both real and perceived public capacity. Such expectations will probably increase at the personal level as individual affluence increases. Figure 2.7 leaves little doubt about the relative and absolute growth in spending power of the Californian compared with that of other Americans. It is quite likely that such increases will sustain the public's hope that rising affluence will continue after recent economic setbacks are overcome, and such hope will contribute to an impatience about unresolved social, economic, and resource problems.

In the context of a society taking on the character we have outlined, what might be expected about its politics? We suggest that it is the *politics of psychic reassurance*, a politics taking on the paradoxical cast of promise and reassurance *and* latent uncertainty.[20] Perhaps it is almost the politics of anxious hope, hope that the system can in fact be run efficiently enough to ensure the realization of the things we now believe are possible. But such is the mantle cloaking a contradictory undertone of latent confusion associated with complexity beyond comprehension. Public figures try to assure us that confusion can be moderated; they try to persuade the citizenry that all is well and that the machines of government and industry really do operate as advertised— or can be made to if only a change of administration is won.

With widespread perception of improved capacity to produce, distribute, and serve the public, expectations of both elites and the public escalate, and planning units and regulatory agencies proliferate to assure that potential capacity is realized. At the same time, a sense of potential breakdown rears its head, stimulating a complementary enthusiasm for ever more rational decisions and organizational actions. In the scenarios of writers on Postindustria, the emphasis on the rise of a technocratic elite and on the increased importance of knowledge-based action suggests that the quality of theoretically based knowledge is adequate and will be put to effective use. Thus, one gets the sense from much of the literature that all will be relatively well in our postindustrial future.

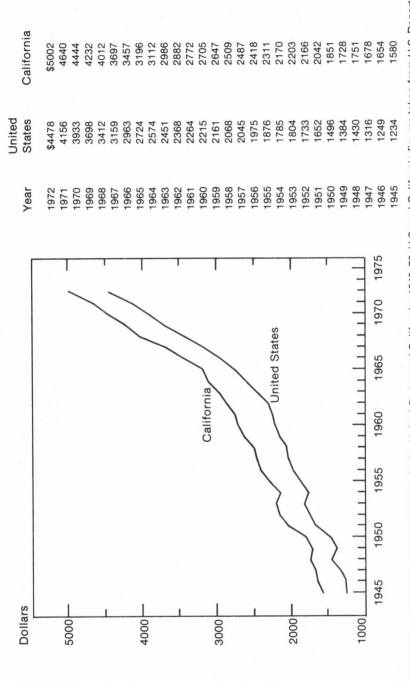

Year	United States	California
1972	$4478	$5002
1971	4156	4640
1970	3933	4444
1969	3698	4232
1968	3412	4012
1967	3159	3697
1966	2963	3457
1965	2724	3196
1964	2574	3112
1963	2451	2986
1962	2368	2882
1961	2264	2772
1960	2215	2705
1959	2161	2647
1958	2068	2509
1957	2045	2487
1956	1975	2418
1955	1876	2311
1954	1785	2170
1953	1804	2203
1952	1733	2166
1951	1652	2042
1950	1496	1851
1949	1384	1728
1948	1430	1751
1947	1316	1678
1946	1249	1654
1945	1234	1580

Figure 2.7. Per Capita Personal Income in the United States and California, 1945–72. U.S. and California figures taken from U.S. Department of Commerce, Bureau of the Census, *Long-Term Economic Growth, 1860–1965*, series C1 and C58, pp. 210, 217. See Appendix for further information.

In such a future, planners and leaders could have a clear under-standing of the wants the public has been able to articulate reasonably well *and* these leaders could have adequate causal knowledge about the socioeconomic dynamics of the system. That being the case, there would be some assurance that the problems associated with economic growth, system coordination, and institutional development can be kept minor. Such a situation would naturally lead to the ascendency of the new "knowledge elite" coming to power perforce of its special capacities for using knowledge effectively, thus winning devotion from leaders and the public. *The crucial and assumed condition in this description of stable postindustrial dynamics is the ability of this new knowledge elite to develop significantly improved causal knowledge about the behavior of social and economic systems and to act upon it.* If this ability proves out, presumably continued affluence will result; and new sociocultural patterns may emerge, engendered by affluence and freedom from eco-nomic scarcity. Cultural developments, relatively untroubled by great social and political surprises, might well become based on the "new scarcities" of information, coordination abilities and time that Professor Daniel Bell discussed recently.[21] New value orientations would emerge, and perhaps they are emerging. In a sense this interpretation could be applied to the Swedish case as described by Hancock in chapter 6 of this volume.

We have attempted thus far to show the plausibility of considering California as a society which exhibits many of the structural characteristics of "postindustrialism." We have depended heavily upon the indicators other writers have used in charting changes in societies they say are associ-ated with developments "beyond industrialism." We have also nominated a set of relationships making explicit some of our notions about the under-lying dynamics of this development. Two things can be said thus far. First, it appears that California as a society is, indeed, well beyond simple in-dustrialism. If we can put much confidence in the indicators others have used, California is well into a postindustrial condition. Therefore, it ap-pears to be an excellent candidate for intensive study. Second, the scheme outlining some of the dynamics of stable postindustria, derived largely from the literature, rests heavily upon the assumption that advances in knowledge have paralleled and will continue to parallel the swift changes in social interaction prompted by the multiple social complexes we have noted. We question whether this is a viable assumption.

What follows is a departure from other visions of the postindustrial future. It is much more speculative than our preceeding discussion and is, in a sense, in the prehypothesis stage. A good deal of the impetus for our effort comes from a deep uneasiness about applying the stable post-industrial notion to the California experience. It may be that those notions cannot be appropriately applied to the society of the West Coast, but in the spirit of attempting to understand the changes "out there" which seem to go beyond the conditions of industrialism, we present the concluding part of this paper.

Unstable Postindustria

In the "stable" postindustrial society, experts may indeed be said to be expert, for the causal knowledge upon which they base action is in a significant sense correct; knowledgeable policies *could* shape events in desired directions. The condition of adequate causal knowledge and effective implementation *could* be met. In the face of rapid and extreme social change, however, an equally plausible condition may obtain; one in which leaders and their knowledgeable assistants have great difficulty in determining what is desired by a population afflicted with a mild state of disorientation. This difficulty is compounded when the validity of the cause-effect beliefs held by these experts for predicting the dynamics of economic, social, and political life diminishes. That their validity *will* diminish is extremely likely if the character of the social science theory relied upon by these experts derives mainly from simple social systems. These theories will prove grossly inadequate when applied to highly complex systems.[22] We argue that to the degree that the beliefs about causality underlying the construction and implementation of policy are mismatched with the economic, social, and political conditions to which they are applied, the dynamics of stable postindustrial societies begin a process leading them ultimately to instability. In a sense, "unstable" Postindustria is the second stage of postindustrial development. An alternative pattern of political development associated with advanced industrial society, it is directly related to the *quality of knowledge* about social operations, organization, and coordination.

Our conception of Unstable Postindustria, drawn schematically in figure 2.8, was in the main developed in our attempt to understand what seems to be happening within California's society. It bespeaks our uneasiness in directly and definitively applying the "normal" postindustrial notion to this experience, even though its vestiges are clearly present within it. Something in the application jars us. A number of indications that the promise of the postindustrial condition has not been realized confronts those of us who live in California.

A postindustrial system approaching an unstable condition retains certain features of Stable Postindustria noted above: (1) increasing apparent organizational capacity to deal with social problems and production demand; (2) increasing public expectation to consume; and (3) increasing importance attributed to the knowledge producing and using classes in dominant institutions. But accompanying this continuity is the emergence of two additional tendencies: (4) increased perception of

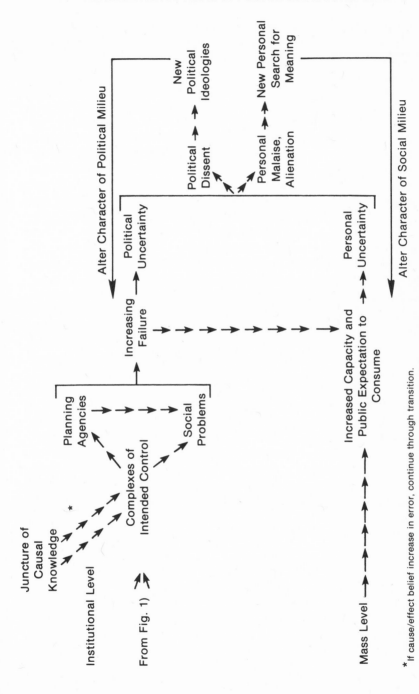

Figure 2.8. Transition to Unstable Postindustria.

*If cause/effect belief increase in error, continue through transition.

the growing number of social, economic, and management problems; and (5) an increased sense that the failure of social, economic, and political programs is *unjustified.*

These two latter conditions issue from the widening disjuncture between the character of the social and environmental problems associated with social complexes of production, distribution, and services and the established institutions of coordination and control designed by an older order for coping with these problems. In the very act of attempting to solve social and production problems, government and industry, operating on erroneous assumptions about the social dynamics behind these problems, promote programs that increase organized complexities and reduce the potential for effective control. Thus, the large-scale programs of government and industry designed to promote social benefit and stability lead in fact to an increasing number of unpleasant surprises, for decision makers, for citizens, and for consumers. The issue here has nothing to do with questions about the malevolence, self-interest, or incompetence of industrial or governmental leaders. Rather, we are contending that the cause-effect beliefs they hold and upon which their institutional processes are developed correspond less and less to what is actually happening in the world. To the degree this is the case, the knowledge elite falters, its promise unrealized. Then experts are expert only on what is past, on matters of relative simplicity applicable to an older scheme of things. These leaders, then, cannot predict or speak rightly of the future, yet they must continue to prescribe for it somehow.

We are suggesting that events and actual conditions have outrun the capacities of experts, both public and private, to understand them well enough to plan reasonably effectively. Policy making and implementation are as much error making as they are productive of desired outcomes. To be sure, many things cause policy failure and exacerbate social problems.[23] That notwithstanding, the futuristic vision of the post-industrial writers implicitly asserts that knowledge-based policy produced with the backing of cadres of science-rooted experts probably suffices for anticipating disruptive external forces or at least for responding to them in ways flexible enough to prevent an increase in social problems. But that vision does not appear fulfilled at present, or is there much reason to believe that it will be in the *near* future. The increase in emphasis on planning and policy studies can in fact be seen as an indicator of significant past failure in these areas. It is possible, indeed probable, that an increasing number of presently constituted policy studies and plans will *not,* as some apparently believe, lead to the resolutions of the problems stimulating the policy studies and plans in the first place. Thus, it is quite possible to have a situation in which there are parallel increases in perceived policy failure, in the number and intensity of social problems, and in public expectation that we should be able to overcome them.

In combination, then, the major characteristics of Unstable Postindustria amount to an intensification of the paradox noted earlier, and with it people's heightened perception of that paradox: the bewildering coexistence of society's impressive potential for dealing with its problems but its equally impressive inability to do so effectively. Whatever the methods we employ in the high hopes of solving our problems, they seem to produce many new ones, often without solving the original ones. Still, we must act; and our official actions are of necessity based on what we think we know. A deep confidence in the generally held perspectives on economic and social problems and in the institutions that have been developed to deal with them almost by definition must inform the actions of leaders and their planners. What other conceptual basis do they have upon which to rationalize their acts? But what if there is a growing number of negative social surprises and apparent policy failures?

It is reasonable to assume that continued and increasing perceived policy failure and negative surprises will result in fundamental uncertainties about the orthodox bases for political decision making and about the sociopolitical ideologies and the institutions they have spawned. If this uncertainty grows sufficiently intense, some kinds of measures for reducing it will be taken. Similarly for individual responses regarding one's own personal future: If one encounters increasing numbers of negative surprises in the events of everyday life, it is likely that, after a time, he or she may become infested with doubt about his or her basis for experiencing the world. As this uncertainty grows more intense, it is certain that a way must be sought to deal with it.

Many and varied are the sources of political and personal uncertainty. How much of this uncertainty may be traced to the planning and policy failures of large institutions is, of course, an empirical question. Yet in an increasingly interdependent economic and social system, the behavior of large institutions and the leadership prompting their action clearly have a significant influence on events. While planning or policy failure may not be the only or the single most important source of uncertainty, we assert that it is one of growing importance. Certainly the experience of living in California leads one to resist putting much confidence in the acumen of public or private leaders, their planners or policy programs.

The San Francisco and Los Angeles areas as well as rural California have been witness to a series of social and political phenomena we might understand to be manifestations of social discontinuity. These phenomena are also evidence of response to increasing levels of political and personal uncertainty. Instances of political tumult evident in California's recent past and the emergence of extremism on both the Right and the Left are testimony to this discontinuity and uncertainty. A great deal has been written about the consequences of this kind of political disaffection. In California the visible results have been social upheaval and dissent. Political extremism on the Right has been evident in the enthusiasm for the Christian anti-Communist Crusade, the development of the John Birch Society, and paramilitary groups such as the Minutemen. These movements have issued principally from Southern California. Somewhat parallel, leftist-tinged movements in the North have also been evident: the rise of the New Left, the Yippies, the Free Speech Movement and its various student progeny in the long saga of campus unrest, and other groups engaging in the "politics of confrontation," much of which took the form of antiwar demonstrations. All such factions have attempted to prompt fundamental changes in the political structure; their ideologies are a scattering of neo-Nazism, extreme nationalism, pacifism, environmental radicalism, and Gay Liberation.

Concurrent with political dissidence, personal alienation and malaise have also increased among many sectors of California's society. These are perhaps less visible but equally important socially. In Southern California periodic renewals of neofundamentalist religious movements have occurred, now particularly evident in the growing numbers of zealots known as "Jesus Freaks." The San Francisco area for its part has seen a significant turn to Oriental religions. Buddhist communities have attracted many disillusioned with the materialism of Western values. The Hare Krishna youngsters are a more evangelistic example. Another type of response may be seen in the mystic cults which extend even to devil worship. Such have found a surprisingly large following among the displaced. In both Northern and Southern California, the encounter-group mystique, the drug culture, and other loosely organized manifestations of the search for alternative life styles have been sufficiently in evidence to prompt a rash of popular commentary. In a sense, Northern California and Southern California might be seen as two visions of the future, each with its lessons of development amid confusion. Each region has responded dramatically to massively induced social change. What may develop in the future is difficult to foresee.

Both the search for new patterns of social and political life and the attempt to recover the familiarities of older forms seem a natural consequence of increased leisure time newly available to individuals. We have developed an economy which has freed people from tight attachment to agriculture and factory labor. Indeed, *most* of our population is freed of those activities which over long hours sap physical and psychic energies, thus precluding for the citizenry both motivation and time for introspection and reflection on public matters. *But* the forms of response to this affluence in time and energy seem to be born more from *uncertainties* about the public order and personal relations than from an image promising an exciting, self-actualizing future within a social order that distributes its wealth in just fashion. California's response, echoed in many other parts of the United States, has been a search at two levels: a search for altered political ideologies and a search for new patterns of personal meaning. These searches have not had the optimistic undertone implicit in the views of many of the "stable post-industrialists." Instead, there has been much to suggest the slightly frantic tone of Toffler's notion of "future shock." Even the hopeful strivings of the various ethnic groups in California have this quality, and their search is characterized more by disillusion and bewilderment than by a sense of promise.

Our recognition of the disparity between these widespread negative-tinged reactions and the positive promise at least *potential* in the bounties of an advanced industrial society underlies our conception of Unstable Postindustria.

There is some evidence that in California political activism has become much less attractive and that the doctrines of neofundamentalist and mystical religious movements have increased their drawing power. But whatever the forms popular movements take, if they are followed by sufficiently large numbers of people, they will alter the political and social milieu within which technological development and government operate. It is likely that new forms of social organization will emerge—perhaps they are already emerging—that are not simply extrapolations of familiar forms. The dynamics of this process in the recent past and its probable extension into the near future are the focus for a series of research questions set forth below.

THE STUDY OF CALIFORNIA AS AN ADVANCED INDUSTRIAL SOCIETY

We believe that the Californian experience since, say, about 1940, can provide an apt setting for examining the more detailed dynamics of technological development and sociopolitical change. The series of relationships hypothesized in figures 2.1 and 2.8 is intended to be seen as a network of linkages tracing a sequential, chronological development and positing significant causal relationships. As such, they can be put to the test in the context of the Californian experience whether or not the experience proves to be a prototype of the future changes expected to occur in societies a bit slower in industrial and technical development. Whatever turns out to be the case for California, two levels of research problems confront us, one descriptive, the other analytic.

A much better description of the relationship between technological development and industrial-distributive-service development is needed in order that more finely detailed indicators may be developed. Without such indicators, hypotheses will be difficult to test. An important *initial hypothesis* is that as technological developments have become more complex and more sophisticated, the organizations associated with their development and with the consequent distribution of technical output have themselves become more complex internally and more interdependent with other organizations. Thus, the first order of business should be an exploration of the character of technological development and the patterns of stimulus/response shown by various industrial and service organizations. A *second* and related hypothesis asserts that, meanwhile, with some time lag for learning, the public's level of expectation about "normal" services begins to increase. In other words, a higher and higher level of service and rate of consumption becomes considered an allowable minimum.

A *third* hypothesis is one more in keeping with the conventional way of conceptualizing the postindustrial phenomenon with the connection made between the type of employment (and/or the type of employing organization) and the sort of values likely to be held by the employee. A much better understanding of the process by which divergent deeply held social values are shaped by *industrial* as opposed to *service* activity is necessary if we are to continue to use this gross occupation indicator with much confidence. Examination of these major hypotheses adds up in a sense to methodological research aimed at increasing the confidence we can place in the meaning of indicators which, on their face at least, seem rather indirect signs of the behavior under scrutiny. Such a project may be possible for the California case, though the outlines of the effort are not clear at present.

The relationship between those holding knowledge and their consequent participation in planning and advisory councils is also crucial for the whole postindustrial argument. A *fourth* hypothesis asserts that as the complexity of techno-organizational development increases, there is increasing need felt by institutional leaders to include those who have knowledge in determining the policies of industrial-governmental complexes. A corollary to this hypothesis is that the use of knowledge enables an improvement of complicated institutional relationships, sufficient for the system to continue operating without undue surprise or difficulty.

An expectation of stability and limited surprise, however, does not make much sense any longer for those of us who live in California; too many things seem out of control. But the effective coordination of the system with the assistance of a knowledge elite may well *have been* the case at some time in the recent past. The question becomes one of the *degree* to which knowledge-based policy has been closely related to stability. What were the characteristics of the situation and the state of knowledge and its use that prompted this alliance of knowledge-based coordination? When, if ever, did this condition begin? To what degree is it still the case? Has there been an erosion of expert effectiveness in institutional guidance? To what factors might such a decline in effectiveness, if not in participation, be attributed?

This line of research points straightaway to the second part of our schema—to the transition to "Unstable Postindustria" charted in figure 2.8. There are many indications that the promised improvements in the "quality of life" implicit in writings on postindustrialism have not been realized in California's society. There is widespread uncertainty and controversy about the role of government, the costs of public services have skyrocketed, systems of welfare run amuck, and medical programs do not function well. In one area of production and services after another, the system flounders. In short, the state does not strike people as nearly so attractive as it once did.

The series of relationships outlined in figure 2.8 might partially describe what is happening. A *fifth* hypothesis is that as the quality of knowledge about system dynamics declines, there is in fact an increasing number of policy failures; programs do not work anywhere nearly as well as the public has been led to believe they should. As a result, there is more investment in the planning function and at the same time there is a growing recognition of numerous social problems. Some way of testing this hypothesis may be worked out, though the problems of gathering data on such sensitive materials are bound to be considerable. Indirect indicators may have to fill the gap. Yet such a test is crucial to the argument. If the quality of cause-effect beliefs has not declined, and there is still erosion in public and private programs, another story is implied. On the other hand, the sense of program failure may not adequately reflect what has, in fact, happened; then some way of accounting for that perception is in order.

Our last observations involve the patterns of value and ideological changes apparently abroad in our society. The argument can be summarized in a *sixth*, summary hypothesis: that for citizens and consumers, simultaneous perceptions of increasing failure in government and private programs, of increasing social capacity to deal with public problems, and an increasing or constant expectation to consume products and services leads to feelings of uncertainty about their personal futures. Granted, such a relationship may not exist in fact; if it does not, then there can be no direct connection between perceptions of capacity, consumption, and social failure and political or personal malaise. But if it does, it must be explored and its affinity to the emergence of new political ideologies and to the significant increase in the number of people following alternative life styles established.

Let us say that all the relationships we have asserted about reality are so. Our task is not over; we have merely taken the descriptive steps. New obligations come forth. If our notions have merit, it is in their usefulness in *ordering* a series of relationships in sensible ways. But that feat does not *explain* what has been going on. Explanation must await a more searching series of studies, studies which can be put into perspective by our final set of questions:

What is it about technological development that prompts the increased organized complexity of social, economic, and political institutions?

What is it about the character of social science knowledge that prompts an erosion of quality in the face of such increased organized complexity?

What is it about the sense of uncertainty that results in an impulse to search out either a new political ideology or a new religious emphasis or orientation?

Finally, what *would* it be about an altered political or social milieu that would shape future technological development in ways different from those of the past when, unconstrained by social and political values, such development was seemingly driven by a simple faith in progress through technology?

NOTES

1. See, for example, Walton Bean, *California, An Interpretive History* (2nd ed.; New York: McGraw-Hill, 1973); David Lavender, *California: Land of New Beginnings* (New York: Harper & Row, 1972); Robert G. Cleland and G. S. Dumke, eds., *From Wilderness to Empire—A History of California* (New York: Knopf, 1959); Ralph J. Roske, *Everyman's Eden: A History of California* (New York: Macmillan, 1968); and Michael Rogin and John L. Shover, *Political Change in California: Critical Elections and Social Movements 1890-1966* (Westport, Conn.: Greenwood Press, 1970). For the more popular literature concerning recent events see, for example, John Brooks, *The Great Leap Forward—The Past Twenty-Five Years in America* (New York: Harper & Row, 1966); Michael Davie, *California, The Vanishing Dream* (New York: Dodd Mead, 1972); Curt Gentry, *The Last Days of the Late Great State of California* (New York: Putnam, 1968); Dennis Hale and Jonathan Eisen, eds., *The California Dream* (New York: Collier Books, 1968); and Carey McWilliams, ed., *The California Revolution* (New York: Grossman, 1968). See also Neil Morgan, *The Westward Tilt: The American West Today* (New York: Random House, 1963); Neal R. Pierce, *The Megastates of America* (New York: Norton, 1972); and Kevin Starr, *Americans and the California Dream* (New York: Oxford University Press, 1973).

2. From the perspective of comparative politics, California may be viewed as a society whose political system has a high degree of internal integration but is yet tightly bound to the society to its east through economic and political ties. Accordingly, the effects of exchange between the two societies can be examined, as well as can the impact of external influences upon California emanating from the East.

3. Particularly dramatic examples (and ones drawn from the extreme ends of our chronological spectrum) are (1) the "Bloody Thursday" confrontation on the San Francisco waterfront in 1934 between ILWU dockworkers and the National Guard, which triggered a general strike in the Bay Area; and (2) the frequent clashes in the late 1960s between antiwar demonstrators and city police, county law-enforcement personnel, and the militia.

4. We accept the term "postindustrial" with some uneasiness. It has come to mean many things to many people, and in a descriptive sense it discloses more ambiguities than it clarifies. We adapt it here in part heuristically—as an exercise—and in part metaphorically—as symbolic of the situations facing highly advanced industrial societies.

5. Limitations of space do not allow us to mention all those who have contributed to the concept of postindustrialism. Some of the seminal ideas were provided by Daniel Bell, "Notes on the Post-Industrial Society" *Public Interest* 1, nos. 6, 7 (Winter and Spring 1967); "The Measurement of Knowledge and Technology," in *Indicators of Social Change*, Eleanor Bernet Sheldon and Wilbert E. Moore, eds. (New York: Russell Sage Foundation, 1968); and *The Coming of Post-Industrial Society* (New York: Basic Books, 1973). See also Norman Birnbaum, *The Crisis of Industrial Society* (New York: Oxford University Press, 1969) and "Is There a Post-Industrial Revolution?" *Social Policy* 1, no. 2 (July/August 1970); Zbigniew Brzezinski, *Between Two Ages: America's Role in the Technetronic Age* (New York: Viking Press, 1970); Amitai Etzioni, *The Active Society* (New York: Free Press, 1968); Victor C. Ferkiss, *Technological Man* (New York: Braziller, 1969); Victor R. Fuchs, *The Service Economy* (New York: National Bureau of Economic Research, 1968); John Kenneth Galbraith, *The New Industrial State* (Boston: Houghton Mifflin, 1967); Bertram Gross, "Planning in an Era of Social Revolution" *Public Administration Review* 3 (May/June 1971): 259–97; Robert Heilbroner, *The Limits of American Capitalism* (New York: Harper & Row, 1965) and "Economic Problems of a 'Postindustrial' Society," *Dissent* (Spring 1973): 163–76; Ronald Inglehart, "The Silent Revolution in Europe" *APSR* 65, no. 4 (December 1971): 991–1017; Herman Kahn and Anthony J. Wiener, *The Year 2000* (New York: Macmillan, 1967); Sheldon and Moore, *Indicators of Social Change;* and Alain Touraine, *The Post-Industrial Society* (New York: Random House, 1971).

6. We are grateful to our colleague Martin Landau for discussing this vital point with us.

7. For an association of affluence with postscarcity values see Inglehart, "The Silent Revolution in Europe," pp. 991–1017. For an argument challenging the idea that new "social experiences and needs" are traceable to the disappearance of the old industrial work milieu, on grounds that the industrial milieu is not being appreciably reduced, see Heilbroner, "Economic Problems of a 'Postindustrial' Society," pp. 164–65.

8. Heilbroner adds transportation and utilities (usually grouped in the tertiary or service sector) and mining (usually grouped in the primary sector) to the secondary or manufacturing sector as well (ibid., p. 164). We note that Daniel Bell follows the same grouping of tertiary industries as we do here; see *The Coming of Post-Industrial Society.*

9. Whether the shift in employment has been neatly patterned after this scheme (i.e., from agriculture to manufacturing during the industrial revolution and from manufacturing to services during the "postindustrial revolution") or whether it has been one from agriculture to services and manufacturing is a debated matter. Heilbroner, "Economic Problems," and Kenneth Boulding, "Is Scarcity Dead?" *Public Interest* (Fall 1966), suggest that the shift has been from

agriculture to services. We present data in the following section which bears on this debate.

10. The literature is replete with discussions of the difficulties of measuring these indicators. Also, the problem of measuring productivity in the service industries is complicated by inflationary spirals and depletion of resources which ultimately militate against affluence and abundance. For a discussion which bears on this point, see Boulding (ibid.).

11. Thomas Kuhn, *The Structure of Scientific Revolutions* (Chicago: University of Chicago Press, 1964).

12. This conception of technology and organization builds on the assumption that technology must be embodied in social organization before the promise of the physical concept and machines of the technology can be realized. It also means that without widespread distribution of the technology little social change will result. Thus, it is not technical potential or theoretical capacity which makes a difference in a society's operation, but the combined action of new capabilities with the organizations to carry out technically based operations on the physical world in sufficient volume to alter experience for large numbers of people. For a full discussion of this point, see T. R. La Porte, "Technology as Source," in La Porte et al., *Interactions of Technology and Society—Impacts of Improved Airtransport: A Study of Airports at the Grass Roots* (Berkeley: Institute of Governmental Studies, University of California, Berkeley, Report to the National Aeronautics and Space Administration, December 1974), chap. 1.

13. As with other indicators used in this paper, increased productivity is, in a sense, a surrogate indicator. A more straightforward indication would be a careful charting of the actual degree and magnitude of technical innovation's active introduction into the work processes. But we are not blessed with such data and will have to settle for the less precise and the indirect data available from economic statistics. We are equally handicapped in measuring other aspects of postindustrial dynamics. To wit: A rough indicator of innovative efforts (and hence of general productivity) can be found in federal, state, and private sector expenditures for research and development. A review of relevant data shows that California compares favorably with the patterns for the whole United States both in the degree of increase and in the relative proportion of R&D efforts. See, for example, National Science Foundation, *Federal Funds for Research and Development and Other Scientific Activities*, Surveys of Science Resources Series NSF 72-317, vol. 21, p. 154 ff.; National Science Foundation, *Research and Development in State Government Agencies—Fiscal Years 1967-1968*, Survey of Science Resources, NSF 70-22, p. 62 ff.; National Science Foundation, *Research and Development in Industry, 1970*, Surveys of Science Resources Series NSF 72-309, pp. 50-51; and National Science Foundation, *Resources for Scientific Activities at Universities and Colleges, 1971*, Surveys of Science Resources Series, NSF 72-315, pp. 30-39; 43-51. See also Jay D. Starling, "Extra Incrementalism in Science Spending: Toward an Understanding of Exceptional Policy Outcomes" (University of California, Berkeley, Space Sciences Laboratory Internal Working Paper no. 115, May 1970). Preliminary investigation suggests that California commands a disproportionate share of the nation's research and development activities in all fields and on all counts (expenditures, professionals, etc.).

14. See Appendix for numerical tables supporting figures 2.3 and 2.4. Based on U.S. Census data, these categories could be constructed reliably from 1910 for the United States, from 1920 for California.

15. The term *"organized* complexity" as opposed to *un*organized complexity distinguishes the type of structural complexity based on relatively tight internal interdependence from that describing the complex interaction and behavior of atomic particles, voters, and buyers in a market system. The essential difference is in the degree of internal interdependence among individual com-

ponents. This distinction, originally advanced by Warren Weaver, "Science and Complexity," *American Scientist* 36 (1948), became the initial basis for a series of related studies in the effects of "organized social complexity"; see Todd La Porte, ed., *Organized Social Complexity: Challenge to Politics and Policy* (Princeton, N.J.: Princeton University Press, 1975).

16. There are no effective measures of interdependence at this time. Patterns of internal interdependence are most difficult to chart; adequate measures of this intuitively sensible phenomenon must await developments both in concept and statistics. See ibid., chaps. 1, 6, and 7.

17. See note 15.

18. See Galbraith, *New Industrial State*.

19. One early manifestation of this situation in California government was Governor Edmund Brown's attempt to enlist the aerospace industry in seeking solutions to social problems like welfare, waste disposal, and crime. See Ida Hoos, "Systems Analysis as a Technique for Solving Social Problems" (University of California Space Sciences Laboratory, Reprint no. 88, 1968).

20. For a more complete discussion of the emergence of the politics of psychic reassurance, see T. R. La Porte, "Complexity and Uncertainty: Challenge to Action," in La Porte, *Organized Social Complexity*, chap. 10.

21. *The Coming of Post-Industrial Society*.

22. La Porte, "Complexity and Uncertainty."

23. One of the more important factors for both the United States and California is the close economic and political bonds each has with other societies. In varying degrees each is only modestly in control of its own future.

APPENDIX
TECHNICAL NOTES AND STATISTICAL TABLES

TECHNICAL NOTES

FIGURE 2.2 Data for the United States 1966–72 are not readily available in "output per man-year" form; so, using the definition of output provided by *Long-Term Economic Growth*, Series A158 and A159 ("Output per Employee," p. 143), figures were derived by dividing the 1966 GNP in 1958 dollars by the total employment for 1966. The same procedure was used for 1967–72. The GNP in 1958 dollars for 1966–72 is from *Survey of Current Business*, October 1973, table A, "Alternative Measures of Constant Dollar GNP," p. 9. Employment figures were taken from *Statistical Abstract of the U.S., 1972*, p. 216.

FIGURE 2.5 Data on the proportion of employed with coordinative skills to total employed in the United States and California, 1940–70 are taken from U.S. Department of Commerce, Bureau of the Census publications as follows: For U.S. data, *Population 1970*, vol. 3, *The Labor Force*, pt. 1, table 58, pp. 75–76; *Census of the Population 1960*, vol. 1, pt. 1, table 202, pp. 1–528 and 1–529; *Detailed Characteristics*, U.S. Summary, pp. 725–27. For California data, *Population*, Third series, *The Labor Force*, table 2, pp. 25–27; *Census of Population 1960*, vol. 1, *California*, table 120, pp. 6–660 and 6–662; and *Detailed Characteristics, California*, sect. 1, table 171, pp. 1539–41.

Table A. Distribution Among Sectors of Employment in Industry for United States and California[a] 1910–70 (in percent)

		1910	1920	1930	1940	1950	1960	1970
Primary Sector Industries								
All categories	U.S.	34.98	28.90	23.97	21.03	14.11	7.74	4.53
	Cal.	00.00	19.67	14.98	12.90	8.41	5.09	3.58
	Cal. % U.S.	.84	2.54	3.20	3.37	4.00	5.87	7.73
Agriculture, forestry, fishing	U.S.	32.46	26.28	21.90	18.99	12.46	6.73	3.71
	Cal.		18.04	13.40	11.05	7.64	4.65	3.12
	Cal. % U.S.		2.55	3.12	3.20	4.24	6.16	8.23
Mineral extraction	U.S.	2.50	2.60	2.00	2.00	1.60	1.00	.82
	Cal.		1.63	1.58	1.85	.80	.50	.46
	Cal. % U.S.	2.42	2.27	4.04	4.99	3.26	3.97	5.45
Secondary Sector Industries								
Manufacturing and construction[b]	U.S.	27.90	30.80	28.90	28.31	32.10	33.00	31.88
	Cal.		28.60	25.45	22.99	27.22	30.42	26.98
	Cal. % U.S.	1.08	3.36	4.51	4.46	5.85	8.22	8.31
Tertiary Sector Industries								
All categories	U.S.	36.45	40.26	47.12	50.66	52.69	57.94	63.58
	Cal.	00.00	51.85	59.15	64.11	64.36	64.47	69.44
	Cal. % U.S.		4.68	6.43	7.02	8.53	9.89	10.81

Table A continued

Trade, transportation, communication	U.S.	21.00	25.10	28.60	26.87	29.98	29.29	31.86
utilities, clerical, finance	Cal.		30.86	35.55	35.14	35.17	30.70	34.09
insurance, real estate	Cal. % U.S.		4.46	6.37	7.18	8.12	9.32	10.46
Professional services	U.S.	4.50	5.20	6.70	7.50	8.51	11.70	18.47
	Cal.		7.69	9.41	8.75	9.70	12.70	20.08
	Cal. % U.S.		5.36	7.23	6.39	8.92	10.90	10.63
Public service/administration[c]	U.S.	1.10	1.80	1.80	3.10	4.50	5.00	5.49
	Cal.		3.01	2.42	3.81	6.30	5.90	6.49
	Cal. % U.S.		6.19	7.09	6.66	9.79	10.61	11.55
Domestic, personal, business, and	U.S.	9.80	8.10	10.10	11.52	9.36	9.29	7.75
repair services; entertainment,	Cal.		10.23	11.75	14.99	12.00	11.80	8.77
and recreation	Cal. % U.S.		4.58	5.94	7.15	8.92	10.15	11.07
Grand Total[d]	U.S.	100.01	99.88	100.00	98.29	98.51	96.01	99.98
	Cal.		100.06	99.48	98.58	98.83	96.67	99.98

[a] Data compiled from U.S. Department of Commerce, Bureau of the Census, *Census of Population* (Washington, D.C.: Government Printing Office, 1910–70). Percents do not add to 100% due to rounding. Data for California before 1920 are sketchy and not strictly comparable.
[b] Construction under 8% of secondary sector since 1940.
[c] Public administration as an employment category has been in use since 1940.
[d] Percentage discrepancies 1940–60 in grand total are due to industry-not-reported.

Table B. Distribution of Employment Among Major Industry Groups in the United States and California, 1910–70[a]

Industry Group	Region	1910	1920	1930	1940[b]	1950[b]	1960[b]	1970[c]
Agriculture, Forestry, Fishing	U.S.	12,388,309	10,936,026	10,722,467	8,559,134	7,033,591	4,349,884	2,840,488
	Cal.	88,197	272,947	334,968	273,488	298,119	267,760	233,850
Agriculture	U.S.[d]		10,665,812	10,471,988	8,449,463	6,908,647	4,256,734	
	Cal.[d]			332,024	265,871	286,642		
Forestry, fishing[e]	U.S.	241,806	270,214	250,469	109,671	124,944	93,150	
	Cal.			12,944	7,617	11,477		
Mineral Extractions	U.S.	965,169	1,090,223	984,323	918,853	930,968	654,006	630,788
	Cal.[d]	23,358	24,698	39,743	45,892	30,308	25,973	34,379
Manufacturing	U.S.	10,656,545	12,831,879	14,110,652	10,670,087	14,685,482	17,513,086	19,837,208
	Cal.[d]	115,296	430,631	636,564	415,721	763,680	1,391,166	1,614,687
Construction	U.S.				2,087,564	3,457,980	3,815,937	4,572,235
	Cal.				153,310	298,675	361,691	404,350
Trade[f]	U.S.	3,633,265	4,257,684	6,081,467	7,497,743	10,507,331	11,792,645	15,372,880
	Cal.		209,399	436,619	552,160	872,608	1,081,730	1,575,721
Transportation, Communication Utilities[g]	U.S.	2,665,269	3,096,829	3,843,147	3,143,227	4,449,861	4,458,147	5,186,101
	Cal.		124,848	199,228	198,221	318,913	393,804	533,119
Transportation, communication	U.S.				2,588,226	3,664,504	3,559,562	
	Cal.				156,393	254,300		
Clerical, Financial, Insurance[h]	U.S.	1,718,458	3,111,836	4,025,324	1,474,681	1,919,610	2,694,630	3,838,387
	Cal.		133,405	253,320	119,959	179,417	291,367	443,165
Professional Services[i]	U.S.	1,711,275	2,171,251	3,253,884	3,390,427	4,238,789	6,723,318	14,142,397
	Cal.		116,412	235,386	216,510	378,012	732,864	1,503,263
Public Service and Public Administration[j]	U.S.	431,442	738,525	856,205	1,415,283	2,514,469	3,202,890	4,201,652
	Cal.		45,579	60,741	94,298	246,230	339,826	485,453
Domestic and Personal Services	U.S.	3,755,798	3,379,995	4,952,451	3,903,884	3,464,991	3,858,494	3,536,576
	Cal.		154,841	294,075	237,522	263,043	326,688	339,314
Business and Repair Services	U.S.				883,313	1,307,669	1,610,728	2,394,487
	Cal.				69,778	130,260	197,717	317,389
Repair services	U.S.				636,974	949,543	849,298	
	Cal.				246,339	358,126	761,430	
	U.S.							

Table B continued

Entertainment and Recreation	U.S.			396,529	493,433	502,879
Services	Cal.			63,700	76,795	81,864
Industry Not Reported	U.S.			729,540	843,335	2,608,085
	Cal.			35,022	46,218	268,983
Grand Total All Occupations[k]	U.S.	38,167,366	41,614,248	48,829,920	45,070,315	56,435,273	64,639,247	76,553,599
	Cal.	1,512,760	2,500,644	2,475,581	3,902,278	5,761,433	7,484,690

[a] Further information on sources, methods of computation, and lacunae may be obtained from the authors.

[b] U.S. figures taken from summary in U.S. Department of Commerce, Bureau of the Census, *Census of Population* (Washington, D.C.: Government Printing Office, 1960), pt. 1, pp. 1–223.

[c] The most recent U.S. data are less reliable for comparative purposes, because of census category proliferation and collapse, than data of previous decades when categories remained more parallel from census to census. Neither U.S. nor California 1970 figures for Entertainment and Recreation are available from census sources.

[d] Number employed in Agriculture in California in 1910 categorized as "farmers" in 1910 California census data source. See U.S. Department of Commerce, Office of the Census, *Statistics for California 1910* (Washington, D.C.: Government Printing Office, 1914), p. 638. This source differentiates "farmers" from "wage earners," the category containing the figures shown here for Manufacturing and Mineral Extraction (Mining).

[e] California figures for 1960 and 1970 not entered because most up-to-date source available combines figures for Forestry, Fishing, and Agriculture. But see table A above for percent distribution.

[f] Calculations for the United States in this category for 1940, 1950, and 1960 based on 1960 census figures for a wide variety of wholesale and retail activities and outlets.

[g] U.S. figures for 1940, 1950, and 1960 calculated from 1960 U.S. census data. California figures for 1940 and 1950 from 1950 census data (17th Census), *Census of Population*, vol. 2, pt. 5, "California." U.S. and California figures for Transportation and Communication, 1970, not separable from overall total which includes Utilities.

[h] The 1960 U.S. census data, the source providing the U.S. figures for 1940, 1950, and 1960, also include Real Estate and other fields not counted here in their Clerical category.

[i] The 1960 U.S. census source distinguishes Professional Services as either "government" or "private." The present table combines those figures for this category, which for 1940 includes figures based on welfare, religious, and nonprofit organizations and for 1940, 1950, and 1960 on hospital and other related services.

[j] In the 1960 census data which provides the U.S. figures here for 1940, 1950, and 1960 Public Service figures are derived from number employed in public administration.

[k] Figures for 1940 and 1950 taken from California census data in the 17th Census of the U.S. (see note g), table 31: "Industry Group of Employed Persons by Sex for the State 1950 and 1940," pp. 5–70.

A detailed list of the 2a occupational categories considered to require coordinative skill is on file with the authors and available to interested readers. Occupations so designated were totaled and compared to the entire labor force including the military. Census data for 1940–70 are not strictly comparable because of major shifts and extensions of occupational categories occurring from census to census. For example, "accountants, auditors, bookkeepers" comprised a nonprofessional category in the 1940 census; but in the two subsequent censuses "accountants" were designated professionals while "auditors" and "bookkeepers" remained nonprofessional categories. Later changes in census categories make it difficult to determine for our purposes in what areas of "business administration," for example, coordinative skills are requisite. Figures in table 5 are to be taken as more-or-less accurate indicators of the correlation of coordinative skills to other skills throughout the labor force.

FIGURE 2.7 Data for the personal income per person for the United States and California 1966–72 were gathered from the *Statistical Abstract of the United States* as follows: 1966 figure from 1968 edition (no. 468, p. 322); 1967 and 1968 figures (the 1968 figure is termed preliminary) from 1969 edition (no. 469, p. 320); 1969 figure from the 1971 edition (no. 497, p. 314); and 1970–72 figures (preliminary for 1972) from the 1973 edition (no. 529, p. 326).

3

THE NATURE OF VALUE CHANGE IN POSTINDUSTRIAL SOCIETIES

RONALD INGLEHART

As many Western countries emerge into a postindustrial phase, the basic value priorities of their publics may be changing. Such changes could have a major impact on the kinds of issues that will be salient in politics; and to a certain extent, they will shape the policies adopted by the countries' political elites.

Are the value priorities of Western publics changing? As we shall see, the evidence suggests that they are. A still more complex question is, *How* are they changing: what kinds of goals are likely to be emphasized by Western publics in the postindustrial era?

A rather exceptional data base is available for our investigation. In 1970, and again in 1971, the European Community carried out public opinion surveys in France, West Germany, Belgium, the Netherlands, and Italy; comparable data are also available from Great Britain.[1] These surveys focused mainly on attitudes toward European integration, but they also included a series of questions designed to investigate intergenerational value change. We wanted to know which values an individual would rank highest when forced to choose between "Materialist" or security values, such as economic stability, and expressive or "Postmaterialist" values.[2] We hypothesized that those who had been socialized under conditions of peace and relative prosperity would be most likely to have Postmaterialist values.

Given this hypothesis, we should find substantial differences in the values held by various age groups. One of the most pervasive concepts in social science is the idea that people tend to retain a certain basic character, once it has been formed in childhood and youth, throughout adult life. If this is true, older European age groups should show value priorities that reflect the relatively insecure material conditions which prevailed during their formative years. On the other hand, since World War II virtually all the countries of Western Europe have experienced an unprecedented period of continuous economic growth. And they have all been free from invasion. We would expect, therefore, that younger groups—particularly those brought up since World War II—would be much less likely to have Materialist values.

It would be ridiculous to argue that *no* change in basic values occurs during adult life. Our point is simply that the likelihood of such change diminishes after one reaches adulthood, and probably continues to decline thereafter. To the extent that adult relearning takes place, it would tend to even out the differences among age groups. Moreover, we would not expect to find Postmaterialist values totally absent even among the oldest cohorts. At least a small stratum of economically and physically secure individuals have always given top priority to nonmaterial values. But this stratum should be smallest among the oldest cohorts, if values actually tend to reflect the conditions prevailing within a given society during a given cohort's pre-adult years.

By the same token, the distribution of these values preferences should vary cross-nationally in a predictable fashion. We would expect the amount of apparent value change across a given nation's age groups to reflect that nation's history during the lifetime of the people in the sample. Germany, for example, has undergone extreme changes in the conditions that prevailed during the pre-adult years of her respective age cohorts. Older Germans experienced famine and slaughter during World War I, followed by severe inflation and the Great Depression; devastation, invasion, and massive loss of life was their lot during World War II. Younger Germans have been brought up in relatively peaceful conditons in what is now the richest of the six European countries under study. If one's value type reflects one's formative experiences, relatively large value differences should be found between the older and younger German age cohorts—probably even larger than those between older and younger Frenchmen.

Great Britain represents the opposite extreme from Germany. The wealthiest country in Europe prior to World War II, she alone escaped invasion during the war—but has had a relatively stagnant economy ever since. For the last twenty-five years, the growth rate of the other five countries has been about twice as great at Britain's. One after another, they have moved ahead of Britain in gross national product per capita, with the result that by 1970 Britain ranked fifth among our six European countries in per capita wealth. We would expect to find a relatively small amount of value change in Britain.

In order to test each of these predictions, we must be able to measure the priority an individual gives to various politically relevant goals. A set of items in the 1970 survey seems to provide a reasonably accurate indicator of such value priorities. Representative national samples of the population over fifteen years of age in Great Britain, Germany, Belgium, the Netherlands, France, and Italy were asked the question:

> If you had to choose among the following things, which are the *two* that seem most desirable to you?
> Maintaining order in the nation
> Giving the people more say in important political decisions
> Fighting rising prices
> Protecting freedom of speech

Two choices were permitted; thus, aside from nonresponse, it was possible for a respondent to select any of six possible pairs of items.

Before we examine the way different age groups respond to these items, we need to know whether they tap an underlying dimension which is so pervasive that it might be said to reflect basic values. We also want to know the *meaning* of this dimension, exploring in some detail the attitudes linked with it. But first of all, we must examine the structure of the four items themselves.

Choice of the first of these four items ("order") presumably reflects a concern with physical safety; choice of the third item ("prices") presumably reflects a high priority for economic stability. We expected that people who chose one of these items would be likely to choose the other item also. We would expect this because economic insecurity and physical insecurity tend to go together. If a country is invaded, for example, there is likely to be both economic dislocation and loss of life. Conversely, economic decline may be associated with severe and protracted domestic disorder, as was the case in Weimar Germany.

Emphasis on order and economic stability might be described as a Materialist set of value priorities. By contrast, choice of the "free speech" and "political participation" items reflects emphasis on Postmaterialist values. These items we expected, would also tend to go together. On the basis of the choices made among these four items, therefore, we might classify our respondents into six value-priority types, ranging from a pure Materialist type to a pure Postmaterialist type, with four mixed categories in between.

We do *not* view the Postmaterialist type as necessarily placing a negative value on order and economic stability, or the Materialist type as being opposed to political participation and free speech. On the contrary, other evidence from the 1970 surveys indicates that most respondents consider all four goals desirable. Indeed, the Postmaterialist type tends to have a higher standard of living and higher economic expectations than the Materialist—but the Postmaterialist tends to assume that he will get what he wants, materially. Consequently, he worries more about other things.

It is not a question of valuing one thing positively and the other negatively. But in politics it is sometimes impossible to maximize one good without detriment to another; frequently, this is where the real crunch comes. In such cases the relative *priority* one gives to valued objects becomes a vital consideration. For this reason, our questions were asked in forced-choice format, where the respondent has to decide which goals get chosen above others.

Our hypothesis that the older age cohorts would be more likely to choose Materialist values can be explained quite simply: People tend to place a high value on whatever needs are in short supply. This concept is similar to that of marginal utility of the consumer in economic theory. Moreover, they tend to retain a given value orientation throughout adult life, once it has been established in pre-adult years.

If we wish to go beyond this simple explanatory scheme, the work of Abraham Maslow is particularly suggestive. Maslow argues that people act to fulfill a number of different needs, which are pursued in a hierarchical order according to their relative urgency for survival.[3] Top priority is given to the satisfaction of physiological needs as long as they are in short supply. The need for physical safety comes next; its priority is almost as high as that of sustenance needs, but a hungry man will risk his life to get food. Once an individual has attained physical and economic security, he may begin to pursue other, nonmaterial goals. These other goals reflect genuine and normal needs—although people deprived of sustenance or safety needs may fail to give them attention. When at least minimal economic and physical security are present, the needs for love, belonging, and esteem become increasingly important; later, a set of goals related to intellectual and aesthetic satisfaction looms large. There seems to be no clear hierarchy within this last set of needs (which have been called "growth needs," "being needs," or "self-actualization needs"). But evidence suggests that they became most salient only after an individual has satisfied the material needs and belonging needs.[4]

Our analysis does not depend on the correctness or falsity of the entire Maslovian theory; the simpler, nonhierarchical conceptual framework will do. But Maslow's theory is interesting because it generates a set of expectations about the direction in which values may be changing in postindustrial society.

More immediately, Maslow's work suggests that responses to the four value-priority items described above should fall along a single dimension corresponding to the need hierarchy. As an indicator of concern with economic needs, the "rising prices" item would be at the base of the hierarchy. "Order" (an indicator of the safety needs) would come next, followed by "political participation" and "free speech" (which are assumed to be linked with needs for belonging and self-expression). If we had a perfectly unidimensional hierarchy, *all* of those who made "rising prices" their first choice would choose "order" as their second choice. Conversely, everyone who chose "free speech" in first place would select "political participation" in second place. Needless to say, in the real world, survey data rarely if ever fit so simple a pattern.

Our four items are only rough indicators of Maslow's concepts. Moreover, we attach considerable importance to World War II as a watershed event which may have linked relative economic and physical security rather closely for many West Europeans. Consequently, we anticipate that the two Materialist choices will be rather closely related to each other, but will be separated from the two other items by a relatively broad Postmaterialist threshold that only the postwar age groups are likely to have crossed.

Do people actually choose among our four items as if they were located along this dimension? The data give a fair approximation of this pattern. Among the people surveyed in our six West European countries, those whose first choice is "rising prices" are at least twice as likely to make "order" their second choice as are the other respondents. Conversely, the two "expressive" items are relatively close together; those whose first choice is "free speech" are about twice as likely to choose "political participation" in second place as are the other respondents.

This set of items was administered to national samples in six countries in 1970, and was used again in five of these countries in the European Community's 1971 survey.[5] The results of these eleven surveys are summarized in table 3.1. Virtually all the correlations shown are negative; since once a given item has been chosen, there is only one chance in three that any particular other item can be chosen. The correlation coefficients for each of the six possible pairs of items give an indication of how far apart any two items are: the lower the negative correlation, the more likely two items are to be chosen together.[6] If the choices among these items were made purely at random, all the entries in table 3.1 would be −.333; that is, all four items would be equally distant.

Since there are six pairs of choices among the four items, each survey produces a matrix of six correlations. The pattern is remarkably

Table 3.1.   Correlations among Items in Materialist/Postmaterialist Index, 1970 and 1971

Results of 1970 Surveys:

	Germany			Italy		
	Order	Partic.	Prices	Order	Partic.	Prices
Order						
Participation	−.513			−.403		
Prices	+.030	−.539		−.017	−.379	
Free Speech	−.520	+.022	−.466	−.432	−.021	−.402

	Netherlands			France		
	Order	Partic.	Prices	Order	Partic.	Prices
Order						
Participation	−.531			−.443		
Prices	−.050	−.384		−.094	−.390	
Free Speech	−.414	−.031	−.528	−.484	−.010	−.510

	Belgium			Britain		
	Order	Partic.	Prices	Order	Partic.	Prices
Participation	−.432			−.537		
Prices	−.091	−.426		−.144	−.265	
Free Speech	−.509	−.017	−.462	−.324	−.190	−.439

consistent across the eleven surveys. In every case, the correlation between the two Materialist items is far above the −.333 value generated by random answering; in most instances, it is near zero. The same is true of the correlations between the two Postmaterialist items in each of the eleven surveys. The four "mixed" pairs, by contrast, tend to have negative correlations that are stronger than the random-answering level; that is, they are relatively *unlikely* to be chosen together. Consequently, about half of each national sample fell into one of the two polar types, with the other half distributed among the four "mixed" types. If we map the distances between these items, they fit readily into two dimensions, producing a long, narrow configuration not unlike the one-dimensional model suggested by Maslow's work. If people were responding to these items at random, we would get a three-dimensional pyramid, with the four items roughly equidistant at the apexes.

Various other sets of four items, in similar forced-choice format, were included in the 1970 and 1971 surveys. In no case did the internal structure of the other sets of items approach the clarity shown in table 3.1. The degree of constraint found among these items is unusually strong for survey data.[7] More remarkable is the fact that this pattern

Results of 1971 Surveys:

	Germany			Italy		
	Order	Partic.	Prices	Order	Partic.	Prices
Participation	−.522			−.535		
Prices	−.041	−.437		−.048	−.417	
Free Speech	−.467	−.048	−.485	−.471	−.071	−.452

	Netherlands			France		
	Order	Partic.	Prices	Order	Partic.	Prices
Participation	−.535			−.434		
Prices	−.164	−.342		−.011	−.509	
Free Speech	−.342	−.164	−.450	−.596	−.010	−.436

	Belgium			Mean, 11 Surveys		
	Order	Partic.	Prices	Order	Partic.	Prices
Participation	−.464			−.498		
Prices	−.077	−.418		−.064	−.408	
Free Speech	−.475	−.120	−.437	−.458	−.060	−.459

persists across eleven surveys carried out at two points in time, in six different countries.

It seems justifiable to group our respondents into Materialist, Postmaterialist, and "mixed" types, for further analysis. I hypothesize that these categories reflect the value priorities of given individuals. But do they? By one definition, "values differ *operationally* from attitudes only in being fewer in number, more general, central and pervasive, less situation-bound, more resistant to modification and perhaps tied to developmentally more primitive or dramatic experiences."[8] If these items do indeed tap *values*, they should enable us to predict a much larger number of more specific attitudes. And, as we have argued, the value types of given age cohorts should tend to persist over time, reflecting the fact that they are tied to important early experiences.

Let us examine the former question first. Do the Materialist/Postmaterialist value categories reflect a central aspect of the individual's outlook on life, with pervasive ramifications among his political attitudes? Yes, quite impressively. Our value typology seems to constitute a sensitive indicator of a broad range of political preferences, some of which have a fairly straightforward relationship to the face content of the four items on which our typology is based, and some of which seem completely unrelated.

For example, on the basis of an individual's value type, one can make a pretty accurate prediction of his response to the following item from our 1970 surveys:

Within the last couple of years, there have been large-scale student demonstrations in (Britain) and other countries. In general, how do you view these? Are you

Very favorable
Rather favorable
Rather unfavorable
Very unfavorable

Table 3.2 shows the respective levels of support for student demonstrations in each of the six countries. While the majority in each country is unfavorable, there is a wide variation in support levels according to value type; a mean difference of fully 55 percentage points separates the Materialist and Postmaterialist respondents. In every country, those who choose the Postmaterialist pair are the most favorable to student demonstrations. Overall, they are more than four times as likely to favor the demonstrations as are the Materialist respondents. With only one exception among the six value types in six countries, respondents choosing the Materialist value pair are *least* favorable to the student demonstrations (in the one exceptional case, the Materialist respondents are within 3 percentage points of the least favorable group).

These value types also show significant relationships with numerous other attitudes that have no apparent similarity in face content. For example, they serve as good predictors of attitudes toward supranational European integration; this goal was supported by 30 percent of the Materialist and 61 percent of the Postmaterialists.

Similarly, in each country, the Materialists were far more likely to give high priority to having a strong army than either the Postmaterialist or mixed types; in each country, the Postmaterialists were more likely to give a high priority to economic aid to less-developed countries; and, the Materialists consistently gave a higher priority to national prestige. For each of these items, there is a mean difference of about 25 percentage points between the Materialists and Postmaterialists—with the mixed groups falling between the two theoretical polar types. Marked differences were found in connection with various other attitudes. For example, the Postmaterialists in each country showed more concern for women's rights than did the Materialists; in the five 1971 surveys as a whole, 49 percent of the Postmaterialists chose this goal, as compared with 29 percent of the Materialists.

Table 3.2. **Attitude Toward Student Demonstrations, By Value Pairs Chosen**
(Percentage Favorable to Student Demonstrations)

Nation	Order and Prices (Materialist)	Order and Free Speech	Order and Participation	Prices and Free Speech	Prices and Participation	Free Speech and Participation (Postmaterialist)	Overall
Netherlands	21	33	42	37	47	70	39
Italy	19	29	36	42	54	77	36
Belgium	18	29	36	32	60	65	35
Germany	14	35	29	35	46	83	32
France	12	18	23	38	41	66	27
Britain	12	22	9	22	60	65	17
Mean	16	28	29	35	51	71	

The foregoing figures give only a sampling of the variety of attitudes that show significant and cross-nationally consistent relationships with the Materialist/Postmaterialist value types.

The correlations between value type and attitudes were generally strongest among the German respondents and weakest among the British; the other four countries fall between these extremes. This suggests that the world view of the German public tends to polarize on a Materialist/Postmaterialist basis to a greater extent than that of the British and other publics.[9] Probably more than any other country in our sample, Germany has experienced cataclysmic change during the last several decades. As a consequence of these changes, many ideas that were accepted by earlier generations are rejected today. Britain, of course, has undergone change also, but at a somewhat slower pace. The British public has not been confronted with cultural change in such a dramatic form; the German public has been *forced* to think about these issues. These cross-national differences may reflect differences in the extent to which two distinct subcultures have confronted one another.

There are differences in the amount of constraint among responses of the various nationalities. But the basic configuration of the items is strikingly similar in all six countries. In dimensional analysis, various attitudes tend to fall into two distinct clusters, one linked with Materialist goals and the other with Postmaterialist goals. As we shall see, the value types also show some rather striking relationships with social structure and political party preference. This highly structured pattern would scarcely emerge from random or superficial responses. The Materialist/Postmaterialist index seems to tap a central and pervasive aspect of the individual's outlook on life. I believe it provides an indicator of certain basic value priorities.

But it is only a rough indicator. Based on an extremely parsimonious ranking of four basic goals, it can be regarded only as a first step toward developing more broadly based multi-item indicators of relevant values. The four items provide a better measure than a single item. And a large battery of properly designed questions should provide a more accurate measure than our present simple tool.

Imperfect though it may be, we seem to have an indicator that taps a wide range of preferences related to the Materialist/Postmaterialist theme. We are in a position to test our hypotheses concerning value change. Our first prediction was that the old would be more likely to have Materialist value priorities than the young; conversely, the Postmaterialist type should be more prevalent among the young. Table 3.3 shows the distribution of value types by age group in each of the six European countries.[10] To simplify a complex table, only the two polar types are shown: the column headed "Mat" gives the percentage of Materialists and the column headed "P-M" the percentage which is Post-

Table 3.3. Value Types by Age Cohort: Combined 1970 and 1971 Data
(Percentages Materialist and Postmaterialist)

Age Range of Cohort in 1971	Germany			Belgium			Italy			France			Netherlands			Britain [a]		
	Mat	P-M	N	Mat	P-M	N	Mat	P-M	N	Mat	P-M	N	Mat	P-M	N	Mat	P-M	N
16–25	22	22	(544)	20	26	(487)	28	21	(757)	25	20	(754)	26	20	(770)	29	13	(508)
26–35	36	14	(895)	29	16	(429)	37	13	(650)	38	13	(726)	25	14	(696)	28	10	(680)
36–45	47	9	(768)	29	16	(473)	39	9	(735)	40	12	(697)	38	11	(717)	31	8	(556)
46–55	47	7	(663)	30	11	(378)	46	6	(710)	43	10	(649)	34	12	(547)	35	6	(796)
56–65	58	4	(593)	36	9	(409)	48	6	(571)	50	5	(533)	39	7	(455)	41	6	(662)
66+	55	4	(474)	46	5	(474)	55	3	(400)	52	3	(700)	45	5	(324)	47	4	(748)
Difference between youngest and oldest groups	-33	+18		-26	+21		-27	+18		-27	+17		-19	+15		-18	+9	
Total point difference	51			47			45			44			34			27		

[a] Results from a survey carried out in 1971 by the British Social Science Research Council are combined with those from our own British sample in this table.

materialist within each age group (if one wishes to know the percentage falling into the mixed types, one can simply add the figures for the two polar types and subtract from 100).

The general relationship between age and value type clearly bears out our expectations. In France, for example, there is an immense preponderance of Materialists over Postmaterialists among the oldest age group: 52 percent are Materialists and a bare 3 percent are Postmaterialist. As we move up the columns—following the historical sequence of the respective age cohorts—the percentage of Postmaterialist types increases. When we reach the youngest cohort (those who were 16 to 24 years old in 1971) the two types are almost equally numerous: 25 percent are Materialist and 20 percent Postmaterialist. Our interpretation that France's 1968 crisis was linked with intergenerational value change may well be true.

But the phenomenon does not apply to France alone; the same general pattern appears in each of the other five countries. In every case, the Materialists greatly outnumber the Postmaterialists among the older age cohorts; but the balance shifts in favor of the Postmaterialists as we move to the younger cohorts.

This pattern could reflect historical change, as we hypothesized, or it could be a life-cycle effect. Conceivably, the young might tend to be relatively Postmaterialist simply *because* they are young; free from responsibilities, rebellious or idealistic; when they become older, they will have the same preferences as the older groups. We must not ignore this possibility. The only way to be absolutely certain that long-term value change is taking place would be to measure a population's values, wait ten or twenty years, and then measure them again. Such data are rare. In the meantime, however, certain indirect tests can give us a clearer sense of whether these striking age-group differences reflect intergenerational change or life-cycle effects.

The hypothesis that links expected age-group patterns with the historical experience of a given country points to a revealing test. There seems to be no particular reason why one would expect the life cycle of Englishmen, for example, to differ greatly from that of Germans or Frenchmen. But the economic and political history of these countries *does* differ in important respects. If the age-group differences in a given country correspond to changes in the conditions prevailing during a given generation's formative years, we would seem to be on relatively firm ground in attributing these differences to historical change rather than life-cycle effects.

Our expectations were that the British public would show a relatively small amount of value change: Britain alone among these countries escaped invasion in World War II; and she was comparatively wealthy prior to World War II but subsequently has had an economic growth rate about half as large as that of the other five countries. In respect to both physical and economic security, change has been less pronounced in Britain. The difference between the formative conditions of younger and older groups has been greater in *all* the continental countries, but one might expect Germany to show a particularly large amount of value change. The contrast between conditions prevailing in 1930 and 1970—or between 1945 and 1970—is especially dramatic in the German case.

The figures at the bottom of table 3.3 sum up the differences in distributions of value types for the six respective countries. Britain stands out clearly as the country in which the smallest amount of apparent value change has taken place. The difference between the youngest and the oldest British cohorts totals 27 percentage points across the two value types. The amount of apparent change across the German age cohorts is nearly twice this size: a total of 52 percentage points. The other four countries fall between these two extremes, most of them being closer to the German pattern than to the British pattern. Our index of value change is based on the sum of four different cells in the tabulation of value type by age group; we must allow a large margin for sampling error which might accumulate as we construct our index. But the spread between Britain (on one hand) and Germany, Italy, Belgium, and France (on the other) is so great that we can safely conclude that it reflects a real difference in the populations being sampled. The amount of change in value types across a given country's age cohorts *does* seem to correspond to the amount of economic and political change that country has experienced. This suggests that the pattern in table 3.3 might be attributed to the impact of historical events, rather than life-cycle effects. If this is true, our value types seem highly resistant to modification during the lifetime of an individual; the distinctive responses of a given age cohort may reflect experiences of a generation or more ago.

In 1972 and 1973, a number of additional surveys were carried out. As a result, data are available from several more countries, which permit further exploration of value change. Our new cases include Denmark, Ireland, Switzerland, and the United States.[11] The modern history of these countries has distinctive features which give rise to certain expectations about the amount of value change we might find across age cohorts.

In our 1970–71 data, Germany, Belgium, Italy, and France showed a relatively larger amount of value change across age groups; Britain showed relatively little. We now have four countries that should, logically, make up an intermediate group: Switzerland, Denmark, the Netherlands, and Ireland. We might expect them to occupy an intermediate position for the following reasons:

Table 3.4. Value Type by Age Cohort in Eleven Countries, 1972–73[a]
(Original 4-item index, tabulated by age cohorts used in 1970 survey)

Ages	Germany Mat	Germany P-M	France Mat	France P-M	Italy Mat	Italy P-M	Belgium Mat	Belgium P-M	Ireland Mat	Ireland P-M
19–28	24	19	22	20	26	16	18	23	24	13
29–38	39	8	28	17	41	8	20	17	31	9
39–48	46	5	39	9	42	7	22	10	41	6
48–58	50	5	39	8	48	6	25	10	37	6
59–68	52	7	50	3	49	4	39	3	45	2
69+	62	1	55	2	57	5	39	5	51	4
Total point spread across cohorts	56		51		42		39		36	

[a]Swiss data are from 1972; U.S. data are combined results of surveys in May 1972, November–December 1972, and March–April 1973.

[b]Because of the small size of the Luxembourg sample, it is broken down into only three age groups (15–38, 39–58, and 59+).

1. The oldest cohort has experienced less of the devastation of World Wars I and II than the German, French, Belgian, and Italian publics. Switzerland was neutral in both world wars; Denmark and the Netherlands were neutral in World War I; Ireland was neutral in World War II. In varying degrees, this should place them near the British end of the spectrum, showing relatively little value change.

2. In the period following World War II, these four countries have had "intermediate" rates of economic growth—well below the German, French, and Italian rates, but appreciably above the British rates. Insofar as economic change influences rates of value change, this would tend to rank them above the British but below the Germans, Italians, and French.

Recent American history is similar to that of Great Britain in some respects. Like Britain (only more so), the United States had the advantages of geographic isolation and escaped invasion and devastation during the world wars. But more recently, she has experienced relatively great foreign and domestic conflict. Until 1973, she was at war in Vietnam. The war, together with racial problems, have contributed to domestic turbulence. Moreover, crime rates in the United States are far higher than those of Western Europe. During the formative years of the older

Neth.		Denmark		Switz		Lux.[b]		U.S.		Britain	
Mat	P-M	Mat	P-M	Mat	P-M	Mat	P-M	Mat	P-M	Mat	P-M
27	14	33	11	27	15	26	19	24	17	27	11
22	17	34	9	26	17			27	13	33	7
28	9	47	4	30	15	40	7	34	13	29	6
40	10	44	5	35	9			32	10	30	7
41	12	48	4	34	6	44	8	37	6	36	5
51	5	58	2	50	6			40	7	37	4
35		34		32		29		26		17	

cohorts, America was a haven of relative tranquility compared with most of Europe; today the positions seem to be reversed. In regard to physical security, there has been less difference between the formative experiences of America's older and younger cohorts—which should be reflected in a relatively small amount of value change across age groups, as compared with Europe.

The United States resembles Britain in another way: she was relatively wealthy at the turn of the century, ranking far ahead of the other countries in our sample. Like Britain (only less so), America's postwar economic progress has been slower than that of other Western nations. In sum, one might expect the American population to show less change across age groups than any of the European populations except, perhaps, the British or Swiss.

The data conform to these expectations. Table 3.4 shows the distribution of the two "pure" value types in each of the eleven countries surveyed in 1972 and 1973.[12] The American sample shows less value change than any country except Britain. While the *oldest* American cohort has a higher proportion of Postmaterialists than any European nation, the youngest American cohort ranks below the corresponding group in three countries (Belgium, France, and Germany). Recent conditions may have retarded value change on the American scene.

Table 3.5. Amount of Value Change Across Age Cohorts: 1970–71 vs. 1973

	1970–71			1973	
Rank	Country	Point Spread Across Cohorts	Rank	Country	Point Spread Across Cohorts
1	Germany	51	1	Germany	56
2	Belgium	47	2	France	51
3	Italy	45	3	Italy	42
4	France	44	4	Belgium	39
5	Netherlands	34	5	Netherlands	35
6	Britain	27	6	Britain	17

In apparent value change, the Irish, Dutch, Danish, and Swiss form an intermediate group—as we anticipated. And the Germans are at the high end of the scale, with the British at the opposite end, as was the case in 1970–71. If we compare relative amounts of value change in the six countries surveyed in both the earlier and later periods, we find a remarkable stability of relative positions. As table 3.5 indicates, four of the six countries have identical ranks at both points in time. The two exceptions are Belgium and France. In 1970–71, Belgium, Italy, and France all were clustered within 3 percentage points of each other; in 1973, Belgium and France exchanged positions, with Italy retaining third place.

Our four-item index seems to provide a surprisingly good measure of something pervasive and enduring in one's outlook. But we must not overlook this index's shortcomings. Probably its most serious weakness is the simple fact that it is based on only four items. Consequently, it may be excessively sensitive to short-term forces. For example, one item concerns rising prices. Western countries have experienced extraordinary inflation in the past few years. It seems more than likely that the proportion of respondents giving high priority to "fighting rising prices" would go up, not as the result of any fundamental value change, but simply because this is a serious current problem. This type of instability would probably be greater if we simply asked the respondents to rate the importance of rising prices by itself; in the index we use, one's choice of this item is constrained by the fact that it must be ranked against *other* desired goals. Nearly everyone would probably acknowledge that rising prices were a more serious problem in 1973 than in 1970; by no means all of those who ranked "free speech" above "rising prices" in 1970 would be willing to change this ranking in 1973. As noted, four items provide a better measure than one—but a more broadly based index would spread the risk over a still larger number of items, making it less likely that an individual's score would be unduly distorted by any particular recent event. Furthermore, it may help reduce the amount of error in our measurement—something that is always a major problem in survey research. In reply to any given question a substantial number of respondents in a mass survey are likely to give superficial answers, more or less at random or "off the top of their heads." With a single item, it is difficult to separate out those whose answers reflect a genuine attitude from those whose response is essentially meaningless. But a set of consistent responses to a large series of related questions probably *does* reflect a genuine underlying preference.

In our 1973 surveys, we attempted to develop a broader indicator of an individual's value priorities. Analysis of the results should not only give us a more reliable measure of whether value change is taking place, but a more detailed knowledge of the respective world views of the Materialist and Postmaterialist types.

The questions asked about value priorities in these more recent surveys included the four items from the original index but went beyond them—including eight additional goals. The questions asked were as follows:

"There is a lot of talk these days about what the aims of this country should be for the next ten years. (*Hand respondent Card A.*) On this card are listed some of the goals which different people would give top priority. Would you please say which *one* of these you, yourself, consider most important?"

CARD A

A. Maintaining a high rate of economic growth

B. Making sure that this country has strong defense forces

C. Seeing that the people have more say in how things get decided at work and in their communities

D. Trying to make our cities and countryside more beautiful

"And which would be the next most important? (*Hand respondent Card B.*) If you had to choose, which one of the things on this card would you say is most desirable?"

CARD B

E. Maintaining order in the nation

F. Giving the people more say in important government decisions

G. Fighting rising prices

H. Protecting freedom of speech

"And what would be your second choice? Here is another list. (*Hand respondent Card C.*) In your opinion, which one of these is most important?"

CARD C

I. Maintain a stable economy

J. Progress toward a less impersonal, more humane society

K. The fight against crime

L. Progress toward a society where ideas are more important than money

"What comes next?

"Now would you look again at all the goals listed on these three cards together and tell me which one you consider the *most* desirable of all? Just read off the one you choose.

"And which is the next most desirable?

"And which one of all the aims on these cards is *least* important from your point of view?"

This series of questions enabled us to obtain relative rankings for twelve important goals. These items were designed to permit a fuller exploration of Maslow's need hierarchy; figure 3.1 indicates the basic need which each item was intended to tap. The four items from the original index appear in capital letters. Six of the items were intended to tap emphasis on the physiological or Materialist needs: "rising prices," "economic growth," and "stable economy" being aimed at sustenance needs and "maintain order," "fight crime," and "strong defense forces" being aimed at safety needs. The remaining six items were intended to tap various Postmaterialist needs.[13] We view the latter needs as genuine and potentially universal: every human being has a need for esteem, a certain inherent intellectual curiosity, and a need for aesthetic satisfaction; he or she will act on these needs unless circumstances force him to stifle them. Put another way, "Man does not live by bread alone"— particularly when he has enough bread. Our expectation, therefore, is that emphasis on the six Materialist items will tend to form another distinct cluster. A still more specific—and far more demanding—expectation would be that the three sustenance items would tend to cluster at one

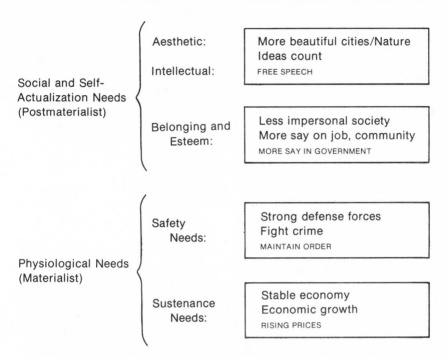

Figure 3.1. Items Used in 1973 Surveys and Needs They Were Intended to Tap.

end of a single dimension, followed by the safety items, with the "belonging" items next and the "aesthetic" and "intellectual" items at the opposite end of the continuum.

In order to test the former hypothesis, we performed conventional factor analyses of the rankings of these goals in each of the ten countries.[14] The loadings on the first factor in each country are shown in table 3.6.

The results show a cross-national consistency that is simply breathtaking. In each case, five items—the *same* five items in every country—cluster near the positive end of the continuum. Six items—again, the *same* six in every country—cluster near the negative pole. The remaining item falls near the midpoint.

The items that cluster toward the negative pole are the six Materialist items. And five of the six Postmaterialist items fall into the opposite cluster. A single item—"more beautiful cities" ("protect nature from pollution" in the American sample)—does not fit into either cluster (although in the American sample it comes close). For eleven of the twelve items, the polarities are perfectly consistent cross-nationally; the item intended to tap aesthetic needs, however, not only fails to fit into the Postmaterialist cluster, but has a slight negative polarity in three

Table 3.6. The Materialist/Postmaterialist Factor in Ten Countries
(Loadings of value-priorities items on first factor)

Goal	France [a] (23%)	Ger. (22%)	U.S. (20%)	Belg. (20%)	Lux. (20%)	Den. (20%)	Italy (20%)	Neth. (19%)	Brit. (18%)	Ire. (17%)
More say on job	.636	.562	.451	.472	.659	.604	.599	.568	.611	.636
Less impersonal society	.592	.675	.627	.532	.558	.566	.553	.451	.498	.393
Ideas count	.499	.498	.508	.562	.476	.577	.577	.539	.482	.453
More say in government	.400	.483	.423	.478	.434	.464	.566	.514	.506	.572
Free speech	.486	.575	.409	.564	.527	.330	.499	.338	.210	.401
More beautiful cities	.087	.092	.278	.040	-.089	.181	-.100	.141	.197	-.073
Fight rising prices	-.305	-.440	-.334	-.511	-.342	-.154	-.386	-.306	-.238	-.395
Strong defense forces	-.498	-.359	-.464	-.324	-.322	-.366	-.326	-.414	-.295	-.375
Economic growth	-.412	-.398	-.397	-.297	-.497	-.517	-.245	-.442	-.536	-.152
Fight crime	-.457	-.418	-.484	-.417	-.347	-.387	-.490	-.405	-.233	-.465
Stable economy	-.441	-.451	-.435	-.407	-.345	-.523	-.322	-.410	-.574	-.202
Maintain order	-.558	-.376	-.491	-.497	-.488	-.440	-.462	-.549	-.346	-.459

[a] Percentage of total variance explained by first factor for each national sample appears in parentheses.

cases, Italy, Ireland, and Luxembourg. This one item clearly does not behave according to our expectations—a fact we must explore in more detail. But the other eleven items live up to expectations to an almost uncanny degree. The consistency of responses to these items cannot be attributed to such common sources of spurious correlation as response set; the items were asked in a "cafeteria-style" format, which gives no cues to the "right" answer and does not set up a pattern where the respondent agrees or disagrees with a whole series of similarly worded items. The respondent had to select each item from a mixed pool of possibilities, on the basis of the given item's content.

Eleven of the twelve items fall into two separate clusters, reflecting Materialist and Postmaterialist priorities respectively, as indicated in figure 3.1. Figure 3.2 maps the relative position of each item on the Materialist/Postmaterialist dimension in the ten countries as a whole. The results are mixed. Within the Materialist cluster, the loadings of "sustenance" and "safety" items are interspersed; "belonging" and "self-actualization" items are similarly interspersed within the Postmaterialist cluster. But factor analysis does not tell us anything about the absolute distribution of preferences. In a moment we will examine the extent to which choice of these items as hierarchical (or scalar) as predicted by Maslovian theory. The present analysis does make it clear that the Materialist items tend to be chosen together—and that those who choose them are unlikely to choose the Postmaterialist items. But there is one exception: the item designed to tap aesthetic needs

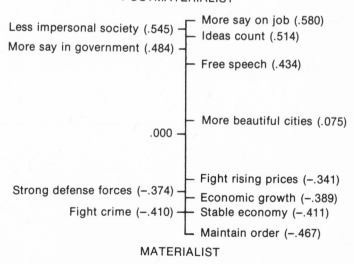

POSTMATERIALIST

Less impersonal society (.545) ⌐ More say on job (.580)
More say in government (.484) ┤ Ideas count (.514)

⊦ Free speech (.434)

.000 ┤ ⊦ More beautiful cities (.075)

⊦ Fight rising prices (−.341)
Strong defense forces (−.374) ┤ Economic growth (−.389)
Fight crime (−.410) ┤ Stable economy (−.411)
└ Maintain order (−.467)

MATERIALIST

Figure 3.2. The Materialist/Postmaterialist Factor. Mean loadings on first factor in analyses of surveys from ten countries, 1973.

actually fits into neither cluster. With the same consistency by which the eleven other items *did* fit into their expected places, this item fails to show a loading above the .300 level in any of the ten countries. Why?

The answer, apparently, is that the item concerning "more beautiful cities" does not primarily evoke aesthetic needs. Above all, it seems to tap an industrial/anti-industrial dimension on which collective economic development is seen as conflicting with one's personal security; it shows a surprising strong relationship with the safety needs. An examination of the second factor that emerged from our analysis illustrates this point. As table 3.7 shows, there is considerable cross-national variation in the makeup of this second factor, by contrast with reuniformity of the first factor. And this cross-national variation reflects the developmental level of the respective countries. Our countries now fall into three distinct groups. The first is composed of Germany, France, and the Benelux nations; the second of Great Britain, the United States, and Denmark; and the third of Ireland and Italy. This third group is particularly interesting. In the first two groups, "more beautiful cities" has strong negative loadings; overall, it is the highest-loading item on this factor. In Ireland and Italy, "more beautiful cities" is only weakly related to the second factor (or to a lesser third factor, which is not shown).

Ireland and Italy happen to be the two poorest countries among the ten being analyzed. What may be even more to the point, they are also the only two countries in which more than half the population still lives in rural areas. In the Netherlands, Britain, and the United States, the percentage living in rural areas ranges from 20 to 27 percent (needless to say, they are not all farmers). In Belgium, Germany, France, and Luxembourg, the proportion ranges from 31 to 38 percent; Denmark still has a relatively large rural population (42 percent) but in Italy and Ireland the figures are over 50 percent.[15]

The theme of this second dimension varies from group to group, but broadly speaking, it seems to involve a reaction against the problems of urban industrial society. In the countries of Type 1, it pits a concern with "more beautiful cities" and crime against emphasis on political activism and economic stability; in Ireland and Italy, the pattern is similar to that of Type 1—except that concern for "more beautiful cities" is not present among the key items. If this factor reflects different responses to urban-industrial problems, it seems significant that a concern for "beauty" is intimately involved only in those countries where economic development and urbanization are relatively far advanced—sufficiently advanced that the public is relatively sensitive to the lack of *beauty* in the environment. In such countries, ugliness may be seen as an integral part of the urban problem—linked with the crime and disorder that seem to be economic development's seamy side.

Table 3.7. The Economy vs. the Environment in Ten Countries
(Loadings of value-priorities items on second factor)

Goal	Country (Type 1)				
	Belg. (14%)	France (13%)	Lux. (13%)	Ger. (12%)	Neth. (12%)
More beautiful cities	-.621	-.587	-.416	-.606	-.516
Fight crime	-.479	-.485	-.501	-.534	-.504
Fight rising prices	-.312	-.467	-.494	-.450	-.279
Ideas count	-.056	-.029	-.153	-.133	-.116
Maintain order	-.046	.061	.055	.089	.193
Less impersonal society	-.029	.054	.238	.059	-.121
More say on job	.038	-.011	-.165	-.043	.150
Free speech	-.047	.079	.062	.055	.208
Strong defense forces	.083	.128	.112	.102	.047
More say in government	.329	.377	.287	.287	.293
Stable economy	.564	.466	.418	.448	.597
Economic growth	.685	.583	.563	.535	.560

Goal	Country (Type 2)			Goal	Country (Type 3)	
	Brit. (13%)	Den. (12%)	U.S. (13%)		Italy (12%)	Ire. (14%)
More beautiful cities	-.508	-.491	-.551[a]	Fight crime	-.567	-.500
Maintain order	-.574	-.498	-.375	Fight rising prices	-.429	-.385
Free speech	-.395	-.407	-.378	Strong defense forces	-.023	-.446
Strong defense forces	-.139	-.215	-.215	More say on job	-.229	-.217
Less impersonal society	-.259	-.209	-.089	Ideas count	-.107	-.167
Ideas count	-.176	-.055	-.292	More beautiful cities	-.127	-.108
Fight crime	-.138	-.138	.022	Less impersonal society	-.002	-.025
Economic growth	.109	.306	.202	Free speech	-.052	.039
Stable economy	.314	.320	.239	More say in government	.261	-.013
Fight rising prices	.456	.446	.215	Maintain order	.044	.225
More say on job	.398	.284	.574	Stable economy	.576	.627
More say in government	.453	.456	.559	Economic growth	.669	.756

[a] This loading is based on the item "Protect nature from being spoiled and polluted" in the American sample.

In poorer, less urbanized societies such as Ireland and Italy, economic growth is prized relatively highly. There is only a weak tendency to feel that it may be detrimental to the beauty of the environment—which is given relatively low priority in any case. The Irish and Italians give "economic growth" a higher priority than any other public except that of Luxembourg, and rank "beautiful cities" lower than any public except the Germans (see table 3.8). In Ireland and Italy (as in all these countries) an anti-industrial dimension is present—but a concern with environmental beauty does not play a significant part in it. On the contrary, among the Irish and Italians emphasis on more beautiful cities is slightly more prevalent among people who have *Materialist* values than among other types (as is shown by table 3.6).[16] In the other eight countries, a concern with beauty forms part of the anti-industrial syndrome; but while it is negatively correlated with emphasis on economic growth and stability (as we would expect), it tends to be *positively* linked with a concern for the safety needs. Its position is ambiguous: emphasis on "More beautiful cities" goes with a high priority for a "less impersonal, more humane society," and a "society where ideas count more than money." But it is *also* linked with a high priority for the "fight against crime." The net result is that "beautiful cities" shows only a weak overall association with the Postmaterialist cluster.

There are two versions of the anti-industrial dimension among the wealthier, more urbanized countries. Both of them pit the defense of physical security and beauty against economic gains. But in Type 1 (which prevails in France, Germany, and the Benelux countries) the anti-industrial reaction emphasizes *personal* security against collective economic goals: the fight against crime is salient, together with "beauty" at the anti-industrial end of the continuum. The second version (which prevails in Britain, Denmark, and the United States) has more of a political tone: the still-pervasive polarization between environment and economy is reinforced by a concern for the defense of public order and free speech, on the former side, and an emphasis on political and social activism, on the latter side. In both versions, "beauty" shows an unsuspected linkage with law and order.

Overall, the item concerning "more beautiful cities" seems to take on a nostalgic tone, evoking not only aesthetic gains, but also the idea of a more peaceful, slower-moving society. And, unlike the five other items intended to tap Postmaterialist needs, this item tends to be given relatively high priority by *older* respondents.[17] On balance, this item leans toward the Postmaterialist pole—in the more developed countries, at any rate. But its linkages with Postmaterialist items are all but neutralized among mass publics by the certain connotations of anti-industrial reaction.

There may be an additional reason why our indicator of aesthetic concerns did not, in fact, form part of the Postmaterialist cluster. Most of the countries covered in our surveys have not yet reached a level of affluence at which aesthetic needs per se are a really salient public concern. As we move from poorer to richer nations, there is a tendency for the loadings of our environmental item to rise, moving it into the Postmaterialist cluster. In the Irish and Italian samples, this item has negative loadings on the first factor. The loadings are positive in all other countries—approaching the .300 level in the wealthiest one, the United States. Whether at some future time of higher affluence and security this item will show strong positive correlations with the five Postmaterialist items is a question we cannot answer. There are faint hints that this might be the case.

For the present, only a limited number of people give a high priority to "more beautiful cities." This item ranks in a tie for tenth place among the publics of the nine European Community countries. Table 3.8 shows the manner in which the top two choices of Western publics are distributed over the twelve items.

This table gives a portrait of the goals most valued by each public. There are some fascinating cross-national differences. For example, the American public places a good deal less emphasis on fighting rising prices and maintaining economic growth than most European publics— perhaps a reflection of the relative economic security that Americans have enjoyed in past decades. The German public, on the other hand, is distinguished by an exceptionally strong concern for economic stability—an attitude that may reflect lingering traces of the incredible inflation and exceptionally harsh depression of the Weimar era. There are numerous other cross-national variations, but certain common features stand out starkly—the most significant, perhaps, being the fact that the items dealing with economic (or "sustenance") goals comprise three of the four most widely chosen items. These items are indicated by an E in table 3.8. Moreover, among the five top goals, *both* of the two remaining ones are indicators of the safety needs (designated as S in table 3.8). The next three goals are indicators of the needs for belonging (indicated by B); they are followed by the three items aimed at expressive and intellectual needs (indicated by A).

Thus far, our items have an excellent fit with what the need-hierarchy concept would lead us to expect among a predominantly materialistic public. The sustenance and safety needs are most likely to be given top priority, while needs for belonging and self-actualization are given least emphasis. There is one exception, however; the item "strong defense forces," which theoretically should have ranked in fourth to sixth place, is given *lowest* priority in most of the European countries. In the United States it gets significantly greater emphasis, ranking sixth among the twelve items. In the three decades since World War II, the European publics have come to deemphasize the importance of safety against foreign threats to an astonishing degree. Only in the United States—

Table 3.8. Goals of Western Publics, 1973
(Percentage choosing given goal as first or second most important out of twelve)

Goal	Belg.	France	Lux.	Ger.	Neth.	Den.	Brit.	Ire.	Italy	Mean, Nine Eur. Countries	U.S.
Fight rising prices (E)[a]	52	43	29	44	26	24	50	44	41	39	25
Economic growth (E)	19	18	33	24	14	23	29	29	31	24	16
Fight crime (S)	21	20	9	21	26	21	17	25	37	22	22
Stable economy (E)	12	12	22	39	16	28	25	24	16	22	21
Maintain order (S)	10	21	28	18	18	31	11	16	17	19	20
More say on job (B)	18	13	22	12	24	20	15	20	9	17	16
Less impersonal society (B)	17	28	11	11	26	17	12	8	14	16	12
More say in government (B)	11	9	19	9	14	8	15	15	11	12	16
Free speech (A)	17	14	7	11	13	11	11	6	9	11	10
More beautiful cities (A)[b]	15	9	7	4	10	7	6	5	3	7	18
Ideas count (A)	7	11	9	3	10	7	4	3	5	7	8
Strong defense forces (S)	2	3	3	5	4	2	6	6	7	4	16

[a] Letters in parentheses indicate category of the given goal: (E) = Economic, (S) = Safety, (B) = Belonging, (A) = Self-actualization.
[b] In the United States, this item was "Protect nature from being spoiled and polluted."

which was still at war as recently as 1973—do military priorities retain a moderately high rank.

We now have two sets of evidence concerning the extent to which the priorities of ten Western publics correspond to a Maslovian model:

1. Factor analysis indicates that eleven of these twelve items tap a common dimension, which might correspond to the need hierarchy; those who choose the Materialist items tend not to choose Postmaterialist ones, and vice versa.

2. The marginal distribution of choices among these items fits Maslovian expectations in eleven out of twelve cases (although the nonconforming item is not the same one in both instances).

Let us now submit the data to a third test. The Maslow model implies that a hierarchical scale should underlie the items, with the sustenance items being the "easiest" to choose, followed by the safety items and the belonging items, and with the self-actualization items most "difficult." Do people actually choose among these items in hierarchical fashion?

To answer this question, we attempted to form Guttman scales.[18] With the data from the nine European countries, we used the ten items for which both factor loadings and percentage distributions correspond to expectations derived from the need-hierarchy model. With the American data, where both the dimensional configuration and the percentage distributions came closer to Maslovian expectations, we used all twelve items.

In both instances, the fit is rather good. For the nine European samples treated as a whole, the ten items form a Guttman scale having a coefficient of reproducibility of .88. This is slightly below the .90 level usually considered to be the criterion of a good scale; still, it is surprisingly high when we consider that, theoretically, one would not *expect* any specific order among the three "economic" items, for example. Insofar as they tap the same need, one's preference order among these three items would be unpredictable, tending to inflate the number of "errors" made in ranking the items. We allowed a maximum of two "errors" per respondent; those for which more than two responses did not fit the scalar pattern were classified as nonscalar types. Among the 13,484 respondents in our pooled European sample, 71 percent were scalar types on the ten-item scale. And the scalar order of the items conforms very well to Maslovian expectations. The Materialist items, ranked from "easiest" to most "difficult," are:

1. Fight rising prices
2. Economic growth

3. Stable economy
4. Fight crime
5. Maintain order

In other words, the three "sustenance" items are easiest, followed by the two "safety" items. The Postmaterialist items, of course, have opposite polarity from the Materialist items. They were reflected in this analysis, with high priority for a Postmaterialist item becoming equivalent to low priority for a Materialist item. The order among the Postmaterialist items, from "easiest" to most "difficult," is:

1. More say on job
2. Less impersonal society
3. More say in government
4. Free speech
5. Ideas count

In other words, the three "belonging" items came first, followed by the two "self-actualization" items.

Analysis of the American data produced a scale having a coefficient of reproducibility of .89, although only 54 percent of our respondents were scalar types. Two of the three "easiest" items were indicators of sustenance needs ("fight rising prices" and "stable economy") "Fight crime" was second "easiest," and "maintain order" was fourth. At the opposite end of the scale, two of the three most "difficult" items were indicators of self-actualization needs ("ideas count" and "free speech"). There are anomalies among the American data, however; the *most* difficult item was a "less impersonal society." Furthermore, "strong defense forces" ranked as fourth most "difficult."

But on the whole, the average ranking for the three sustenance items falls at the "easy" end of the scale, followed by the "safety" items, the "belonging" items, and finally, the "actualization" items.

Technically, we obtain even better results if we limit ourselves to a four-item scale consisting of only one indicator of each of the four need categories—in which case we do not have to cope with theoretically tied items. A scale based on the four items from the original values index, for example, has a coefficient of reproducibility of .93, with 87 percent of our combined European sample being scalar types.[19] And the order among these items fits the Maslovian hierarchy without anomalies.

We cannot regard our findings as an empirical verification of Maslow's theory. Some items do not fit as one might expect, and these are a considerable number of non-scalar individuals. But most items and most respondents do conform to Maslovian expectations; our findings seem to provide a considerable measure of support for the idea that human needs tend to be hierarchically ordered. If this is true, it means that we hold specific expectations about long-term changes in the types of needs that will be most salient, under given conditions of need satisfaction. Changes in emphasis along the need hierarchy, in turn, are likely to bring political change. For the political outlook of those with Postmaterialist priorities seems to differ greatly from the outlook of Materialist types.

Before exploring the political implications of value change, we need to answer one more question about the nature of value change in Western societies. The items used to measure one's value priorities refer to broad societal goals. This is intentional; we wished to tap one's long-term preferences in the widest possible perspective. But our theory implies that these choices tend to reflect one's personal goals. Do they?

In order to test this assumption, our respondents were asked:

> Here are some of the things people usually take into account in relation to their work. Which one would you personally place first?... And which next?
>
>> A good salary so that you do not have any worries about money
>> A safe job with no risk of closing down or unemployment
>> Working with people you like
>> Doing an important job which gives you a feeling of accomplishment

This item refers to much more immediate and personal concerns than the societal goals dealt with earlier. The first and second alternatives were intended to tap Materialist personal goals: cash and security. The third and fourth alternatives were designed to tap "higher order" needs in the Maslovian hierarchy. And as one might expect, the respective pairs tend to be chosen together. Are our respondents merely giving lip service to goals that are fashionable in their milieu and age group but unrelated to their personal preferences? Apparently not. We cross-tabulated the responses to this question by an index of Materialist/Postmaterialist value priorities based on responses to the broader pool of items used in 1973. Scores on this new index range from zero (those who made nothing but Materialist choices) to 5 (those who made a maximum of Postmaterialist choices).[20] Figure 3.3 shows the relationship between value type and job priorities.

In each country, Materialist respondents tend to choose "a good salary" and "a safe job," while the majority of Postmaterialists choose "working with people you like" and "a feeling of accomplishment." In the nine nations as a whole, the Postmaterialists are more than twice as likely to choose the two latter items as are the Materialists. And with very few

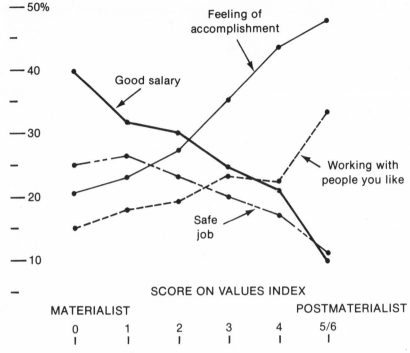

Figure 3.3. Job Goals, by Value Type. First choice among "things which are most important in a job" in combined nine-nation European sample, 1973 (*N* = 13,484).

exceptions, there is a monotonic increase in emphasis on needs for belonging and self-actualization as we move from the pure Materialist type across the four intermediate types to the pure Postmaterialist type. As we move from Materialist to Postmaterialist, between types 2 and 3, a transition point occurs at which a sense of accomplishment begins to outweigh emphasis on salary; and congenial co-workers begins to outweigh emphasis on job security. We might regard the first three types as predominantly Materialist and the last three types as predominantly Postmaterialist.

One's choice of long-term societal goals tends to be integrated with one's immediate personal goals. This indicates that if Postmaterialist types are becoming increasingly widespread, in the long run changing demands will be made on employers—and, indeed, various indications are that this is already occurring to a limited extent. But value change in Western societies has a number of other implications, some of which have an even more direct political relevance. Let us consider them.

In a theoretical and empirical analysis of the Maslovian need hierarchy, Knutson concludes that the basic needs could be viewed as points along a continuum which runs from "concern with one's self" to "concern with the environment (and self in relation to it)."[21] As long as an individual is preoccupied with needs for sustenance and safety, he or she is likely to have little energy available to deal with more distant concerns. It follows that the Postmaterialist types should have broader horizons than the Materialist types; they should be less parochial, more cosmopolitan in a basic sense. We have already seen evidence of this: Postmaterialists are relatively likely to support European integration. But this is a specific issue, not necessarily a basic attitude, and it is very much a matter of partisan debate in some countries. In Britain when Labour was in power and backing British membership in the Common Market prior to 1970, British respondents who supported Labour were more pro-European than the Conservatives; later, when the Conservatives came to office and were negotiating membership, the Conservative electorate was the more pro-European of the two. Clearly, this sort of rapid change cannot be attributed to one's basic values, which would (presumably) change very slowly in an adult population.

In an effort to tap a more basic sense of political identity, our European respondents were asked:

Which *one* of the following geographical units would you say you belong to first of all? And the next?

> The locality or town where you live
> The region or province where you live
> Great Britain, France, etc., as a whole
> Europe
> The world as a whole

For American respondents, we substituted "the Western world" for "Europe." Cross-tabulation of one's first and second choices revealed that this item has a very strong tendency to tap a parochial/cosmopolitan dimension. Those whose first choice was the town or locality in which they live were most likely to choose their region or province as second choice; those who identified first of all with the world as a whole were most likely to name Europe (or the Western world) as their second choice.

Figure 3.4 shows the relationship between value type and identification with some geographic unit larger than the nation. There are large cross-national variations, with the Germans, Italians, Dutch, and Americans relatively likely to have a cosmopolitan sense of identity; and the Danes and Irish least cosmopolitan.[22] But within any given nation, the Postmaterialists are far likelier than the Materialists to have a sense of identity which transcends national boundaries. The political implications are important, particularly in the European case. If there is a

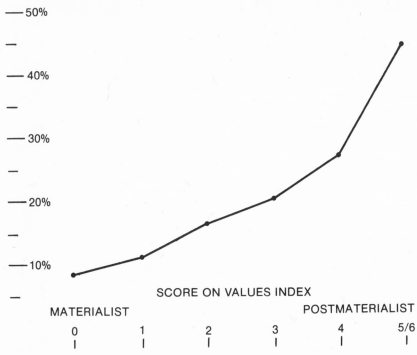

Figure 3.4. Geographic Identity, by Value Type. Percentage identifying with "Europe" or "World as a Whole" in combined 9-nation European sample. Value type based on 12-item index.

gradual but persistent ongoing shift toward Postmaterialist value priorities, this process should enhance the potential support for supranational integration. In Europe, it should tend to favor European integration in the long run—although partisan disputes may more or less neutralize its effects in the short run. In a still longer time perspective, it might be expected to work in favor of still broader forms of integration, such as an Atlantic Community or eventual world government. For the Postmaterialists are markedly more likely to feel that they belong to such broader political units.

By the same reasoning which led us to expect that Postmaterialist types would be more likely to have a cosmopolitan sense of identity, we might expect them to be relatively open to innovation in general: responsive to ideas rather than immediate circumstances, and to things that are relatively remote in time rather than those which prevail at present. Logically, one might expect Postmaterialists to take a relatively change-oriented position on political issues, and to support the more change-oriented political parties. Yet this expectation conflicts with two facts: Postmaterialists are likely to come from relatively affluent social backgrounds; and those with relatively high incomes and high-status occupations tend to support the more *conservative* political parties. To what extent do the personal values of the Postmaterialist types tend to offset the influence of their predominantly middle-class milieu?

The answer is that it varies from country to country. In some nations, established political loyalties are relatively deep-rooted and persistent; in others, the structure of macropolitics is relatively fluid, allowing an easier translation of individual values into political position. Moreover, the process of value change is not equally advanced in all societies.

But despite these important qualifications, Postmaterialists tend to take a less conservative, more change-oriented stand in politics than the Materialist types. Let us deal with issue positions first.

Any specific issue is likely to carry somewhat different connotations from one nation to another. Furthermore, what may be a burning political question in one society may be irrelevant in another. Nevertheless, in each of our European countries most people are able to place themselves on a Left-Right scale, which apparently summarizes their political stance in a broad, general fashion; and in the United States most people are willing to describe themselves as falling somewhere on a continuum ranging from "very liberal" to "very conservative." Perhaps more than any single issue could, this kind of continuum may help us to classify the political views of the publics of these ten nations in more or less comparable fashion.

Our European respondents were asked: "In political matters, people talk of 'the Left' and 'the Right.' How would you place your views on this scale?" The respondent was handed a horizontal scale divided into ten boxes, with the word "Left" at one end and "Right" at the opposite end. In the United States, our respondents were asked a similar question, except that the alternatives were "very liberal," "liberal," "conservative," and "very conservative." Figure 3.5 shows the percentage placing themselves on the "Left" or "liberal" half of the continuum for each of the six value types.[23]

In each of the ten countries, a decline in Materialist values is associated with a rise in support for a Left or liberal political position. On the average, about 46 percent of the respondents belonging to the pure Materialist type place themselves on the Left; 80 percent of the pure Postmaterialists do so. The strength of the relationship varies from a maximum in France and Italy to a minimum in Ireland and Belgium, but in every case the pure Postmaterialist type is located to the Left of any other group.

This pattern applies not only to one's sense of affiliation with the Left or the Right, but to voting intention as well. Our European respondents were asked, "If there were a general election tomorrow, which party would you support?" In the United States, respondents were asked how they voted in the 1972 presidential election. For cross-

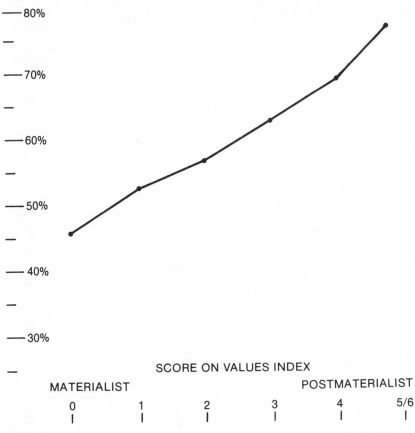

Figure 3.5. Left-Right Self-Placement, by Value Type. Percentage placing themselves on Left in combined nine-nation European sample.

national comparison, we grouped the political parties of each country under two headings; one might think of the two respective groups as the Left and the Right, although the precise labeling is unimportant. In two-party systems, the dichotomization was automatic; in multiparty systems, we followed the prevailing public perceptions of which parties were on the Left and which on the Right.[24]

In every one of our countries, the Postmaterialists were substantially more likely to vote on the Left than were the Materialist types. Table 3.9 shows the results. The *strength* of the relationship (as indicated by the gamma coefficients at the foot of each column) varies substantially from country to country; it is greatest in France and Italy, weakest in Belgium and Ireland. I will not undertake a detailed country-by-country discussion of these findings. Let me simply suggest that the cross-national differences reflect the degree to which the political institutions of the given country have realigned themselves along the

Table 3.9. Left/Right Voting Intention, by Value Type
(Percentage voting for the Left)[a]

Value Type	France	Italy	Neth.	U.S.	Lux.
Materialist	37	34	34	28	32
Score = 1	50	54	47	37	38
2	64	51	57	41	40
3	71	67	59	45	48
4	69	73	65	42	71
Postmaterialist	79	76	76	75	70
Gamma	−.443	−.416	−.373	−.327	−.324

Value Type	Ger.	Ire.	Brit.	Den.	Belg.
Materialist	51	51	51	41	38
Score = 1	60	60	66	43	48
2	66	67	59	56	46
3	59	63	62	57	49
4	74	71	67	60	57
Postmaterialist	78	77	88	64	62
Gamma	−.274	−.243	−.236	−.228	−.186

[a]In the United States, percentage reporting that they voted for George McGovern in 1972.

Materialist/Postmaterialist dimension. Some of the factors that facilitate or inhibit such realignment have already been suggested.

In each of our ten countries, the Postmaterialist types seem significantly more likely to support relatively change-oriented political parties. Does this mean that each election will bring an automatic increase in the percentage voting for the Left? Of course not. Political elites are generally characterized by a strong desire to win elections. We can assume that they will, through a process of trial and error, tend to adjust their parties' positions to new distributions of political preferences. And this process of readjustment will not always necessarily favor the Left. The breakup of the Democratic party in the United States in 1972 apparently reflected a premature readjustment toward a Postmaterialist position: at that point in time, Postmaterialist elements had become highly visible and active but were still far from a majority of the electorate. In the long run, however, their numbers seem likely to increase.

If the proportion of Postmaterialists continues to increase, we would expect an irregular but long-term shift toward increasing emphasis on the quality of life rather than quantitative gains, and on expressive values more than those instrumental to economic and physical security. Their preferences among the twelve items used to identify them give an idea of the specific kinds of change the Postmaterialists are likely to emphasize.

The respective value types display distinctive and coherent world views across such diverse fields as attitudes toward one's work, one's sense of geographical identity, and one's political preferences. Our new index, based on choices among twelve items, provides a more accurate predictor of these attitudes than the original four-item index. While both indices seem to tap the same phenomenon, the twelve-item one gives a more powerful explanation of variance in each of the domains we have discussed; in some instances it accounts for two or three times as much variance as does the original four-item index.

This holds true of the relationship with age, as well. The new index consistently shows a *stronger* linkage with age group than the one shown in table 3.4. The distribution of value type by age cohort is shown in table 3.10 using the new index. The changes across age group are striking and very nearly monotonic. But the question remains: Do these differences reflect a process of value change, or are they simply a reflection of different stages in the human life cycle?

If the latter is true, we would seem to have uncovered a remarkably powerful life-cycle effect, and further analysis of it may help us understand the clash of generations which occasionally occurs. But if this pattern reflects a process of historical change, then politics in

Table 3.10. Value Type, by Age Group
(New 12-item index for combined ten-nation sample, 1973)[a]

		Value Type					
Ages	Materialist	Score 1	Score 2	Score 3	Score 4	Post-M	(N)
15–28	36%	18%	16%	10%	9%	10%	(3880)
29–38	49	17	13	9	6	5	(2693)
39–48	55	18	12	7	5	3	(2455)
49–58	57	17	11	8	3	3	(2096)
59–68	61	17	12	5	3	3	(1913)
69+	67	16	8	5	1	1	(1313)

[a] The 12-item index was not included in the Swiss survey or in the American surveys in 1972. Otherwise the data base is the same as in table 3.4.

Western countries will probably be quite different in the future from what they have been in the past; the cohorts now entering the electorate (and eventually the decision-making posts) seem to want very different things from those already there. Needless to say, we *cannot* be certain whether the pattern in table 3.10 reflects historical change, the life cycle, short-term effects, or a mixture of all these things until we have data covering twenty or thirty more years. Nevertheless, it seems worthwhile to attempt to reduce our uncertainty as much as possible.

It was suggested earlier that economic growth was one of the forces underlying the hypothesized process of value change—not the only force, certainly, but an important one. If this is true, then in the long run, a country's rate of value change should correspond, roughly, to its rate of economic growth. Table 3.11 shows a test of this hypothesis. In the column on the left, each of our nine European countries is ranked according to the strength of the relationship between values and age group in 1973; in the column on the right, the same countries are ranked according to their rates of economic growth during the period 1950–65, allowing a certain time lag for the effects of economic change to become manifest in the values of a national population. The rank orders in the two columns correspond very closely. Eight of the nine countries have either the same position in the second column as in the first, or an adjacent position. We must point out that the United States does not fit into table 3.11; although the U.S. economic growth rate for 1950–65

Table 3.11. Economic Growth and Value Change

Correlation Between 12-Item Values Index and Age		Average Annual Growth of GNP per capita, 1950–65[a]	
	Gamma		**Percent**
Germany	−.315	Germany	5.5
Italy	−.310	Italy	4.7
France	−.301	France	3.6
Denmark	−.267	Netherlands	3.5
Ireland	−.267	Denmark	3.0
Belgium	−.254	Belgium	2.9
Netherlands	−.203	Ireland	2.6
Luxembourg	−.198	Britain	2.4
Britain	−.134	Luxembourg	2.0

[a]SOURCE: *U.N. Yearbook of National Account Statistics, 1966*, cited in Charles L. Taylor and Michael C. Hudson, *World Handbook of Political and Social Indicators* (New Haven: Yale University Press, 1972), pp. 314–15.

would fall near the bottom of the range, in strength of the relationship between value type and age group America would rank third. But the American value index is not identical to the one used in Europe; one of the twelve choices offered to the American sample dealt with "polluting" nature rather than "beautiful cities and countryside." Whether this accounts for the discrepancy or not cannot be determined with the data now available. However, even if we assume that the United States is a deviant case, there seems to be a close relationship between rates of economic change and value change for the ten nations as a whole.

Unfortunately, we are not in a position to make sure-fire projections about the value priorities of Western publics two or three decades from now; even assuming that the differences in value types from one age group to another *do* reflect a process of historical change, we cannot be sure that the process will continue. If rising affluence contributed to the emergence of relatively numerous Postmaterialists among the younger cohorts, it would be logical to expect that the disappearance of prosperity would lead to the disappearance of the Postmaterialists. And at the time of this writing, the Western world is undergoing its most serious economic crisis since the Great Depression.

The years 1971–73 were a period of exceptionally severe inflation in both North America and Europe. Unemployment rates were rising, aggravated by a serious energy crisis in late 1973. These factors clearly had an impact on the attitudes of Western publics. In December of each year, a national sample of the German public is asked, "Do you enter the new year with hopes or fears?" In December 1968 optimism was at an all-time high: 65 percent felt hopeful. Confidence remained almost equally high in December 1969, just before our first survey: 63 percent felt hopeful. A marked deterioration of confidence is evident in subsequent years. By December 1973 (about the time of our own survey), only 30 percent of the sample expressed hope. Confidence among the German public was at its lowest level since 1950.[25] Surveys of American consumer confidence indicated a similar low point in late 1973. Throughout 1972 and up to October 1973, when our own surveys were executed, heavy pluralities of the publics of Germany, France, Italy, Belgium, and the Netherlands were of the opinion that the economic situation had deteriorated during the previous year.[26]

If such conditions persisted for long, we would expect them to reshape the priorities of Western publics in an increasingly Materialist direction. But the question is, "*How* long?" If the items we have been discussing really do tap an individual's basic value priorities, we would expect them to be reasonably resistant to short-term forces—even forces as powerful as the economic crisis of the 1970s. The publics would, eventually, become increasingly Materialistic—but only gradually.

We now have data on individual value priorities which cover a

Table 3.12. Changes Over Time in Distribution of Value Types[a]
(February/March 1970 vs. September/October 1973)

	Britain		Germany		France	
	1970	1973	1970	1973	1970	1973
Materialist	36%	32%	43%	42%	38%	35%
Postmaterialist	8	8	10	8	11	12

	Italy		Belgium		Netherlands	
	1970	1973	1970	1973	1970	1973
Materialist	35%	40%	32%	25%	30%	31%
Postmaterialist	13	9	14	11	17	13

[a]1970 figures are from "The Silent Revolution in Europe," *American Political Science Review* (December 1971): 995. The original 4-item index is used for both years.

three-and-a-half-year time span. Our four-item index was first administered in February/March 1970 and was last used in September/October 1973. Let us examine the distribution of value types in the six countries for which we have data at both points in time. Table 3.12 shows this comparison. There is some indication of an increase in the proportion of Materialists in these six countries—but the trend is very weak. In most instances, the differences are so small that they could be attributed to normal sampling error. In several cases, the proportion of Materialists seems to have *declined*, not increased; and in one case, the percentage of Postmaterialists shows a slight increase rather than a decline. The overall change moves in the direction we would expect under recent economic conditions; but when we compare it with the precipitous drop in consumer confidence registered for this period, it seems almost incredibly small.

When attempting to deal with the future of industrial society, any conclusions are bound to be tentative. Perhaps next year or a few years from now, the Postmaterialist type will have withered away. But it seems doubtful. Assuming, as some argue, that Western society has passed its peak years of economic growth, we might expect the number of Postmaterialists to dwindle—though only gradually. But if—as seems quite possible—the West experiences a revival of prosperity, we would anticipate a continuing increase in the proportion of Postmaterialists, bringing a distinctive outlook and a distinctive set of priorities to the politics of Western nations.[27]

NOTES

1. These surveys were part of an ongoing program of public opinion research carried out under the direction of Jacques-René Rabier, special adviser to the European Community. I am indebted to him for sharing these data, and for his encouragement and openness to suggestions over a period of several years during which the surveys analyzed here were planned, tested, and executed. The earlier fieldwork was carried out in February and March 1970 by Louis Harris Research, Ltd. (London), Institut für Demoskopie (Allensbach), International Research Associates (Brussels), Nederlands Instituut voor de Publieke Opinie (Amsterdam), Institut français d'opinion publique (Paris), and Institut per le Ricerche Statische e l'Analisi del' opinione Publica (Milan). The respective samples had Ns of: 1975 (Britain), 2021 (Germany), 1298 (Belgium), 1230 (Netherlands), 2046 (France), and 1822 (Italy). The surveys in the European Community countries were sponsored by the European Community Information Service; a much shorter questionnaire used in Great Britain was sponsored by funds from the University of Michigan. The brevity of the latter questionnaire reflects the fact that limited funds were available for this purpose. The 1971 fieldwork was carried out in July by Gesellschaft für Marktforschung (Hamburg), International Research Associates (Brussels), Institut français d'opinion publique (Paris), Demoskopea (Milan), and Nederlandse Stichting voor Statistiek (The Hague). The respective numbers of respondents were: 1997, 1459, 2095, 2017 and 1673.

2. In earlier publications, I used the terms "Acquisitive" and "Post-bourgeois" to describe the two polar types on this value-priorities dimension. These terms tend to overemphasize the purely economic basis of value change. Both our analytic framework and the way we have operationalized our measurement of value priorities give an equally important role to the importance of the safety needs. The term "Materialist" should be understood to denote relative emphasis on *both* economic and physical security.

3. See Abraham H. Maslow, *Motivation and Personality* (New York: Harper & Bros., 1954); see also James C. Davies, *Human Nature and Politics* (New York: Wiley, 1963); and Robert E. Lane, *Political Thinking and Consciousness* (Chicago: Markham, 1970), chap. 2. A somewhat different analysis of human behavior as goal-seeking activity following a regular hierarchy of needs is presented in Karl W. Deutsch, *The Nerves of Government* (New York: Free Press, 1963).

4. See Jeanne M. Knutson, *The Human Basis of Polity* (Chicago: Aldine, 1972). Allardt, however, questions whether there is any hierarchy among needs. He finds no relationship between income level and scores on subjective indices of loving and being; on the other hand, his data indicate that a sense of social support tends to be a prerequisite to self-development. See Erik Allardt, *About Dimensions of Welfare: An Exploratory Analysis of a Comparative Scandinavian Survey* (Helsinki: Research Group for Comparative Sociology, 1973).

5. The five countries were Germany, Belgium, France, Italy, and the Netherlands.

6. The correlations in table 3.1 are based on dummy variables, with code 1 being used if the respondent *did* choose a given item (in either first or second place) and code 0 being used if he didn't. Virtually all the correlations in this table are negative, since each individual gets only two choices. Once he has chosen a given item he has only one choice left, and his likelihood of choosing one of the other three items is reduced accordingly.

7. For a definitive discussion of "constraint" in public opinion survey data, see Philip E. Converse, "The Nature of Belief Systems in Mass Publics," in *Ideology and Discontent*, ed. David E. Apter (New York: Free Press, 1964), pp. 202–61.

8. John P. Robinson and Phillip R. Shaver, *Measures of Social Psychological Attitudes* (Ann Arbor: Institute for Social Research, 1969), p. 410.

9. One might also argue that the political attitudes of the German public have a relatively high degree of constraint *in general*, that they are more interested in politics than other nationalities and consequently spend more time thinking about politics and organizing their ideas in coherent form. The German public does, in fact, tend to report relatively high levels of political interest. It is somewhat paradoxical that these items seem to work least effectively in Britain. This can hardly be attributed to faulty translation of the concepts into English; most of these items were originally written in English. Unless the translations are better than the original, there seems to be a genuine cross-cultural difference.

10. To obtain greater reliability, table 3.7 is based on the combined data from the 1970 and 1971 surveys. This table also incorporates data from a 1971 British survey carried out by Mark Abrams and Alan Marsh of the British Social Science Research Council's survey unit. I am grateful to Abrams and Marsh for furnishing the relevant cross-tabulation. Breaking the data down into six age groups reduces the number of cases on which a given percentage is based and therefore tends to increase the margin of error. But in general, the 1971 pattern was quite similar to that of the 1970 data.

11. We also have 1973 data from Luxembourg. But the small size of the sample (N = 330) makes any conclusions based on age-group analysis less reliable than for the other countries. For comparative purposes, findings for Luxembourg are included in table 3.4, and elsewhere, but they are to be interpreted with caution.

12. The Swiss survey was carried out by the Universities of Geneva and Zürich, supported by a joint grant from the Swiss National Fund. Fieldwork was performed by KONSO (Basel), January–June 1972, with a total of 1917 interviews. I am grateful to Dusan Sidjanski and Gerhard Schmidtchen for making these data available. Ten other surveys were carried out in 1973, all sponsored by the European Communities Information Service. The first was executed in March–April by the Gallup Organization (Princeton, New Jersey) with an N of 1030. The publics of the nine member countries of the European Community were all surveyed in September–October; the survey organizations and number of interviews for the respective countries was as follows: France, IFOP, N = 2227; Belgium, INRA, N = 1266; the Netherlands, Nederlandse Stichting voor Statistiek, N = 1464; Germany, Gesellschaft für Marktforschung, N = 1957; Italy, DOXA, N = 1909; Luxembourg, INRA, N = 330; Denmark, Gallup Markedsanalyse, N = 1200; Ireland, Irish Marketing Surveys, N = 1199; Great Britain, Social Surveys, Ltd., N = 1933. Here, again, I wish to thank Jacques-René Rabier for enlisting my participation in the design of these surveys and making the data available. Interested scholars can obtain data from all the European Community surveys from the Inter-University Consortium for Political Research.

13. In the American survey, the item "protect nature from being spoiled and polluted" was used instead of "trying to make our cities and countryside more beautiful." As we shall see, neither of these items was very effective in tapping the intended dimension.

14. For this analysis, each item was recoded as a separate variable with codes ranging from 1 to 6. If the given item was chosen as the "most desirable" among the entire set of twelve items, it was coded 1; if it ranked second overall, it was coded 2; if it ranked last overall, it was coded 6. If chosen first among its set of four items (but not first or second overall) it was coded 3; if it ranked second in its set of four, it was coded 4. Items not singled out for either high or low rankings were coded 5.

15. For the European countries, these figures are from *A Survey of Europe Today* (London: Reader's Digest Association, 1970), p. 14; for the United States, from *Reader's Digest Almanac, 1973*, p. 121.

16. Surprisingly enough, the "beautiful cities" item also has a slightly negative loading in our analysis of data from Luxembourg—which is considerably wealthier and more urbanized than Ireland or Italy. We should bear in mind the small size of the Luxembourg sample in evaluating this fact, however.

17. This is not true of the corresponding item used in the United States. "Protecting nature from being spoiled and polluted" is given a significantly higher priority by young than by older respondents. This item also has a relatively strong tendency to be linked with the Postmaterialist cluster.

18. We used the OSIRIS II Guttman Scale Scoring computer program for this purpose.

19. We allowed a maximum of one "error" per respondent in this case.

20. Our index of Materialist/Postmaterialist value priorities was constructed in two stages. The respondent received a score of +2 if both his first and second choices overall were "Postmaterialist" items, and a score of +1 if only one was; we then added an additional point if the *lowest* priority overall was given to a "Materialist" item ("more beautiful cities" or "protect nature from being polluted" was treated as neutral in this stage). Scores at the end of the first stage ranged from zero to 3. We next added one point to this score for each pair of two Postmaterialist items chosen within the three sets of four items; and we deducted one point for each pair of Materialist items chosen among the four-item sets. Negative scores were coded zero and scores of 5 and 6 were merged, to avoid an excessive number of categories. Our final index thus has scores ranging from zero (the Materialist extreme) to 5 (at the Postmaterialist pole). We use this index rather than the Guttman scale scores because we can score virtually all our respondents on this index; on the Guttman scale about 30 percent of our sample are nonscalar types.

21. Knutson, *Human Basis of Polity*, p. 28. Knutson undertakes an empirical test of the Maslovian need hierarchy and finds evidence that tends to confirm its applicability. Her analysis is valuable and provocative, but her data base (like mine) is limited.

22. In the Danish case, a sense of Scandinavian identity may be widespread, but it is not tapped by our question.

23. Those who could not place themselves on the Left/Right scale are excluded from the percentage base in Figure 3.4.

24. The Communist, Socialist, Social Democratic, and Labor parties in every country were perceived by the respective publics as located on the Left and were coded accordingly. Other "Left" parties were: Democrats, 1966, and Radicals (Netherlands); and the Radicals of the Left (rather than those in the Reform Movement) in France; and Fine Gael (Ireland). Parties of the "Right" were: Conservatives (Britain); Fianna Fael (Ireland); Christian Democrats (Germany and Italy); Christian Social (Belgium and Luxembourg); Radicals, Conservatives, Liberals, and Progress party (Denmark); Catholic People's party, Christian Historical Union, and Anti-Revolutionary party (Netherlands); Liberals and neo-Fascists (Italy); and the Gaullists and Reform Movement (France). To reduce ambiguity, the following parties were excluded from this analysis: Liberals (Britain and Belgium); Free Democrats (Germany); Flemish and Walloon nationalist parties (Belgium); Democratic Socialists, 1970 (Netherlands); and Republicans (Italy). In the United States, a Democratic presidential vote in 1972 was coded as "Left" and a Republican vote as "Right."

25. Institut für Demoskopie, annual greeting card (Allensbach, December 1973).

26. See Commission of the European Communities, "Information Memo: Results of the Fifth Survey on Consumers' Views of the Economic Situation" (Brussels, February 1974).

27. The sources and probable consequences of value change are explored in much greater detail in my book, *The Silent Revolution: Political Styles Among Western Publics* (Princeton, N.J.: Princeton University Press, 1977).

JAPAN AS A
POSTINDUSTRIAL SOCIETY

TAKETSUGU TSURUTANI

There is little doubt that, on the basis of certain economic criteria commonly used, Japan already is, or has just about become, a postindustrial society. For instance, by 1970, 48 percent of her labor force was employed in the tertiary economic sector, according to the Japanese government.[1] Another source reports that tertiary-sector employment reached 52.9 percent of the total labor employment as early as 1968.[2] For another example, the level of capital accumulation in Japan is such that "scarcity is no longer a major social problem."[3] Japan, however, is "postindustrial" beyond an economic sense. Put a bit differently, the term postindustrial suggests something more than, or quite apart from, certain economic features; for, as Aron argues, what is referred to as postindustrial society in economic terms depends, after all, for its maintenance upon the "industrial" foundation and, therefore, is unavoidably "industrial" in its basic activity and character.[4] In this paper "postindustrial" is used, therefore, primarily in reference to political rather than economic phenomena that seem unique to Japan in the 1970s and, as we might venture to suggest, incipient in other nations that are also postindustrial in those economic terms.

The following pages limit our discussion to only four of what I consider to be significant political phenomena caused by Japan's emergence as a postindustrial society. These selective phenomena are basically four aspects of political change that seem to be taking place in Japan today. They arise from certain industrial and technological dynamics that Japan shares with other advanced industrial nations, and for this reason, their variations may well be detected in these nations as well. These four selective aspects of change in postindustrial Japan are: (1) the rise in salience of cross-stratal issues, (2) a new pattern of political participation, (3) a new type of elite-mass strain, and (4) popular demand for new legitimacy.

It must be stressed here that the political phenomena to be examined in this paper are by no means definitive either in clarity of manifestation or prospect for viability. It may well be that they are only passing phenomena that will decline as suddenly as they apparently rose. Their mutual coherence and the logic that seems to underlie it clearly suggest, however, that these phenomena are symptomatic of certain change that is definitely taking place in Japan. In short, they are not mere happenstances, but rather societal responses warranted by the changing environment. The rise of these phenomena, increasingly noticeable though they are, does not mean, of course, that certain key political phenomena characteristic of "industrial" society have disappeared. Indeed, the latter persist with varying degrees of recalcitrance. The confusion, the stress, and the apparent volatility that have become major features of politics in Japan (and elsewhere with different variations) are the function precisely of the sharpening conflict between forces that seek some fundamental change and those that resist it. Such conflict, it is suggested here, is a political symptom of the coming of postindustrial society.

Certain difficulties accompany any comparative study of postindustrial societies in terms of political phenomena. One of them is caused by what might be called "differential manifestation." Different societies respond to the same stimulus differently, and thus the same phenomenon manifests itself in divergent forms in these societies. This difference is caused, among other things, by the variation among these societies in the extent to which various functionally comparable institutions and organizations are entrenched and routinized, as well as in sociopolitical tradition and cultural environment. Expanding affluence, for instance, produces leveling effects on consumption patterns and life styles among various classes and groups in modern industrial society. Such leveling effects, objectively ascertainable cross-nationally, nevertheless readily engender one form of politically relevant manifestation in one nation and an altogether different form, or none at all, in another.

This difference may well be accounted for by these nations' respective sociopolitical traditions.[5] Where the political party system is deeply institutionalized and the pattern of popular political participation appropriate to it is highly routinized, the emergence of critical issues unique to postindustrial society would not readily cause ascertainable changes in the operation of the party system or in the patterns of participation, while it will quickly engender noticeable changes in these political dimensions in another society where both the party system and popular political participation are of relatively recent origin. Institutionalization signifies, among other things, imperviousness to environmental change and disturbance. Differential manifestation largely accounts for the fact that certain political phenomena that can be associated with postindustrial society are more readily observable in Japan than, say, in America and some of the other advanced industrial states. Japan has a relatively short history of democracy and political parties as well as a long tradition of socioeconomic stratification and mutual group insulation.[6]

One consideration closely related to differential manifestation is what we may term "residual behavior." Various institutions in society, as well as groups and individuals, long accustomed to thinking and behaving in certain ways, tend to persist in thinking and behaving in the same way even when circumstances have changed. The acuteness of this problem has, we have noted in the past, been especially manifest in the so-called developing nations, but we are now witnessing it in many an advanced industrial society that is, in more senses than one, a paradigmatically "developed" society. At any rate, there is always a gap between the rate of change in the environment and the rate of change in thought and behavior, and the greater the gap, the more strain society is likely to experience. In the words of Emery and Trist, "the postindustrial society is structurally present but culturally absent."[7] In any event, the tenacious phenomenon of residual behavior creates serious problems of adaptation in postindustrial society that are fundamentally akin to those we have long noted in relation to developing nations. In postindustrial society, the patterns of thought and behavior that are appropriate in industrial society persist, and they necessarily inhibit processual and functional changes that are warranted by the requirements of the changed or changing environment.

Consider, for example, group political activity. In a nation such as the United States, where there is a long tradition of occupationally and/or functionally based associational groups and, moreover, a long experience of effective political input functions performed by these groups, not only their organizational imperatives and institutional inertia but also the thought and behavior of their memberships tend powerfully to militate against the emergence of the type of organization/group and the tactics of participation that may be deemed more productive in postindustrial society. In contrast, such new modes of participation and new types of group may more readily arise in a society such as Japan, which is not handicapped by overinstitutionalization of the mode of thought and behavior long regarded as characteristic of modern industrial open societies, and thus more readily manifests certain symptoms and phenomena associated with postindustrial society.

THE RISE IN SALIENCE OF CROSS-STRATAL ISSUES

Issues that are salient in modern industrial society are largely segmental, arising out of conflict and competition among social classes and groups each of which seeks to get as much of what can be gotten as it can prevail upon the political system (or decision makers) to give it. Class- or group- or interest-oriented allocations of values thus constitute, at least in one common view, the major function of the public authority. Within this generalized political context (and here we are of course talking about societies that are industrially advanced as well as reasonably open in political process), all or nearly all participating groups and interests are treated as intrinsically equal (or, perhaps more appropriately, plastic) in value and legitimacy. In other words, whether or not one group or one coalition of groups gets more than another depends entirely upon the extent to which it can outperform the other in terms of influencing the decision making. There are basically no other standards.[8] "Pluralist" society does not admit of moral superiority of any single group or coalition of groups. Theoretically, at least, it also rejects the existence of any national, centralized interest organization that would dominate or take clear precedence over all other interests.[9] Only at times of the severest national crisis, such as war, would the groups and interests concerned agree to subordinate themselves to the pursuit of a single overriding national goal or goals, e.g., military victory over an external enemy.

Japan has been no exception to this general pattern of politics of modern industrial open society in the postwar era. Partisan cleavages were determined by participant groups' respective perceptions of which party promised to satisfy their interests most, thus producing certain ascertainable coalitions and alignments among these groups and between them and the political parties. Agriculture, business, and industry, for example, constituted the core of support for the ruling conservative Liberal-Democratic party (LDP). Organized labor, the urban young, and the intelligentsia generally supported leftist opposition parties, especially the Japan Socialist party (JSP). Until very recently, therefore, it was the politics of modern industrial open society, not fundamentally different from its counterparts in other advanced industrial open societies.

Toward the end of the 1960s, however, a rather novel phenomenon gradually emerged: the rise of issues, or rather the rise in salience of issues, that cut across traditional socioeconomic and ideological cleavages. This phenomenon has been generated by the culmination of the singleminded pursuit of economic growth and material prosperity that the nation had engaged in with such uncritical mass devotion. The policy of so-called *kōdo keizai seichō* (high economic growth), while successfully catapulting the nation as a foremost industrial power in the world, ultimately resulted in making ordinary citizens acutely aware of the exorbitant prices they suddenly found themselves having to pay for the impressive international status abroad and the rising prosperity and affluence at home: environmental pollution; an unabated, perhaps even unabatable inflation; urban congestion; housing shortage; etc. To be sure, these problems did not emerge overnight. They were there before, albeit with lesser degrees of seriousness and urgency. But they had been regarded with a degree of stoicism as temporary inconveniences accompanying the collective national endeavor for economic superpowerdom and also as remediable shortcomings that would be effectively resolved as the nation continued to make spectacular economic advances. In short, they had not been the kinds of problems that would arouse public passion and thus become focal points of political conflict. They became politically significant, however, once people began to perceive them as serious political problems.

Political salience of these theretofore latent issues, in the meantime, rapidly increased as people became more and more conscious of the painful fact that the powerful triumvirate of the ruling conservative party, the deeply institutionalized and immobilist bureaucracy, and growth-obsessed industry was incapable of responding to these ills of advanced industrial society which it had been responsible for creating. As more and more concerned citizens and groups approach government agencies for solutions of these issues, they are shocked and angered by the latter's remoteness, inertia, and unresponsiveness, and this maddening discovery on the part of citizens tends further to raise the salience of the cross-stratal issues that threaten them.[10] The combination of the growing popular awareness of the ills of modern industrialism and the new consciousness of popular inability to force the ruling triumvirate to remedy them has resulted in the politicization of the *costs* (external diseconomy or negative externalities) of high economic growth.[11] Politicization of the *costs* of modern industrialism is significant in distinguishing, however arbitrarily, between postindustrial and industrial societies; for, in industrial society, whatever its political arrangement and ideological configuration, the object of general public concern and political struggle is the *benefits*, rather than the *costs*, of economic advances and industrial development, and how such benefits ought to be distributed.

Quite unlike the distribution of the *benefits* of industrialism, which, in the nature of things, is perforce selective, discretionary, and differential, the *costs* of advanced industrialism in the form of increasingly apparent negative externalities tend to be egalitarian, catholic, indiscriminate, hence cross-stratal in impact. In Japan, the rich and poor alike suffocate in the polluted air, at least when they are outdoors; are sickened or disgusted by contaminated water when they go to rivers, lakes, and ocean beaches; and suffer from urban congestion whether they travel by private cars or by public transportation. Wage and salary increases that the blue- and white-collar workers annually obtain, which by American standards seem so phenomenal and enviable, are all but wiped out by rapid rises in living costs. Farmers and city dwellers alike are witness to the denaturing process that is being perpetrated upon their surroundings by giant real-estate conglomerates and high-powered developers. As their concern with these worsening problems becomes more acute, citizens also become increasingly aware of their powerlessness in this presumably democratic society. In short, the costs of modern industrialism have in an important sense become greater than the benefits it is able to provide. Today, seven times as many people in Japan regard environmental protection as the top-priority task for the nation as those who consider further economic growth to be the most important national business.[12] The number of consumer protests registered through the Japan Consumers Association (*Nihon Shōhisha Kyōkai*) rose twenty-seven fold between 1962 and 1970, and protests and petitions about pollution doubled during a recent three-year period.[13]

The increasing salience of cross-stratal issues does not in itself signify that the kind of issues predominant in industrial society has disappeared. What we see, instead, is a popular ambivalence in this regard. That citizens are acutely aware of the *costs* of modern industrialism does not mean that they are also rejecting the *benefits* of industrial society. In fact, Japanese people by and large still do desire more of the good things that advanced industrialism can allegedly provide: better highways (which necessarily leads to *more* highways, hence *more* denaturing of the natural environment, if not more air and noise pollution); better housing (which inevitably means also *more* housing, requiring the cutting of *more* trees, leveling of *more* hills and fields for development, among other things); more creature comfort and luxury at home and at place of work (meaning, in the end, among other things, more energy, especially electricity in Japan which in turn requires building of *more* dams for hydroelectric power plants despoiling the natural beauty of *more* rivers and lakes, and increases the demand for such items as petrochemical products when the petrochemical industry is perhaps the worst culprit for perpetrating environmental pollution and other forms of what the Japanese call *kōgai*—public harms); and higher wages and salaries and more fringe benefits for more abundant *dolce vita* (which could be generated only through increased productivity and/or higher rates of profits when the urgent need is to scale down or at least retrench industrial activities and to force industry to divert more of its profits into necessarily costly antipollution devices and measures). What Inglehart calls the "materialist" value[14] still seems to dominate the Japanese national psyche. Virtually everybody desires the benefits of industrialism while decrying its costs more and more vocally. Few are entirely willing consciously to forsake or forgo some of the benefits they already enjoy in their affluence. Thus, traditional competition among various groups for what can be gotten—that is, the politics of industrial society—continues.

What is significant in Japan today, however, is that the customary issue of distribution of *benefits* of industrialism is no longer solely predominant, as it was until very recently. The issue of industrial *benefits* has come to be challenged by the clear politicization of industrial *costs*, which were until recently taken more or less for granted as unfortunate but necessary sacrifices to be tolerated and borne for the all-important national goal of growth and prosperity. The costs are no longer taken for granted or tolerated, and despite the clear persistence of the popular desire for industrial benefits and the corresponding continuity of "industrial" political competition (as an instance of residual behavior), there has emerged in the center of the political arena this growing popular concern with the seriousness of the costs that individuals and groups, regardless of their traditional socioeconomic positions and ideological preferences, are now more or less universally forced to pay. The extent to which the cross-stratal impact of the costs of modern industrialism has become a central issue of rapidly rising salience may be seen in its corresponding behavioral manifestation. The existing party system, for example, still operates in terms that are fast losing their congruence with the changing environment. The incongruence between the existing political arrangement on the one hand and the nature of new cross-stratal issues that are increasingly becoming dominant in Japanese politics on the other has already resulted in a growing popular frustration with, and an incipient rejection of, the party system and government in general—without, however, any corresponding popular withdrawal from the political arena. It is to this second aspect of Japan as a postindustrial society that we now turn.

NEW PATTERN OF POLITICAL PARTICIPATION

Salience of cross-stratal issues briefly discussed above has given rise to a new pattern of political participation that seems slowly but steadily to be modifying the whole popular input process in Japanese politics.

Historically as well as developmentally, the pattern of political participation is determined largely by the nature of political issues deemed salient in each society. Disregarding for the moment the phenomenon of residual behavior (which, in the developmental process, has very serious implications at each stage of social change), it can be argued, for instance, that, in preindustrial society where the central focus of political conflict is office, i.e., partaking of decision making,[15] political participation takes place on the basis of communal, dynastic, regional, or class divisions and manifests a relatively specific range of methods such as palace coups, assassination, civil war, revolution. In industrial society, the focus of political conflict shifts to economic values (benefits of industrialism and their distribution). Here, political participation is the function of segmental or sectoral calculus of relative material well-being derivable from such participation, thus leading to the proliferation of autonomous interest groups which, in turn, align themselves with political parties allegedly representing alternatives in terms of distribution of those industrial benefits. Partaking of the decision making in itself is no longer viewed as the issue of central operative importance in industrial society.

In industrial society, there are two specific dimensions of political participation: electoral and extraelectoral. And it is in changes in these dimensions that certain features of postindustrial society may be detected. Such, at least, seems to be the case in Japan. Voting, as a means of popular political participation, may be motivated by one of two perspectives that are mutually exclusive. In one perspective, which relates to open industrial society, electoral participation can be viewed as supportive of the existing arrangement and/or the general basic values on the basis of which the government operates. Citizens vote because voting is consistent with, and warranted by, the requirements of the existing arrangement as well as expectations of those autonomous groups to which citizens belong. In the modern industrial context, the existence of a large bloc of nonvoters suggests not necessarily alienation (though that may be the case at times), for these citizens are more likely to be apolitical—politically indifferent—rather than consciously opposed to the existing arrangement (which would suggest an acute political concern). As such, they acquiesce in the existing arrangement and the value it seeks to maximize. In short, in an open industrial society, voting as well as nonvoting can be viewed as symptoms of stability. The existing arrangement admits of communication, articulation, and aggregation at least to the minimum extent deemed necessary.

In postindustrial society (or at least in its early stages), however, voting as well as nonvoting may prove to be the function, not of support for or acquiescence in, but rather an acute frustration with the existing arrangement. Why vote if frustrated? Partly, this is a phenomenon of residual behavior inherited from industrial society, for, in one sense, voting arises from the diffuse expectation that candidates and platforms of apparently reformist appeal (based, however, largely upon the basic parameters of old party organization, operation, and process) might in fact bring about the kind of change that the changed or changing environment seems to warrant. In the main, however, voting continues because citizens are now reduced to what Touraine calls "dependent participation," that is, performing a no-longer productive or meaningful participatory ritual precisely because the continuity of the existing arrangement requires it.[16] In the meantime, nonvoters are also becoming alienated and frustrated. They are, therefore, no longer apolitical as in open industrial society, but instead they are acutely political, i.e., frustrated with and opposed to the existing arrangement. This alienative trend is the result of transition from industrial to postindustrial society during which the customary processes of popular input functions deemed productive in industrial society become less and less effective and there subsequently emerges a growing gap between the capacity of such popular input functions on the one hand and the responsiveness and efficiency of aggregative and decision-making processes on the other.

And this is precisely what seems to be happening in Japan these days. The rates of electoral participation during recent general elections were as high as those in earlier ones held in an era of risking economic growth and affluence and of national agreement on the need for continuous material advances. Moreover, participation in local elections has sharply increased, especially in metropolitan and urban districts and prefectures. At the same time, however, there has been a significant and continuous rise in the size of what the Japanese call *datsu seitō* (the disengaged from political parties) within the electorate. *Datsu seitō* today account for one-third of the national electorate, thus rivaling in size the LDP supporters. This sector of the electorate consists of two subcategories: antiparty and "nonparty," and it is significant that the increase in the *datsu seitō* sector has been caused by a radical growth of the "antiparty" voters. At the time of the 1967 general election (which may be viewed as the last of the "industrial era" elections), 9.4 percent of the electorate declared itself antiparty, and this figure increased to 11.4 percent in 1969 and to 15.5 percent in 1972.[17] The same phenomenon of *datsu seitō* is even more pronounced in urban prefectures and metropolitan districts that are more seriously affected by the ill consequences of modern industrialism, and it is noteworthy that this phenomenon is manifesting itself simultaneously with a significant rise in electoral participation in these areas. In Tokyo, for instance, which has perhaps been most devastatingly affected by the cross-stratal problems of postindustrial society,[18] the *datsu seitō* voters constitute over 36 percent of the electorate, the remainder consisting of 27.5 percent LDP, 18.3 percent JSP, 7 percent Japan Communist party (JCP), 6.1 percent Democratic Socialist party (DSP), and 5.1 percent *Komeitō* (or Clean Government party).[19]

One interesting side effect of advanced industrialism in Japan is a significant decline in the traditional urban-rural political dichotomy. Not only is there an increasing similarity in the phenomenon of *datsu seitō* between the urban and rural areas today, but there is also another, largely unanticipated change in the pattern of party support in the two traditionally distinct areas of society: a noticeable drop in rural support for the conservative LDP and an equally manifest decline in urban support for the leftist JSP, and both without any compensating growth in popular support elsewhere.[20] This has been caused by at least two factors relating to the rising incongruence between the existing political arrangement and the postindustrial environment. One factor is that each party in its traditional stronghold has come to be viewed by its customary supporters as inertia-ridden, beholden to special interests of industrialism (LDP to big business, large developers; JSP to dogmatic organized labor, for instance), hence incapable of responding effectively to new critical issues that concern larger constituencies. As people become politically more and more aware of the problems they face locally and nationally, they also become increasingly conscious of the basic outdatedness and unresponsiveness of the parties they have more or less uncritically supported.

The other factor for the rapid decline of the customary rural-urban political dichotomy is the fact that, in Japan at least, a combination of geographical proximity, high population density, a highly developed network of communication and transportation, and population mobility and postwar industrial expansion has rendered the negative impact of the costs of modern industrialism genuinely catholic. Only in the remotest of villages and hamlets could one truly escape from the din, the smell, the chemically polluted river, the sight of smog, the wild-eyed land speculator/developer, the construction site for another industrial plant, the thoughtless and indiscriminate trampings of fields, woods, and forests by those ubiquitous, ill-mannered weekenders from the city, and a myriad of other offshoots of modern industrialism. Today, rural people more or less see and feel the same things that the city dwellers do, and both are increasingly incensed by, hence concerned about, more or less the same things. And one of the feelings they commonly share today is a sense of frustration with and alienation from the parties that have until now taken their support for granted.

The second significant dimension of political participation is extra-electoral. As referred to earlier, the typical activity in this dimension in modern industrial society is interest-group activity, and it is indeed the most highlighted input function performed in modern society on the basis largely of economic or occupational cleavages and interests. This type of input function is presumed to be the most crucial to decision making. Both political participants and political scientists have felt that such patterns of interaction between government and society are appropriate in a modern state and generative of maximum benefits for all concerned as well as for social stability. In comparative politics, such patterns of interaction and input function have long been regarded as an important indicator of the maturity and modernity of political systems, which less modern, less mature nations would be well advised to emulate. The rise of postindustrial society, however, may be casting some serious doubt upon this traditional and comfortable notion.

That the outwardly (i.e., statistically) similar level of electoral participation may be quite different in motivation and purpose in post-industrial society from industrial society can be supported by the difference in the pattern of this second dimension of political participation. The kind of political input activity that has arisen in recent years and is threatening to overshadow the traditional, economic/occupational-interest-oriented group activity is exemplified by *jūmin undō* (residents movements, alternatively called *shimin undō*—citizens movements).[21] This new form of political input activity differs from the traditional one both in motivation and in criteria for participation. It is motivated by the popular perception, not of the government's or political system's ability to distribute positive values to society, but of its inability to reduce the costs of modern industrialism.

As the authoritative *Chūōkōron* noted, the "heightening of citizens' desire for political participation [through *jūmin undō*]" has been precipitated by "a lowering of their expectations toward political parties."[22] The rise of postindustrial problems has exposed the fundamental structural defect of the postwar Japanese political system that had until recently been glossed over by the national preoccupation with the pursuit of economic growth and material affluence. That defect (perhaps not a defect from the perspective of industrial society) consists in the gap between a parliamentary system predicated upon traditional interests-based parties on the one hand and the need for genuine popular participation in politics on the other. Masses have been effectively barred from the substantive process of the political system. Paradoxically, this basic gap in the postwar Japanese political system has until recently been the main source of basic stability and remarkable continuity during the 1950s and the 1960s, enabling the predominance and entrenchment of powerful organized special interests in the nation's politics, and creating and consolidating a serious dichotomy between parliamentary democracy in theory and administrative centralization and bureaucratic elitism in practice.[23]

The fundamental criterion for participation in *jūmin undō* is cross-stratal and geographical, as the word *jūmin* (residents) clearly suggests, transcending traditional socioeconomic and ideological cleavages that have in the past constituted major bases of participation. Estimates of the number of *jūmin undō* range from 1400 to over 3000, spread from one end of the country to the other.[24] Their mode of operation, too, is quite unprecedented: there are sustained "daily activities" (*nichijō katsudō*), thus significantly diverging from the traditional ad hoc voter activities that customarily emerge during election campaigns. The major thrust of these activities is not to lobby legislators and administration officials in the customary sense of the term lobbying. Their targets are specific public agencies as well as private organizations (e.g., a manufacturer, a plant) on specific issues (e.g., local air pollution; exorbitant prices charged in local stores, markets; construction of high-rise buildings or expressways). A typical *jūmin undō*, therefore, is formed in a specific locale (a city, a district, a group of contiguous villages) and consists of volunteer activists from among its residents with an inevitably wide-ranging occupational, social, and economic spectrum who have never before associated or worked together. It attempts to generate public pressure, through boycott, demonstration, marches, public confrontation, sitdown strikes, and other forms of activity upon one institution, organization, or agency or another deemed guilty of such public crimes as emission of pollutants; dereliction in enforcement or observance of environmental laws; charging of excessive prices; footdragging on effective environmental, housing, public health, sanitation, and anticorporate legislations; and so on.[25] On issues of common concern, such as construction of expressways, pollution of cross-prefectural rivers and lakes, or the need for more effective control of certain types of industrial activity, these *jūmin undō* coalesce across geographical lines and become metropolitan, prefectural, regional, sometimes even national.

As might be expected, this new pattern of political participation is more manifest in urban areas where traditional political referents and behavioral inhibitions have been more rapidly eroded. To take just one example, a recent survey shows that more than two-thirds of the Tokyoites either already participate in or intend to participate in *jūmin undō*.[26] In rural areas, too, the rising concern with postindustrial problems has begun to overcome traditional behavioral inhibitions that normally tend to persist longer than in urban areas, and the latest general elections (December 1972) were revealing in this regard not because of the win-loss statistics they produced but more importantly because of the extent to which *jūmin undō* in traditionally quiescent rural areas had begun to alter the basic character of political conflict and competition in those areas.[27]

Another important aspect of the new pattern of political participation is that it is not only those who are customarily active politically, but also those others who are normally regarded as either marginally political or apolitical that eagerly take part in *jūmin undō*, such as housewives and the young.[28] Apart from the growing public concern with the ill consequences of modern industrialism, this obvious politicization of the hitherto apolitical may be attributed to a widespread sense of efficiency concerning the new pattern of political participation, for the typical *jūmin undō* participants' view is: "Direct action in the form of *jūmin undō* is far more effective than voting, and more and more problems are of the kind that could be remedied only through direct action."[29]

The new pattern of political participation has already brought about some significant changes in the style and process of Japanese politics, about which more anon.

ELITE-MASS STRAIN

The elite-mass division notwithstanding, industrial as well as preindustrial societies are characterized, among other things, by what may be termed "vertical value congruence" in one crucial sense: the agreement on the central value deemed desirable and hence controlled to varying extents of explicitness by the dominant class and therefore avidly sought after by the subordinate class or masses. To put the same idea a bit differently, in societies preceding the postindustrial period, both the dominant and subordinate classes collectively prize one essential type of universal value, and the political struggle has to do with who gets how much of what both classes commonly value. In preindustrial society, the central value commonly prized, at least in one basic perspective alluded to earlier, is participation in decision making. The rising middle class or bourgeoisie (and, in today's new nations, masses at large) struggles against the traditional natural or unnatural aristocracy which almost invariably tries to resist the demand from below for a share in that status. The French Revolution was perhaps one paradigmatic historical instance of this struggle in preindustrial society.

In industrial society (which Aron refers to as "post-revolutionary"[30]) where, especially in open society, the issue of political participation has usually been resolved or at least ceased to be central, the primary value universally prized and coveted is economic. Here the most crucial focus of struggle is between those who control the means of production but are unwilling to share the fruits of production, on the one hand, and on the other, those who sell their labor and in exchange demand what they consider to be their just share of the fruits of production. Both, however, are in complete agreement about the central desirability of the fruits of modern industrial production.[31] Their mutual struggle is merely over who gets how much of what they commonly value. It is for this reason that once the aspirant masses acquire an increasing share in this basic value, they too become more and more committed supporters of the existing arrangement: they become politically integrated.[32] When this stage is reached in industrial society, the intensity of ideological differences that have once been regarded as the source of conflict between classes declines,[33] although many of the outward signs and rituals of the ideological differences are likely to persist, owing in part to residual behavior.[34]

In Japan, too, this pattern of development and the nature of conflict obtained throughout most of the postwar era. Despite the surface ideological configuration that was perhaps much wider than that in, for example, America, there was a deep value congruence between the dominant stratum and the masses. The focal point of congruence was the mutual commitment to and united pursuit of rapid economic recovery, growth, and prosperity, i.e., the benefits of modern industrialism. Conflict, as between management and labor or between the ruling conservatives and opposition socialists, was only over the extent of fairness and equity in the sharing of what they all coveted. As more and more of what they coveted became available to the masses, the alleged ideological differences that had seemingly accentuated the conflict gradually declined.[35] One concrete manifestation of this change is the steep drop, since the early 1960s, in the appeal of Marxism within the organized labor and a corresponding decline in worker support for the Japan Socialist party.[36]

The obvious decline in the salience of ideology or ideological differences, however, has not led to any greater harmony between the dominant class and the masses. Instead, as society enters the postindustrial stage, a new kind of strain seems to emerge between the dominant class and the masses at large. And this phenomenon seems to arise from a combination of interrelated factors which are yet obscure. A few of these factors, however, may be speculated on, and certain observable manifestations tend to support such speculation.

One such factor or cause for the incipient elite-mass strain may be a subtle but increasing gap between the two in basic perception of the role of industrialism and technology. The ruling elite has achieved and consolidated its position of power and influence owing largely to the momentum of the development of industry and technology; consequently, its pattern of thought and behavior is deeply embedded into industrial society. In short, it is still industrial-benefits-oriented.[37] The masses, on the other hand, while desirous of the good things that modern industrialization is presumed capable of providing and while their thought and behavior are also conditioned by industrial society, are more and more acutely and daily concerned about a variety of ill effects of headlong industrial and technological progress which they have until recently so uncritically supported. The ruling elite, which maintains its position because of modern industrialism, believes in the continuing efficacy and ultimate benignity of industrialism and technology. The masses increasingly mistrust and fear them.[38] This divergence in perception is reflected in recent election campaigns, for example. Local elections are increasingly conducted on the basis, not of customary *hoshu vs. kakushin* (conservative vs. progressive) differences (which, after all, have to do with how industrial *benefits* are to be distributed), but rather of the newly perceived conflict between *kigyō yogō* (promotion of business and industry) and *seikatsu yogō* (protection of daily life, i.e., defense of human existence from ills of industrialism).[39] And it is this newly perceived elite-mass cleavage that renders *jūmin undō* as a new pattern of political participation relevant and efficacious to increasing proportions of the Japanese population.

A second likely factor contributing to the growing strain between the dominant class and the masses in Japan concerns the unique nature of the central value deemed essential and hence controlled by the ruling elite in the postindustrial era. Quite in contrast to the situation in preindustrial and industrial societies, the centrally crucial value (i.e., what constitutes the basis or instrument of power, such as officeholding in preindustrial society or wealth in industrial society) that the dominant class does or must possess in postindustrial society does not seem to admit of being *shared* by the masses. The central value (i.e., the instrument of power and influence) in societies preceding the postindustrial, as mentioned earlier, is capable of being shared by the masses. The role in decision making, i.e., participation in office, for example, can be extended to the hithertofore unenfranchised by legislation, fiat, or revolution. Whether or not the desired value is available to the masses is not a matter of objective or scientific determination. The value that is the basis of power and influence in industrial society, i.e., material wealth, too, is capable of being shared readily, and whether or not it is in fact widely shared is not the question intrinsic to it, but rather the matter of whether or not society (the dominant class, the masses, the revolutionaries, as the case might be) chooses such sharing. Since power is the function of possession of the central value in each society, it can be shared insofar as, and to the extent that, the central value can be effectively shared.

In postindustrial society, this seems no longer to be the case, if the instrument of power, i.e., the central value, as many students of postindustrialism note, is knowledge. "If property was the criterion of membership in the former dominant class," observes Touraine, "the new dominant class is defined by knowledge and a certain level of education."[40] The kind of knowledge and education that becomes the instrument for dominance by the ruling class in postindustrial society, however, seems to be the kind that rejects distributive egalitarianism. In a sense, it is the kind of value that makes democracy impossible.

For instance, the complexity of government and administration has reached beyond the point of popular comprehension and control, and it is this qualitatively different level of complexity that makes for the increasingly more complete autonomy of the ruling elite.[41] Closely related to this is the heightened necessity in postindustrial society to anticipate and control change, and this necessity inevitably warrants a capacity to manipulate and control actions of citizens, groups, and institutions so as to maximize societal control over natural, human, political, economic, and cultural phenomena, i.e., the totality of the existential environment or ecology of human and social existence. In short, a key ingredient of the kind of knowledge that becomes the underpinning of power in postindustrial society is the capacity to "program."[42] And such programming does not admit of democratic popular participation, for it is in the nature of things that the programmed not know how they are programmed. If true, then, the knowledge and education that constitutes the basic instrument of power in postindustrial society tends to reverse the general though uneven democratizing trend that has obtained during the industrial period. Power that was once thought to be more and more democratically shared in industrial society may now be subtly but rapidly reverting away from the masses.

Popular reaction to this incipient phenomenon is diffuse and still largely unarticulated. In part, this is because, as Birnbaum argues, "the conspicuous fact about the new form of elite organization is that it is not conspicuous."[43] Absence of recognizable culprits renders popular reaction diffuse and unfocused. Nevertheless, a deeply felt popular apprehension already exists that the government and administration (the latter including that of the corporate world) have become too secretive, too autonomous, too impervious to popular needs and expectations, hence dangerously undemocratic. *Jūmin undō* in Japan, much like various movements for participatory democracy elsewhere, are clearly motivated by this growing popular apprehension, for their emergence is predicated upon the recognition that the citizenry can no longer keep the government and administration responsive and responsible, hence democratic, by traditional modes of popular political participation.

DEMAND FOR NEW LEGITIMACY

Major social change is generally accompanied or preceded by change in the nature and type of authority. Max Weber's paradigmatic typology of authority is too well known to warrant repetition. There seems to be a suspicion, however, that authority in modern industrial society is perhaps not quite as rational as it should be, or that, at least, the basis for such rationality may be quite different in postindustrial society. At any rate, in Japan today, the fact of new elite-mass strain discussed above suggests that increasing numbers of citizens are searching for the kind of authority that is more appropriate to the requirements of postindustrial society.[44] This phenomenon is clearly related to the rise of cross-stratal issues and the emergence of *jūmin undō*.

First, the rise of cross-stratal issues signifies that more and more citizens are aware that critical problems of society are those that transcend traditional class differences and socioeconomic cleavages and therefore call for methods of resolution other than those that have perhaps been appropriate for problems of industrial society. Second, the appearance of *jūmin undō* as a new pattern of mass political participation indicates a clear decline in efficacy and effectiveness of the customary methods of popular input activity so favorably and uncritically valued until recently. This, in turn, means that customary parameters, not only of input functions, but also of decision making, hence authority itself, have come under critical review. Third, the growing elite-mass strain suggests more specifically that the basis of the claim of competence and popular support on the part of the dominant class and government no longer enjoys uncritical popular acceptance or acquiescence. The basis of such claim has been a combination of the basic congruence between the elite and the masses in terms of the desired instrument of power, an ability to mobilize existing technology and resources to maximize the acquisition of the instrument, and ideological justifications of the particular manner in which the value that constitutes the instrument of power is allegedly to be shared. The nature of new postindustrial problems and the changing disposition of the masses about them seriously challenge it.

Moreover, the decline in the salience of ideological differences has not been accompanied by each major party's disengagement from its traditional class or sectoral ties, and this failure on the part of political parties as major tools of parliamentary democracy further hinders them from becoming adaptable and responsive to the problems of postindustrial society. The ruling LDP is most intimately enmeshed with the deeply entrenched, increasingly immobilist bureaucracy on the one hand and the growth-obsessed business and industry on the other.[45] The opposition JSP is equally rigidly bound to the ideologically militant *Sōhyō* (the General Council of Trade Unions of Japan) for organizational, personnel, financial and political support as well as to a spate of doctrinaire, "revolutionary-class-struggle" groups such as *Shakaishugi Kyōkai* (the Association for Socialism) and *Ampo Taisei Daha Dōshi Kai* (Comrades for the Destruction of the Japan–U.S. Military Security System) for ideological and theoretical sustenance.[46] At any rate, it is these basically outdated aspects of Japan's party system and government that are already impressing upon the citizenry the growing infirmity and incongruence of the existing arrangement in general and the basis of authority it claims. Citizens are thus compelled to search an alternative basis of authority and competence that would be more consonant with their expectations and more congruent with the requirements of postindustrial society. In short, they are beginning to combat what Lowi calls "the iron law of decadence."[47]

The kind of authority that the Japanese public, exemplified by *jūmin undō*, is seeking is one that is at once more progressively problem-oriented (hence more adaptive and responsive to new problems) and less techno-bureaucratic (hence more accessible, accountable, intelligible, and manageable to the public). And this search has already produced some significant change in the style and process of politics. The political parties as such no longer command mass popular support, as the rise in the size of *datsu seitō* voters clearly indicates. Political candidates are deemphasizing their respective party affiliations in their election campaigns. This is especially true with LDP candidates, whose national leadership is most unavoidably and justly identified with the postwar policy of *kōdo keizai seichō* (high economic growth) and, at least in the eyes of a rising proportion of the electorate, seems utterly incapable of abandoning its tradition of often suspicious collusion with bureaucracy and industry. Many LDP candidates now go to any length to prevent their party leaders and cabinet ministers from visibly helping their campaigns (e.g., by endorsing them or visiting their districts and/or making speeches in their behalf) because they believe that such customary forms of campaign assistance from their party and its leaders turn their actual and potential voters off. Members of parliament that local candidates seek for campaign assistance are instead those younger, unorthodox, antibureaucracy, antigrowth "rebels" with whom the party leadership would have nothing to do.[48] A similar alienative trend between the established leadership and efforts at the local level is observable within the opposition JSP as well.[49]

The search for new legitimacy seems especially advanced and effective in local politics, and particularly in elections of chief executives (mayors and governors) of urban areas. Elections of local chief executives with specifically identifiable policy commitments provide a context in which actual payoffs for *jūmin undō* as sustained mass political action are direct and ascertainable. (And this is precisely the condition that does *not* obtain for national elections since the national chief executive, i.e., premier, is *not* popularly elected.) The linkage between *jūmin undō* and government policies is visible and increasingly strong.

Traditionally, the most telling sales pitch a candidate for governor or mayor could make in election campaigns was a claim of close connections, through national party leadership or "old boy" ties within the national bureaucracy, to the central government (*chūō chokketsu*, i.e., a direct line to the center or national capital).[50] For this reason, throughout most of the postwar period, governors and mayors have been either former high bureaucrats, former M.P.s, or local party notables.[51] The electorate by and large sought these people because they could get things done—things that were deemed desirable in a fast-advancing industrial society, such as highway construction, industrial investment, business expansion, land development, public project, etc. Today, however, the electorate no longer seeks these "benefits" of advanced industrial society, but instead tries to combat and turn back the accumulated "costs" that such heretofore blindly accepted and coveted "benefits" inevitably have entailed. Thus, voters are electing to the post of local chief executive those candidates who have no bureaucratic, old boy, or partisan ties with the party leadership and the administration, but who seek instead to confront and challenge the ever-secretive and unresponsive techno-bureaucratic attitudes and values that dominate both the party and the government.[52]

With the advent of *jūmin undō*, 40 percent of the population in Japan, a large majority of it in metropolitan and urban areas, is already governed by mayors and governors who represent this new trend.[53] These chief executives are collectively referred to as *kakushin shuchō* (progressive chief executives). The term *kakushin* (progressive) in this new context, however, has no relation, either ideologically or programmatically, with the traditional *hoshu* vs. *kakushin* (conservative vs. progressive) dichotomy, although the leftist parties assiduously attempt to cultivate a popular impression that these *kakushin shuchō* are their political allies, if not progenies. *Kakushin shuchō*, instead, is a wholly new term connoting responsiveness to the dangers and requirements of postindustrial society; freedom and independence from traditional political ties, referents, and inhibitions; and a genuine commitment to meaningful popular participation in the decision-making process. The relationship between the rise of *jūmin undō* and the emergence of *kakushin shuchō* seems mutually generative and reinforcing. In Tokyo, for example, it was a *kakushin shuchō* (Professor Minobe) who, through his style and policy commitment, gave impetus to the rise of widespread *jūmin undō* which, in turn, engineered a massive reelection for him which was record-shattering in both the proportion of popular votes he received and the rate of voter turnout. Osaka, on the other hand, is an example in which the rise of *jūmin undō* against a variety of urban ills caused the demise of the powerful, deeply entrenched long-term incumbent governor and the victory of an obscure scholar as his replacement; and the election of this *kakushin shuchō* in turn has since given additional momentum and vitality to *jūmin undō* in the area.[54] The extent to which this search for new legitimacy may be viewed, however tentatively, as an ongoing and viable phenomenon may be seen in the fact that, for every voter who is either opposed to or pessimistic about the prospects of increase in the number of *kakushin shuchō* in the near future, almost nine expect such increases.[55]

The four selective aspects discussed in this paper of political change that seems to be taking place in Japan are by no means definitive, and this assessment of them is perforce tentative. This element of uncertainty springs from a consideration of the phenomenon of residual behavior which might critically inhibit any further growth of these aspects. Moreover, Japanese politics is still at the earliest stage of postindustrialism, and thus is suffering from the uncertainty and volatility that normally characterize society in transition. Available data are far from conclusive as to the viability of such emergent popular attitudes as may be consistent with the requirements of postindustrial society. In the absence of adequate time-series data, for example, any conclusion that might be drawn from the current data should be viewed with great caution.

Nevertheless, there are indications, albeit with differing degrees of plausibility and persuasiveness, that what might be considered "postindustrial" political culture is far from a sociological pipedream. The latest survey conducted by the authoritative Institute of Statistical Mathematics, to cite one such example in conclusion, suggests a growing viability of emergent postindustrial popular attitude and perception in two specific contexts that directly pertain to our discussion in this paper.[56]

1. Industrial Benefits vs. Industrial Costs

One of the questions asked in this extensive survey was whether or not further economic growth should be curtailed in order to combat and eliminate *kōgai* ("public harms," e.g., pollution, environmental decay, congestion, and other associated ills). Findings are interesting, though at times quite ambivalent:

(a) Both *datsu seitō* (the disengaged from parties) and JSP voters favor the curtailment of further economic growth at a ratio of 4.5 to 3, while more LDP supporters oppose it than favor it (42 percent vs. 38 percent). The continuing decline in electoral support for the LDP since 1960 (58 percent then to 46 percent for the latest general election in 1972) would seem to mean that the proportion of "industrial-benefit-oriented" voters is also declining today.[57]

(b) There is, however, a rather unexpected phenomenon of more younger people *opposing* the curtailment of economic growth than older people (35 percent of those below the age of forty vs. 24 percent of those above). Quite contrary to Inglehart's findings in Western Europe,[58] younger, culturally "postwar" generations in Japan appear to be at least as materialist-value-oriented as their elders, or more so. This may be explained by the fact that younger people are familiar only with conditions of advanced industrial society, while their elders can contrast today's congested industrial conditions with yesterday's world of clean air, clear water, and relatively unspoiled natural beauty. If, however, *datsu seitō* (the disengaged from political parties) voters are more strongly in favor of curtailment of economic growth in order to remedy *kōgai*, as (a) above suggests, then it appears that this currently pronounced materialist orientation of younger generations will decline, since the tendency toward the *datsu seitō* phenomenon has been shown in numerous and periodic surveys to be manifestly stronger for the younger generations than for the older, especially for those in their late teens and through the twenties.[59] By and large, therefore, it may not be too unreasonable to assume that more Japanese would prefer better environment to more prosperity, or, to put the same thing a bit differently, they would become more concerned about cross-stratal issues of modern industrial *costs* and less concerned about sectoral-competitive issues of industrial *benefits*.

2. More *Jūmin* Participation vs. The Existing Arrangement

Another illuminating question asked in the survey by the Institute of Statistical Mathematics had to do with popular attitudes toward and perceptions of whether or not more direct, popular-participatory decision making concerning local and regional issues would be warranted. Here, too, findings tend strongly to support the thesis of significant political change in Japan.

(a) LDP voters tend to be more trusting of or content with the existing arrangements than either the opposition JSP supporters or *datsu seitō* citizens, although more LDP voters favor more *jūmin* participation than oppose it. Thus, one out of every seven LDP supporters oppose more participatory system, while only one out of twelve of the JSP voters and one out of fourteen *datsu seitō* electors are antiparticipatory.

(b) On this question, younger people tend to favor such direct participation much more strongly than their elders (78 percent of those under forty years of age vs. 67 percent of those above). This generational difference, however, may not be the function of postindustrial society as such. The younger generations did not experience (except as small children for those close to forty years of age) the authoritarian rule of the period before 1945, while their elders mostly grew up in a society imbued with obedience to government and reverence for elitist authority. In this sense, therefore, the generational difference noted in the findings may simply be the result of differences in political culture in

Japan before and after 1945, thus in itself having no clearly significant relationship to the industrial-postindustrial political and cultural dichotomy.

There is, however, a sense in which the more strongly participatory orientation of the young may be related to postindustrial political change. The *datsu seitō* phenomenon, as noted above, is more pronounced among the younger voters than among their elders; moreover, it is a relatively recent phenomenon related clearly, not to prewar vs. postwar political cultural diversity, but rather to the culmination of certain industrial and technological dynamics alluded to at the outset of this chapter. The rejection of the existing arrangement by young people, then, is at least in part the function of their *datsu seitō* tendency rather than their having grown up in the democratic postwar political system. The clear parallel between the *datsu seitō* phenomenon and *jūmin undō* as a new pattern of political participation suggests, then, that the demand for more participatory political arrangements would continue to rise and spread in the near future. It may also be parenthetically noted that the proportion of "undecided" and "don't know" respondents is much smaller among the younger voters than among their elders (an average of 13 percent for the young citizens below the age of forty compared to an average of 27 percent for those above).

Whatever reservations we may still entertain about the ultimate resolution of tension and volatility Japan is painfully experiencing today, it seems undeniable that certain political phenomena in Japan are entirely novel and becoming more pronounced. With varying degrees of magnitude, explicitness, and dispatch, moreover, they are beginning to challenge the basic arrangement, the patterns, and the preoccupations of the politics that have in the past characterized Japan as a fast advancing modern industrial society. How these new phenomena will bring about the fundamental changes in Japan's political system they seem to point to would depend upon the rate at which the phenomenon of residual behavior can be overcome in that particular society.

NOTES

1. *Nihon Tokei Nenkan* (Tokyo: Sorifu Tokei Kyoku, 1972), pp. 50–51.

2. Ohashi Ryuken, *Nihon no Kaikyu Kosei* (Tokyo: Iwanami, 1972), p. 132. For the definition of postindustrial society based on the predominance of the tertiary economic sector see, for example, Eleanor B. Sheldon and Wilbert E. Moore, "Monitoring Social Change in American Society," in *Indicators of Social Change: Concepts and Measurements*, ed. Sheldon and Moore (New York: Russell Sage Foundation, 1968), p. 13; and Daniel Bell, "Technocracy and Politics," *Survey* 17 (Winter 1971): 4.

3. Christopher Lasch, "Toward a Theory of Post-Industrial Society," in *Politics in the Post-Welfare State*, ed. M. Donald Hancock and Gideon Sjoberg (New York and London: Columbia University Press, 1972), p. 36.

4. Raymond Aron, *The Industrial Society* (New York: Simon & Schuster, 1967), p. 104.

5. In Japan, with a tradition of social stratification and status differentiation, expansion of affluence has produced a phenomenon of more and more people perceiving themselves as belonging to the middle class, while in America, where there is no such tradition, the essentially same condition has failed to generate any significant upward socioeconomic status perception on the part of working-class people. The Japanese worker, traditionally viewed both by himself and by others as inferior in social and career status, has been psychologically anxious to abandon his former status and to move up to middle-class status, while his American counterpart, lacking the bitter experience of humiliating social discrimination and generally imbued with egalitarian social and political ethos, has never considered his status inferior or undesirable, hence does not feel the consuming urge to move up, despite the fact that he now considers his income to be quite high, often higher than his "middle class" white-collar counterpart. For comparison see, for example, *Kokumin Seikatsu Hakusho 1970* (Tokyo: Keizai Kikakucho, 1971), p. 4; Shinohara Hajime, *Nihon no Seiji Fudo* (Tokyo: Iwanami, 1971), p. 4; and David Garson, "Automobile Workers and the Radical Dream," *Politics and Society* 3 (Winter 1972): 167–69. We also note in West Germany a phenomenon similar to the Japanese case. See Ronald Segal, *The Struggle Against History* (London: Weidenfeld & Nicolson, 1971), p. 8.

6. Consider, for example, the view of contemporary Japan as "an open society made up of closed components." Robert Scalapino and Junnosuke Masumi, *Parties and Politics in Contemporary Japan* (Berkeley and Los Angeles: University of California Press, 1962), p. 145. For the general characteristics and structure of Japanese society in English see Chie Nakane, *Japanese Society* (Berkeley and Los Angeles: University of California Press, 1970).

7. E. E. Emery and E. L. Trist, *Toward a Social Ecology: Contextual Application of the Future in the Present* (London and New York: Plenum Press, 1973), p. xiv.

8. For this essential valuational neutrality of groups in industrial society see, for example, Theodore J. Lowi, *The End of Liberalism: Ideology, Policy, and the Crisis of Public Authority* (New York: Norton, 1969), p. 288.

9. For dangers of such centralized organizations from the modern, open, industrial perspective see, for example, William Kornhauser, *The Politics of Mass Society* (Glencoe, Ill.: Free Press, 1969), pp. 94–95 and passim.

10. See, for example, Yokoyama Keiji, "Kono wakitatsu teiko no nami," *Asahi Janaru*, 23 April 1971; and also *Sekai*, April 1971, pp. 129–30.

11. For an interesting discussion of negative externalities see, for example, François Bourricaud, "Post-Industrial Society and the Paradox of Welfare," *Survey* 17 (Winter 1971): 48–51.

12. *Showa 46 nen ban Kokumin Hakusho* (Tokyo: Keisai Kikakucho, 1971), p. 127.

13. Ibid., pp. 153–54, 159. Memberships of consumer organizations nearly tripled in the past year and a half to 10 million. See "Consumerism," *Japan Quarterly* 20 (July–September 1973): 255.

14. Ronald Inglehart, "The Silent Revolution in Europe: Intergenerational Change in Post-Industrial Societies," *American Political Science Review* 65 (December 1971), and "Industrial, Pre-Industrial and Post-Industrial Political Cleavages in Western Europe and the United States" (Paper presented at the 1973 annual meeting of the American Political Science Association, New Orleans, 4–8 September 1973).

15. For political participation in preindustrial society see, for example, John H. Kautsky, ed., *Political Change in Underdeveloped Countries* (New York and London: Wiley, 1962), p. 24.

16. Alain Touraine, *The Post-Industrial Society: Tomorrow's Social History*, trans. Leonard F. X. Mayhew (New York: Random House, 1971), p. 9.

17. These figures are contained in reports in *Asahi Shimbun*, 26 June 1971 and 8–9 December 1972.

18. For the situation in Tokyo see Taketsugu Tsurutani, "A New Era of Japanese Politics: Tokyo's Gubernatorial Election," *Asian Survey* 12 (May 1972): 429-43.

19. *Asahi Shimbun*, 26 June 1971, p. 24.

20. Shinohara Hajime, "Bunkyokuka suru seiji ishiki," *Asahi Janaru*, 22 December 1972, esp. pp. 5–6; Komuro Naoki, "Kakushin jichitai no tohyo kozo," ibid., 29 December 1972, esp. pp. 102–3; Yamamoto Eiji, "Hoshuto o hanareteyuku nomin," ibid., 24 November 1972; and Shinohara Hajime, "70 nendai to kakushin no kanosei," *Sekai*, March 1970.

21. For the genesis of this new input activity, see Shinohara, *Nihon no Seiji Fudo*, pp. 176–78, 188–90.

22. "Shakaito ron wa naze fumo ka," *Chūōkōron*, November 1970, p. 39.

23. For this paradox, see Tsurutani, "New Era of Japanese Politics," pp. 430–31, 433–34.

24. *Asahi Janaru*, 23 April 1971, p. 41; and *Asahi Shimbun*, 21 May 1973, p. 4. According to the latter, about 55 percent of *jūmin undō* have memberships of fewer than 500 volunteer activists, suggesting, in part, fairly cohesive, informal, but communitarian characters of these organizations.

25. For details of these and other features of *jūmin undō* see Tsurutani, "New Era of Japanese Politics," pp. 432–33; and Yokoyama, "Kono wakitatsu teiko no nami," pp. 129–30.

26. Quoted in *Asahi Shimbun*, 15 January 1971, p. 4. For the rising *jūmin undō* orientation of the electorate see also *Shimin Ishikin no Kenkyu: Machida, Kurashiki, Tokyo* (Institute of Statistical Mathematics Research Report No. 31, Ministry of Education, 1973).

27. *Asahi Shimbun*, 30 November, 2 December 1972, p. 4.

28. See, for example, "Shohisha undo wa kitai dekiruka," *Sekai*, April 1971.

29. *Asahi Shimbun*, 12 April 1971, p. 10. Also see ibid., 15 June 1973, p. 21.

30. Raymond Aron, *Progress and Disillusion* (New York: Praeger, 1968), pp. 5–8.

31. "Marxism . . . had ever been an eccentric and quixotic passion. One oppressed class after another had seemed finally to miss the point. The have-nots, it turned out, aspired only to having." Joan Didion, "Women's Movement" (a review essay on women's liberation books), *New York Times Book Review*, 30 July 1972, p. 1.

32. Thus, we can perhaps agree that "[t]he integrating process which is the chief characteristic of industrial society has now encompassed that class whose inability to integrate into the society was once supposed to destroy that society." Norman Birnbaum, *The Crisis of Industrial Society* (New York: Oxford University Press, 1969), p. 8. Also see his *Toward a Critical Sociology* (New York: Oxford University Press, 1971), p. 371.

33. E.g., Daniel Bell, *The End of Ideology* (Glencoe, Ill.: Free Press, 1960). For opposing views see, for example, Joseph LaPalombara, "Decline of Ideology: A Dissent and an Interpretation," *American Political Science Review* 60 (March 1966): 5–16.

34. See Ulf Himmelstrand, "Depoliticization and Political Involvement: A Theoretical and Empirical Approach," in *Mass Politics: Studies in Political Sociology*, ed. Erik Allardt and Stein Rokkan (New York: Free Press, 1970), p. 68; and Segal, *Struggle Against History*, p. 9.

35. For a good description of this phenomenon in Japan see Seki Yoshihiko, "Japan in Transition," *Journal of Social and Political Ideas in Japan* 2 (August 1964): 41–44.

36. Kuwata Koichiro, "Political Parties in the Next Decade," *Japan Quarterly* 17 (April–June 1970): 139; and Robert E. Cole, "Japanese Workers, Unions and the Marxist Appeal," *Japan Interpreter* 6 (Summer 1970).

37. Premier Tanaka's famous thesis of "restructuring the Japanese Archipelago" is really an extension of what Meadows and others criticize as the "growth-forever policy" which totally neglects the need for "change in human values or ideas of morality." Donella Meadows et al., *The Limits to Growth: A Report for the Club of Rome's Project on the Predicament of Mankind* (New York: New American Library, 1972), pp. 156–57.

38. One of the most fearful consequences in this regard has been a series of new diseases for which there is yet no cure. These illnesses are caused by chemical pollutants discharged into rivers and other bodies of water. They include disorder and destruction of internal organs (when water and fish contaminated by pollutants are consumed) and painful bone diseases and malformation. Instances of these diseases are almost daily reported and court cases involving them are increasing both in number and magnitude. For one of the most publicized court decisions that resulted in the awarding of precedent-breaking compensations to victims see *Asahi Shimbun*, 20 March 1973, pp. 1–3, 10–11.

39. See "Hoshu dokusai ka no chiho senkyo," *Sekai*, June 1971, pp. 187–91.

40. *The Post-Industrial Society*, p. 51. For the critical importance of certain types of knowledge in postindustrial society see Daniel Bell, "Technology and Politics," in *The Coming of Post-Industrial Society* (New York: Basic Books, 1973), pp. 112–20.

41. Galbraith, for example, observes "The autonomy of the technostructure is...a functional necessity of the industrial system." J. K. Galbraith, *The New Industrial State* (Boston: Houghton Mifflin, 1967), p. 393.

42. Hence, postindustrial society is a "programmed" society. See Touraine, *The Post-Industrial Society*, p. 3. Futurologists regard this capability as essential to order and stability of society. See, for example, the long passage about "flexibility" in Herman Kahn and Anthony Wiener, *The Year 2000: A Framework for Speculation for the Next Thirty-Three Years* (New York: Macmillan, 1967), p. 3; and Emery and Trist, *Toward a Social Ecology*, passim.

43. Birnbaum, *The Crisis of Industrial Society*, p. 13.

44. A similar phenomenon is apparently taking place in Germany. See, for example, Heinz Hartman, "Institutional Immobility and Attitudinal Change in West Germany," *Comparative Politics* 2 (July 1970): 579–91.

45. See, among others, Chitoshi Yanaga, *Big Business in Japanese Politics* (New Haven: Yale University Press, 1968); and Nathaniel Thayer, *How the Conservatives Rule Japan* (Princeton, N.J.: Princeton University Press, 1969), chaps. 3 and 8.

46. See, for example, George R. Packard III, *Protest in Tokyo: The Security Treaty Crisis of 1960* (Princeton, N.J.: Princeton University Press, 1966); J. A. A. Stockwin, *The Japanese Socialist Party and Neutralism* (Melbourne: Melbourne University Press, 1968); and Taketsugu Tsurutani, "The Japan Socialist Party in Transition" (Paper delivered at the twenty-fifth annual meeting of the Western Political Science Association, 8-10 April 1971, Albuquerque, New Mexico).

47. Theodore Lowi, *The Politics of Disorder* (New York and London: Basic Books, 1971), pp. 5, 53–54.

48. Haga Yasushi, "Datsu seito jidai to yu genso," *Jiyu*, December 1971, p. 36; and "Jiyuto ni kusuburu hanran no hinote," *Sande Mainichi*, 30 April 1972, p. 131.

49. Kawakami Tamio, "Shin no gen'in wa doko ni arunoka," *Sekai*, March 1970; and Kishima Masamichi, "Jibun jishin no tote mitakoto," ibid.

50. Shinohara Hajime, "Bunka henyo to chihoseiji no kadai,"*Sekai*, April 1971, p. 41.

51. Ohashi, *Nihon no Kaikyu Kosei*, p. 92.

52. Tsurutani, "New Era of Japanese Politics," pp. 435–37.

53. About the rise of this new breed of suprapartisan officials, see, for example, Shinohara Hajime, "70 nen dai to kakushin no kanosei," *Sekai*, March 1970; Yokoyama Kenji, "Uragirareta jūmin undō," *Asahi Janaru*, 7 May 1971; Geji Junkichi, "Kakushin chiji no jitsugen to toitsu sensen," *Zen'ei*, January 1973; *Asahi Shimbun*, 24 November 1973, p. 10.

54. Kondo Hitoshi, "Kyosanto wa nani ni kattanoka," *Chūōkōron*, June 1971; and "'Hoshu dokusai' ka no toitsu chiho senkyo," *Sekai*, June 1971.

55. See the Kyodo Tsushin poll reported in Shinohara Hajime, "Bunka henyo to chihoseiji no kadai," *Sekai*, April 1971, p. 39.

56. Statistical data in the following discussion are adapted from *Shimin Ishiki no Kenkyu: Machida, Kurashiki, Tokyo* (Institute of Statistical Mathematics Research Report No. 31, Tokyo, 1973), pp. 22, 32, 63–65, 69–71.

57. *Asahi Shimbun*, 12 December 1972, pp. 1–2.

58. Inglehart, "The Silent Revolution in Europe."

59. For the latest survey see *Asahi Shimbun*, 10 September 1973, p. 2.

TECHNOCRATIC COUNSEL
AND SOCIETAL GUIDANCE

JEFFREY D. STRAUSSMAN

INTRODUCTION: A SAINT-SIMONIAN RESURRECTION?

One of the salient features of what is increasingly being called "post-industrial" society is said to be the preeminence of technocratic modes of politics.[1] Much rancor, though little serious discussion, has been directed at "technologists," "experts," "systems analysts," "social engineers," and, more generally, "technocrats." Naturally, interest in the roles and influence of specialists of various assorted and sordid areas of expertise is hardly new. Technocracy, both as a concept and an assumed tendency, is rooted in the theory and practice of industrial society. In this connection, the political influence of experts as a description of, and a prescription for, the industrial order can be found in the writings of Henri Saint-Simon, Auguste Comte, Karl Marx, Thorstein Veblen, Max Weber, James Burnham, and Raymond Aron.[2] Some of the most prominent theorists of industrial society, then, have grappled with the recurring theoretical, empirical, and normative issues that permeate the relationship between knowledge and power.

Why has this issue been resurrected by some social scientists who probe the futures of industrial societies? In part, the answer must lie in a subtle malaise within the social science community concerning the controversial and inconclusive roles played by experts in the three broad areas that have dominated post-World War II politics in the United States: (1) the techno-political efforts that have been designed to "tame" the business cycle, avoid depression, and more positively, spur economic growth; (2) the politics of the cold war; and (3) the acceptance and implementation of the welfare state. The utilization of experts and their specialized knowledge in these three major domains has not been inconsequential. Yet, the euphoria of the 1960s has given way to the implicit pessimism of the 1970s. Oversold politicians, disillusioned experts, and frustrated segments of the populace search for explanations to understand failures. For many, the causes stem from an overreliance on both technique and experts. For others, the problem lies, conversely, in the underutilization of new knowledge and the "knowledge elites." Experts are both praised and blamed. They have too much power, say some. We should make more use of our wealth of information and expertise, say others. In short, the role of the expert is often a precarious one.

How much influence do experts have in contemporary industrial societies? The question has been raised by several theorists of industrial society. More recently, social scientists concerned with the emergence of postindustrial society have returned to this intriguing, though empirically barren, research problem.

At the risk of oversimplifying a large amount of literature with several divergent strains, it is still possible to discern two major arguments about the nature of technocracy in industrial society that are clearly incompatible. One dominant assessment of the growth of technocracy asserts that industrial society, with its tendencies toward norms of efficiency and rationalization coupled with role differentiation inherent in bureaucratic organization, inevitably leads to a *shift* of power from politicians (in the public sector) and entrepreneurs (in the private sector) to specialists, often characterized as the "new men," the "new class," or the "knowledge elites."[3] The process is said to be gradual, a "slipping away of power," in the words of Jean Meynaud, that is an irresistible by-product of advanced industrial society.

At the other extreme one finds an appraisal of technocracy that stresses the mandarin aspects of experts and their specialized knowledge. This second position, while recognizing changes in the class structure of industrial societies as well as the emergence of new knowledge elites, suggests that these new elites, who pose no threats to entrenched forms of power and property that continue to be based on wealth and privilege, merely *serve* those who have always controlled both the private and public institutions of power in industrial society. Therefore, rather than shifting power from the elites of early industrialism to the new knowledge elites who are supposedly dominant in advanced industrial society, it is argued that powerful establishments are merely bolstered by these new men of knowledge.[4] In other words, the autonomy of decision-making power by various experts, which serves as the major point of focus for the first interpretation of the evolution of industrial society, is rejected by the proponents of this alternative explanation of the role of the knowledge elites. Put bluntly, the second thesis suggests that the interrelationship between state power and the control of wealth is the predominant aspect of political power in capitalist industrial societies. This, it is argued, is not declining simply because one can identify the emergence of technocratic elites. Thus, while both propositions recognize the growth of expertise in industrial systems as an objective element of societal evolution, they differ sharply on the significance of the trend in assessing potential changes in political power.

While both positions are provocative in their rather sweeping interpretations of the structure of power in advanced industrial societies, both are, at best, caricatures of this all too elusive issue which cannot be ignored by social scientists concerned with the futures of advanced industrialism. While the question of power is beyond the scope of this chapter, a few tentative observations should be made in order to place the issue of expertise in its proper structural perspective. It is important to observe that the prince has always had expert counsel. "The first impression that one gets of a ruler and of his brains is from seeing the men that he has about him."[5] Machiavelli's observation has often been lost on those social scientists who, by only concentrating on the numbers and diversity of the experts surrounding the prince, forget that the prince (or more correctly the princes) is still powerful. Images of Galbraithian technostructures that wield power in the private and public sectors obscure this point. The "myth of the technostructure" has been a focal point for the second argument outlined above. But criticisms of the technostructure argument have not been confined to Marxists and neo-Marxists. Paul Samuelson, perhaps the most famous exponent of mainstream economics, has said:

> I find Galbraith's notion that there is a technostructure which really runs our corporations, government, and which represents a convergence of form and function with the technostructure which runs Russia and China, to be a notion bred in part out of exaggerated self-esteem. I'd like to think that our MIT students will inherit the earth . . . but reality keeps breaking in. They, like the large corporation itself, are constitutional monarchs who reign only so long as they don't rule. Just let some computer tell Henry Ford, or for that matter the General Motors Board, that they've got to do something he [the computer] wants but which they [Henry Ford or the GM Board] don't think is in their long-run interest, and see how fast he draws his severance pay.[6]

The essential point Samuelson is alluding to, of course, is the concentration of wealth and power in American society, an area almost entirely ignored or glossed over by the prophets of postindustrial society who place undue importance on the influence of experts. Recent research by Thomas Dye and his colleagues provides some tentative empirical evidence of the extent of this concentration in the United States. In examining formal positions of authority in twelve institutional sectors (concentration was operationalized as those formal positions of authority which control over half of the nation's resources), Dye and his colleagues find that 4100 individuals occupy 5400 positions.[7] They also find that 40 percent of these positions are interlocked; multiple positions tended to be held by the most wealthy. Though the published account of the study does not permit dissaggregation to test the Galbraithian thesis more fully, it is clear that in what they call the "government" sector, few positions are held by experts or technocrats. Older studies of political executives show that as of 1965 there has not been any appreciable increase in the number of experts (defined in terms of high levels of education and occupation prior to appointment) to high policy positions in the executive branch.[8] Richard Barnet and Gabriel Kolko, in their studies of foreign policy decision makers, have identified what might be called a law firm–corporate concentration in this area of national policy.[9] All this sheds considerable doubt on the notion that "new men" are assuming the important positions of power in American society. At best, this argument is premature.

Given these reservations concerning the notion that power is shifting toward the expert in advanced industrial political systems, it is still necessary to note that at least four major developments have occurred which bear on the relationship between political power and the roles of experts in the future. These include: (1) the proliferation of "hard" and "soft" technologies that may have long-range impact on societal development;[10] (2) the commitment to knowledge and its societal uses;[11] (3) the growth of what Daniel Bell calls the "professional and technical class";[12] (4) the institutionalization of specialist roles in the public and private sectors. Taken together, these phenomena suggest that the roles of knowledge and expertise, while rooted in the evolution of industrial society, reemerge as one of the dominant issues of postindustrial society.

One way to probe this complex facet of "postindustrial" futures is through an examination of the requisites of "societal guidance,"[13]— the coordination and utilization of information by policy makers—and the corresponding roles and functions of experts in this process. If we conceive of the relationship between experts and policy makers in terms of a producer-consumer dynamic, the issue of power begins to become a little less obscure than is generally found in the prevailing literature on postindustrialism. The view which accepts the proposition that, in postindustrial society power shifts to the expert, is implicitly based on the assumption that the shift is partially due to "producer sovereignty"—

control over scarce resources, i.e., knowledge or even information. The paradigm, however, is rather weak. Of critical importance is the fact, seemingly obvious though often ignored in much of the postindustrial literature, that the expert-policy-maker dynamic is, what may be called "consumer intensive."[14] In short, policy makers determine, to a large extent, both the conditions under which expertise is sought and the kinds of information desired. If this assertion is correct, then it is misleading to consider expertise and its utilization as a situation where "free-floating intellectuals" have services to sell to policy makers who are all too eager to consume them. Rather, we view experts as "technocratic counsel"[15] operating in settings in which the consumers—i.e., the dominant policy makers—largely determine the actions and activities of the producers.

To explore some of the ramifications of societal guidance and technocratic counsel as they have emerged in the United States, this discussion centers on four guidance areas that have become preeminent since 1960: (1) the political economy of the "new economics"; (2) program budgeting; (3) social indicators; (4) futures research.[16] To pursue some of the relationships between societal guidance and technocratic counsel, the chapter is divided into four sections. The first section discusses some intimations of societal guidance as they have evolved in the United States with regard to these four guidance areas. The second section suggests three general barriers to the development of guidance capacities. The third section examines three dimensions of postindustrial technocratic indicators as they bear on technocratic counsel. The fourth section explores the implications of what appears to be a normative dilemma that is built into the interrelationships between societal guidance and technocratic counsel.

INTIMATIONS OF SOCIETAL GUIDANCE: THE EMERGENCE OF TECHNOCRATIC POLITICS

During the 1960s a pervasive belief centering on the premise that improved information bearing on social problems would necessarily result in better or more "enlightened" public policy permeated political thought and action. This notion was concretized by President Lyndon Johnson on August 25, 1965, in his announcement that the planning-programming-budgeting system employed at the Department of Defense would be spread to the other federal agencies and departments. In Johnson's words:

> It is better to remember one thing: no system, no matter how refined, can make decisions for you. You and I have that responsibility in the executive branch. But our judgment is no better than our information. This system will present us with the alternatives and the information on the

basis of which we can, together, make better decisions. The people will be the beneficiary.[17]

Despite the obvious euphoria and "oversell" in the statement, it is nonetheless indicative of the recurring attempts, since 1945, to improve the guidance capabilities of the executive branch. The purposive acquisition of information was accompanied by an acceptance of planning as a process to guide, manage, and monitor change in the areas of defense, economic, and later, social policy. Within this broad context, the development of a positive orientation toward planning provided the backdrop for the emergence of technocratic politics. *Coordination* of societal information and the purveyors of information—technocratic counsel—established some of the parameters of the "new politics." It is within the context of societal guidance and technocratic politics that both Peter Drucker and Daniel Bell could argue that one of the dominant issues in the future will center around the potential conflicts between politicians and experts concerning the uses of information. According to Drucker: "Altogether the need to think through and set priorities for knowledge, to direct it and to take risks, moves knowledge, its direction, its goals and its results, increasingly into politics. We can no longer maintain the traditional line between 'dirty politics' and 'pure knowledge.'"[18] Stated somewhat differently, Bell noted: "The relationship of technical and political decisions in the next decades will become, in consequence, one of the most crucial problems of public policy."[19]

The comments by Drucker and Bell point to the political precariousness of information and applied social science, in particular, when adapted for purposes of guidance. To illustrate this, it would be useful to recall the attempts to expand the capacities for societal guidance in the United States since 1960. This requires a brief synopsis of: (1) the political economy of "new economics" growthmanship; (2) the institutionalization of program budgeting; (3) the experiences with social indicators; (4) the burgeoning field of futures research. Each to a limited degree is a "case study" in technocratic politics.

The Political Economy of the "New Economics"

In his famous Yale University commencement speech of June 1962, President Kennedy debunked the old economic myths of the past and declared that the main problems were technical—especially the management of the economy—rather than the resolution of ideological conflicts that have lost their relevance. The requisites of economic planning, management, and coordination were the hallmarks of a new age. Keynesian success at "taming" the business cycle and avoiding depression, though significant accomplishments, were not ends in themselves according to the advocates of the "new economics." For some, a full realization of the goals of the Employment Act of 1946 required the acceptance and implementation of neo-Keynesian "growthmanship," first developed by the Council of Economic Advisers under President Truman and later popularized and concretized as part of the "new economics" between 1961 and 1969.

This is not the place for a full review and critique of the political economy of the 1960s. Still, three points concerning the relationship between macro-economic policy and societal guidance should be highlighted. First, growthmanship combined some of the current concepts and information of academic economics with the concrete policy goals of the Kennedy and Johnson administrations.In many ways, the "new economics" represented the consensus and the "state of the art" of the profession in 1960.[20] Second, economic planning, American-style, brought many well-known professional economists into government service. The Council of Economic Advisers became a beachhead for the economics profession. For example, roughly 50 percent of the members of the CEA have been officers in the American Economic Association. Guidance functions for technocratic counsel in the area of economic policy became institutionalized. But beyond this, the council, as the administration's "economic ideologist," in the words of Edward Flash,[21] also frequently took on the additional roles of legitimation and certification of the strategic options that lay behind the administration's economic policies. This third aspect of the role of technocratic counsel became especially pronounced as the Age of the Economist enterd a rather rough period in late 1965 with the buildup in Vietnam. From 1965 to 1969 the new economists were faced with the unpleasant task of justifying policies that they were not satisfied with. This, of course, is inherent in the producer-consumer relationship mentioned earlier. From 1965, fiscal policies were increasingly subjected to a series of political constraints which made the task of guidance more difficult for the new economics.

While the experiences of the new economists between 1961 and 1969 could not be summarized as one of total success, it is generally argued that the major contribution of the new economics, indeed, its lasting contribution, is the fact that it had generated a "revolution" in the way policy makers *think* about macro-economic policy. While the consensus on this is not complete, few would deny that the influence of economists during the 1960s has been substantial. Whether the policies that flowed from their influence were "sound," "wise," or "just" are subjects of debate that are outside this chapter.

"Efficiency" as Doctrine: PPB

The planning-programming-budgeting system, first used at the Department of Defense under Robert McNamara and later expanded to civilian agencies and departments in 1965 by President Johnson, has often been used as the prime example of the technocratic reformism characteristic of advanced industrial political systems. The short history of program budgeting in the United States from its euphoric beginnings in 1961 to its demise, which began in 1969, serves as a preview of the conflict between the technocratic mode and the reality of politics—one of Bell's forecasts of the postindustrial future.

As a tool of guidance, program budgeting—fundamentally an offshoot of the social technology called "systems analysis"—was designed to improve the efficiency and rationality in the planning, formulation, coordination, management, and implementation of government programs through the use of a set of ill-defined analytical techniques that have their origins in cost-benefit analysis, operations research, and later, program budgeting as designed by Rand economists during the 1950s. In McNamara's words: "The basic objective of the management system we are introducing and trying to operate, is to establish a rational foundation as opposed to an emotional foundation for the decisions as to what size force and what type of force this country will maintain. This rational structure, this intellectual foundation for determining the military forces we should build and support is something that is laid out on paper."[22]

Needless to say, such statements by McNamara and his Defense Department "whiz kids" were hardly conducive to dampening the criticism from skeptics and opponents of program budgeting. Still, the much publicized planning-programming-budgeting system initiated at DOD under McNamara could be said to have had the following effects: (1) it created a "model" from which a positive planning orientation evolved; (2) it brought a group of "new men" into the executive branch whose influence was based on a monopoly of specialized knowledge; (3) it helped to create an atmosphere of "great expectations" that were to be unfulfilled; (4) it influenced the structure of power within the executive branch that was a tacit by-product of the planning process. It is perhaps for these reasons that one could agree with Daniel Bell that "McNamara joins Saint-Simon and Frederick W. Taylor as a hierophant in the pantheon of technocracy."[23]

As a planning tool, PPB was much less grandiose than either its critics or advocates implied. Alice Rivlin, former assistant secretary of Health, Education, and Welfare for Planning and Evaluation in the Johnson Administration, argued that this was the most useful aspect of PPB.[24] As a management tool, program budgeting was potentially innovative and inherently conflictual. In particular, this was evidenced in the rather rigid informational structure and information flow that were endemic to the system. From a managerial perspective, PPB implicitly supported the centralization of power in agency and department heads,[25] the coordinating role of the Budget Bureau, and the institutionalization of sectoral planning through the use of analysis and evaluation of alternative programs in prescribed policy areas.

While these innovations may have bolstered the managerial capabilities of federal executives, they invariably underestimated the conflict dynamics that surrounded the implementation of these reforms. In a recent article in which he prepared the "death certificate" for PPB, Allen Schick has written: "PPB died because new men of power were arrogantly insensitive to budgetary traditions, institutional loyalties, and personal relationships."[26] Though overstated, Schick's point suggests that PPB both underestimated the resilience of the political and promised too much. While in its original form, PPB may have witnessed a quiet death; however, it is probable that some form of the experiment will remain. Besides, the *long-term effects of PPB*, insofar as it tried to utilize both the content and flow of information to alter the structure of power in the federal government, could turn out to be more important than the "laundry list" of short-term fiascoes that one could easily make since its implementation in 1965.

From the Quality of Goods and Services to the "Quality of Life"[27]

By the mid-1960s muted criticisms of economic growth and program budgeting began to appear in discussions concerning the content and direction of public policy. The most consistent point made was that guidance tended to be *econocentric:* data and issues that were nonquantifiable were avoided; quantity rather than quality was stressed; and, in general, the important and inevitably normative questions that centered on the "quality of life" in the United States were obscured. As an antidote to econocentrism, two policy-oriented movements, diverse in both the types of individuals who were attracted to them as well as the multiplicity of approaches adopted by practitioners within the movements, emerged with the hope and expectation that additional information that would be forthcoming would redress this econocentric bias. The social indicators movement and the futures movement evolved in this context.

The initial vitality and yet inherent tension within the social indicators movement has been reflected in the multiple currents and cleavages that have persisted since the movement's beginnings in the mid-1960s. Originally begun by a group of social scientists who were critical of the pervasiveness of "economic philistinism," the movement soon included economists who viewed the movement as an opportunity to expand their presumed areas of expertise to include data and issues that went beyond the conventional concerns of economists.

Fundamentally, the social indicators movement took the humanist view that the quality of life rather than the mere quantity of goods and services should be the objective focus of government policy. This called for new conceptual approaches to traditional policy areas such as unemployment, crime, education, and health. The movement gave new life to the underfinanced and overlobbied federal statistical establishment which saw the potential utility of social indicators as a way of gaining political and financial support for new forms of data collection and retrieval. From the standpoint of federal executives, social indicators, particularly when combined with "social reports," were thought to be a useful tool of executive, and more important, *presidential management*. For a few individuals in the social indicators movement, social indicators were nothing less than a fundamental critique of the capitalist industrial order. This radical current, though never stated explicitly, could be extrapolated from the movement's oblique attack on standard financial accounting, the human value of contemporary bureaucracies, and most important, the ability of the market to provide for social welfare. Suggestions for a new "social calculus" and social systems accounting contained this radical current.

The amorphous nature of the social indicators movement allowed individuals of different stripes to coalesce in a rather loose, vaguely defined manner. Most wanted to improve the quality and increase the quantity of information available to policy makers. Differences emerged as to whether this could be done best through normative assessments of the state of society, monitoring social change, refining the evaluative tools of government analysts, or improving managerial effectiveness.

The internal debates within the social indicators movement over the relative importance of each of these approaches coupled with the lack of progress of social indicators construction in general undermined some of its appeal, both within the movement and among policy makers. Still, "managerialism," "broad-band economism," and "statisticism"—each a significant strain within the movement since its beginnings—are continuing to receive much attention. More important, these rather narrow approaches to social indicators seem to be receiving both financial and political support.[28] Thus, social indicators, contrary to the intentions of some of its original leading advocates, may in the future serve as a tool for societal management rather than as a vehicle for more "enlightened" public policy.[29]

The logic of societal planning and macro-management have always been currents within the social indicators movement, particularly among those who called for the adoption of social systems accounting and among those who felt that national goals be identified along with indicators to assess the degree to which the goals are being realized. For some this required a planning horizon of up to twenty years.[30] In this connection, the social indicators movement was certainly future-oriented in several respects. It was assumed, though only implicitly, that societal guidance was premature in the 1960s because policy makers lacked adequate noneconomic information. Descriptive reporting of social phenomena, always a major theme among practitioners in the social indicators movement, would fill this void. The degree to which societal guidance must rest on a social system model (which would presumably integrate information) proved to be one of the thorniest issues that divided the movement. Social systems accounting, and to a lesser extent, the analysis of social goals, tried to solve this problem. Lack of progress to date in this area remains as one of the substantive weaknesses of social indicators.

Nevertheless, the institutionalization of *guidance roles* was proposed in the mid-1960s.[31] Suggestions to expand the "central guidance cluster"[32] to include social indicators either in a Council of Social Advisers or an expanded Council of Economic Advisers[33] met with opposition from the Nixon administration.[34] Limited coordination through the efforts of the Statistical Policy Division of the Office of Management and Budget and the recent Center for the Coordination of Research on Social Indicators of the Social Science Research Council suggest that the management of social indicators information is not an unrealistic future prospect. When combined with some of the recent corporate efforts such as the notion of a periodic social audit of the corporation,[35] designed to polish up the corporate image, and the broad-band economist effort to establish all-purpose indicators of welfare through a readjusted gross national product,[36] one finds that the coordination and management of social indicators information may become an important (and perhaps ominous) tool for the guidance of postindustrial society. While some, besieged by an unhealthy state of premature optimism, will see this as a precondition for "enlightened" public policy, it may also bring about new forms of domination through the use of managed information by societal elites and their technocratic counsel.[37] This alternative scenario is offered merely to counterbalance much of the writing on postindustrial society that seems to adopt the view that "the truth shall make us free."[38]

Forecasting the Future

The height of optimism in the United States was accompanied by a second important policy-oriented movement that has theoretical and practical significance for the development of capacities for societal guidance. Many policy makers and social scientists felt that it was undesirable to continue to "stumble into the future." Despite the fact that social science for the most part lives in a ".3 world," some advancements in "social technology," systems analysis, econometric forecasting, and technological forecasting supposedly made it possible to begin to plan, project, and even "invent" the future. The futures movement, like the social indicators movement, brought together a rather unique blend of technologists and engineers, policy planners, a smattering of social scientists, a few physical scientists, humanists, and dedicated technocrats—all generally agreed that the study and planning of the future was a serious enterprise for those concerned with the "grand alternatives" inherent in the present.

What are some of the societal factors that have tended to encourage futures research? The sources seem to be as varied as the movement itself. They would include:

1. A vast increase in the rate of change.

2. The proliferation of organizational complexity which makes current concepts obsolete. This results in a search for new conceptual and normative approaches to organizational designs and possibilities for change.

3. The recognition of "macro-problems" as illustrated by the controversies surrounding the "limits of growth" and the "energy crisis."

4. The disjunction between specialization/professionalization and the growing need for transdisciplinary approaches to cope with technological and social imperatives of such macro-problems. This has resulted in new areas of interest such as systems theory and the policy sciences.

5. The belief that modern technology could be used to uncover behavioral and societal "laws" as exemplified by Jay W. Forrester's notion of the "counterintuitive behavior of social systems."[39]

6. The realization that some "findings" of futures research are already being confirmed by contemporary experience. For example, the notion that postindustrial society may experience "alienation amidst affluence"[40] has recently been borne out by the Department of Health, Education, and Welfare's report on work in America.

This list could expand greatly. Nevertheless, these phenomena suggest that the climate for the growth of the futures research industry (and it is quickly becoming an industry as illustrated by the fairly rapid growth of profit and nonprofit organizations that receive contracts for futures research) is favorable.

Although a futurist thrust can be found in macro-economic planning, program budgeting and social indicators, with futures research the overt commitment to both the time span and the breadth of issues and areas included in what is conventionally thought of as "planning" is greatest. Thus with futures research planning is often long-range, generally beyond twenty years and sometimes fifty years or more. Naturally the commitment to planning is very high among futurists; this is one of the issues that tends to unite futurists of different political and analytical postures.

At present political acceptance of futures research as a tool for societal guidance is at best partial. Technological forecasting has been employed at the Department of Defense for several years. According to the Hudson Institute's 1972 Report, the Department of Defense was the source of approximately 75 percent of the Institute's funds between 1962 and 1968. Since 1970, this percentage has dropped considerably.[41] The futures research industry may well profit from a generally pervasive "tech-fix" attitude that tends to accept the notion that urban and environmental problems are ameliorable to technological solutions. This view is found in the report by the President's Task Force on Science Policy entitled *Science and Technology: Tools For Progress*, which was made public in April 1970.[42] An uncritical faith in technology is found throughout the report. The Nixon administration's stress on applied rather than basic research also indicates the predominance of this "tech-fix" syndrome. While all futurists would not necessarily favor such an uncritical acceptance of the technological approaches to societal change, the industry as a whole will most likely profit from such an uncritical stance.

At present, much of the support for futures research is coming from the private sector. Several large corporations have full-time futurists on their payrolls. The Institute for the Future has received several contracts from major corporations.[43] Delphi studies are being undertaken by and for some corporations; the Hudson Institute is presently completing a major study, supported by some sixty multinational corporations, which is assessing the "corporate environment in 1975–1985."[44] With the steady blurring of political and economic power, with the boundaries between the public and the private sector becoming increasingly more difficult to see (and perhaps even behaviorally irrelevant), the futures research industry—though receiving more support, both financially and in the looser sense of encouragement, from the "private" sector—may become a viable part of the intellectual and in a more narrow sense, technological, ingredients of a system of societal guidance in postindustrial society. Finally, the recurring demands for "systems synthesizers," or what Theodore Geiger calls *a new kind of scientific integrator or generalist*,"[45] establishes a new role for futurists as technocratic counsel, for the very transdisciplinary nature of futures research makes the growing group of practicing futurists welcome assistants to the versatile societal managers of a postindustrial future.

What do the experiences of the 1960s tell us in regard to the attempts to promote the capacities for societal guidance? The short histories of these four areas of expertise suggest that, at best, our capabilities are "developing" but it is certainly premature to speak of the "knowledge society" as some propagandists of postindustrial futures tend to do. The experiences of these areas of expertise suggest that initial dynamism—a symptom of technocratic politics—often dissipates over time. In some cases the causes may be found in underutilization. More often, as a reading of the literature in all these areas will confirm, controversy emanated from rather strong doses of "oversell." In the words of Ida Hoos, a vociferous critic of systems analysis, policy makers were "dazzled by the panoply of 'Space Age tools' and overcome by the panegyrics of systems analysis enthusiasts who have made public problem solving their business."[46]

But what is the likelihood that current skepticism (which seems to be eroding) will tend to curtail the continued interest in the development and refinement of information for societal guidance as well as the experts that necessarily accompany this process? For Daniel Bell: "The central point about the last third of the twentieth century...is that it will require more societal guidance, more expertise."[47] Is the evidence conclusive? What political barriers might serve to qualify this projection? In the next section, three reasons are offered to suggest that this rather rosy projection of societal guidance and expertise in the postindustrial future of the United States is open to question.

UNDERDEVELOPED CAPACITIES: BARRIERS TO GUIDANCE

From the above it should be anticipated that guidance capacities are neither uniform nor do they necessarily experience uninterrupted growth. At least three reasons seem to suggest why this has been the case in the United States: (1) there is an imbalance in commitment; (2) within given guidance areas the state of knowledge and the available information is inadequate; and (3) there is a predominance of tactical over strategic innovations among technocratic counsel. These issues are discussed in some detail. Taken together, they might lead one to be somewhat skeptical about the notion that postindustrial society inevitably ensures sustained societal guidance through the utilization of highly developed and coordinated information. These indicators imply that such a conclusion is, at best, premature.

The Imbalance in Commitment

The "knowledge shall make us free syndrome" is best seen in uncritical infatuation with research and development figures. If GNP has been our "holy grail," in the words of Stuart Udall, R&D has been used to indicate, prognosticate, herald, and certify the coming postindustrial, or more coarsely, the "knowledge society." A critical look at R&D along with some additional indicators might dampen some of the enthusiasm among our postindustrial prophets who view R&D as a primary measure of the capacity for guidance.

Stated bluntly, R&D is a poor indicator of guidance capabilities and systematic commitment. First, the commitment of the federal government to guidance areas—defense, the economy, physical and environmental policies, and social policies, all broadly defined—has not been irreversible, even in aggregate terms. Total R&D, in other words, after growing steadily since the mid-1950s, reached its zenith in 1967. As figure 5.1 indicates, federal obligations for R&D dropped from 1967 to 1971. In 1972 it began to rise, reaching the 1967 level (inflation since 1967 would make the 1972 level considerably less in terms of actual value).

But R&D, either as an aggregate figure or as a percentage of gross national product, underestimates the imbalance in commitment in the sense that assigned priorities that underlie the R&D aggregate are

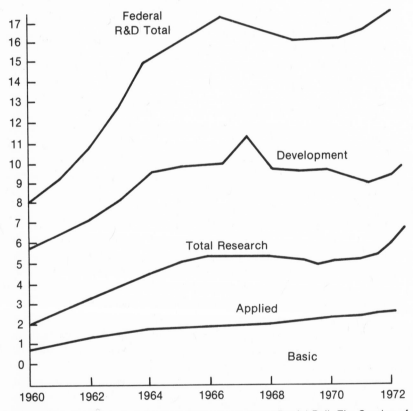

Figure 5.1. Trends in Federal R&D Obligations. From Daniel Bell, *The Coming of Post-Industrial Society* (New York: Basic Books, 1973), p. 259.

minimized. What has been the trend by areas of commitment? As almost every schoolchild knows, R&D has heavily supported defense and space efforts. However, the percentage of R&D allocated to space and defense is decreasing. This is supposed to give solace to those who see a reorientation of our national commitment. In 1960 federal expenditures for research and development for national defense, space research, and technology was 92 percent of total federal R&D. Human resources, natural resources and environment, economic affairs, and miscellaneous made up the rest. While it is true that the percentage for defense and space has decreased steadily, in 1972 it still accounted for 78 percent of the total federal expenditures.[48] The decline has been incremental at best. No claim can be made, based on the available data, that any wholesale change has taken place. On the other hand, a "naive extrapolation" of present trends would suggest that by the year 2000, federal expenditures for research and development will be about evenly divided between defense/space and human resources/economic affairs. Established structures of power along with the present international environment make this likelihood questionable.

If a tinge of optimism could be found in the above description of the change taking place in federal R&D expenditures, further probing of the makeup of R&D illustrates the resiliency of the current imbalance of commitment to guidance areas. If it is true, as many suggest, that our problems are primarily "social" rather than technological, R&D expenditures give no hint that this has been accepted by policy makers. Federal obligations to research in psychology and the social sciences represented 3 percent of total funds for research in 1960 and inched up to 6 percent in 1970, despite the rhetoric of the New Frontier and the Great Society that envisioned crusades in the concerted effort to find solutions to America's social problems.[49] Moreover, if we look at the percentage of federal R&D that went to the Department of Health, Education, and Welfare and the National Institutes of Health as an indication of how serious the effort to improve the "quality of life" actually was, we find a rather large gap between the pronounced goals of the Johnson administration and the actual commitment as reflected in R&D. In 1960 HEW and the National Institutes received approximately 8 percent of total R&D (by agency). In 1965 this increased to 9 percent. In 1970 it declined to 7 percent. Interestingly enough this percentage doubled under the Nixon administration (this despite the fact that the Nixon administration was more reticent in accepting social indicators, particularly in a humanist strain which places emphasis on the "quality of life"). Again, this hardly bespeaks a major redirection of commitment.

What of the notion that postindustrial society experiences a predominance of a professional and technical class whose expertise is essential for sustained societal guidance? Here the evidence confirms the proposition that in the postindustrial society the number of experts and the size of the professional and technical class grows significantly, both in absolute terms and in proportion to other classes—broadly defined. The need for more experts and expertise is not in question. But is the implicit optimism that this is "on the horizon" justified?

If we look at the professional, scientific, and technical personnel in the federal government between 1960 and 1970 we find that scientists made up 34 percent of this group in 1969. By 1970 this percentage increased to 38 percent. However, the percentage of social scientists among all scientists employed by the federal government, which was roughly 8 percent in 1960, did not change for the entire decade.[50] This appears to lend support for the proposition that at present an imbalance in commitment to guidance areas is a fundamental impediment to the development of guidance capacities. Finally, if we look at the output of doctorates as an additional indicator of the gap in capabilities, we find that although the aggregate number of Ph.D.s more than doubled from 1960 to 1968, the percentage of social scientist doctorates, which comprised 14 percent of the total in 1960, remained constant.[51] In other words, no demonstrative shift in the relative proportions, regardless of the optimism of the 1960s and the call for service in the various "wars" against America's social problems, took place.

Taken together, priorities reflected in the relative proportions of R&D expenditures; scientific, professional, and technical personnel employed in the federal government; and the output of doctorates all suggest that there is an imbalance in commitment to guidance areas. The data also suggest that change, if any, has been minimal. If societal guidance is said to be an important feature of a postindustrial future, it is incumbent upon students of postindustrial futures to avoid confusing limited progress in particular guidance areas (as evidenced by the experiences in macro-economics, program budgeting, social indicators and futures research) with a major, nonincremental shift in the system's commitment.

Information Gaps

If we define modernization in advanced industrial political systems as the application of knowledge to increasing areas of social life,[52] and societal guidance as its operational manifestation, then the predominant role of technocratic counsel becomes self-evident. The "knowledge is power" argument, however, tends to gloss over the political vulnerability of experts who invariably have less than complete knowledge in their presumed areas of specialization. The collective experiences with macro-economics, program budgeting, social indicators, and futures research bear witness to the fact that failure to deliver has its political costs. This is certainly true of program budgeting; a good case supporting this point might be developed from the short history of the social indicators movement, and it appears that the more politically astute futurists are softening their claims given the present state of the art. Even the "queen of the social sciences" is wearing a tarnished crown these days, given the present economic problems—"stagflation" and "slumpflation" being the most recent that beset the highly industrialized political systems.

The gaps in knowledge and information are formidable obstacles to sustained societal guidance. One such gap lies in the enormous difficulty in uncovering complex systemic interrelationships. Yet this is crucial if the planning, implementation, and evaluation phases of the policy process are to become integrated. For example, assessing costs and benefits of government programs in nonmonetary terms—a necessity if program budgeting was to be effective as a managerial tool in the administration of social programs—has not been adequately achieved.[53] Rather, the tendency to rely on econocentric indicators and to minimize those data that are complex and nonquantifiable tend to limit the information that would fill this void. Some practitioners felt that social indicators would supplement economic indicators and economic criteria for choice. For some, social indicators were seen as tools for program evaluation.[54] It is in this light that Mancur Olson, former deputy assistant secretary of Health, Education, and Welfare (social indicators) in the Johnson administration, suggested that social reporting was basically an extension of program budgeting.[55]

Besides lacking evaluative information, policy makers also lacked adequate information on the nature of the implementation process. As Walter Williams has pointed out in a review of federal government social agencies, programs designed in Washington took on a much different character (often unrecognizable when compared to the initial "plans") in the "field."[56] Robert Anthony, former assistant secretary of defense (comptroller) during the Johnson administration, states that PPB lacked an accounting subsystem that could have supplied information on how much was spent on specific programs. This is necessary, he argues, if the gap between planning and performance is to be closed.[57] Despite the alleged sophistication of program budgeting, it was unable to provide adequate information on implementation and performance. Little wonder, then, that the initial burst of optimism that accompanied PPB has been completely deflated. Put bluntly, the program budgeteers have failed to deliver. Information gaps were not inconsequential in this failure.

The Predominance of the Tactical

A plethora of information in a given guidance area is, in itself, insufficient to ensure effective societal guidance. What is needed, in addition, is integration of tactical with strategic management. Much of the attention given to the role of new technologies as catalysts of decision-making reforms in postindustrial society is almost exclusively concerned with tactical innovations. The linchpin of Daniel Bell's conception of post-industrial society, though based on an "axial principle" (the centrality of theoretical knowledge) that has strategic implications, becomes operationalized through a series of tactical discoveries. According to Bell: "It is not altogether fanciful to suggest that just as the 100 years before 1945 were dominated by machine technology so the next 100 years may be shaped by a new 'intellectual technology,' which by systems analysis, simulation, game theory, decision theory, programming and other methods hitched to a computer, will lay out a new compass of the rationality of means."[58] To a lesser extent, Zbigniew Brzezinski also seems to stress tactical decision-making innovations.[59]

Unfortunately, focusing on the more visible signs of managerial invention—program budgeting is a case in point—places undue faith in the ability of these tactical innovations to solve large-scale technological, social, and ultimately, political problems. Part of this bias may be due to the continual dominance of the values of efficiency and narrow rationality which limit the development of *strategic* decision making.[60] Mancur Olson stated that social indicators were intended to facilitate movement "toward a system that could provide better information and analysis for strategic decisions on social and economic policy."[61] Fundamentally, a social report was viewed as an instrument of executive, and more specifically, presidential management. From this perspective, indicators provide technical support for strategic planning. But the case of social reporting is rare.

Why have technocratic counsel (and theorists of postindustrial society) tended to ignore strategic reforms? It seems plausible to suggest, after reviewing the short histories of the four guidance areas, that technocratic counsel accept the strategic options supplied by policy makers as given and beyond discussion. This naturally flows from the consumer-intensive nature of the relationship between high policy makers and their experts. Parameters are set by policy makers, not by experts. Once this is established experts can supply information bearing on such questions as the relationship between acceptable levels of unemployment and price stability. In the case of unemployment this is reflected in the debates among economists concerning the operational definition of "full" employment. The late Russell Nixon, commenting on this so-called great debate, once remarked: "If you're in favor of 2 percent, you're a radical, 3 percent, you're a liberal, 4 percent, you're a Democrat, and if you are in favor of 5 percent, you're a Republican." The point here, of course, is that the major conceptual and strategic requirements remain fixed. Willing producers who aspire to some degree of influence in the policy process invariably must accept the strategic positions of the powerful consumers. After all, this is one example of producer-consumer relations where there is little shortage of producers. Technocratic counsel are not in short supply.

The literature on postindustrial futures tends to gloss over the distinction between tactical and strategic change. Yet, an examination of strategic policy making requires a discussion of the complex relationship among institutions responsible for policy guidance. The lack of attention given to problems and prospects of macro-management in much of the literature on postindustrial society creates an aura of sterility and, at times, unreality. Linear projections of the knowledge industry, intellectual technologies, and the professional class are made with little or no reference to the institutional forms they serve. The power of multinational corporations is often ignored or glossed over.[62]

The future of industrial society may witness a growing realization that strategic planning is inevitable. Intimations in this direction are found among the practitioners of futures research. However, governmental institutions are lagging behind corporations in developing capacities for strategic decision making. Closer integration between business and government may provide a setting for strategic management within which technocratic counsel might flourish, particularly at the tactical level. As one possible future, this scenario envisions the emergence of technocratic politics which provides multiple roles for experts as institutions become more complex. In such a setting, the demands for more planning and management may provide more favorable "markets" for technocratic counsel.

POSTINDUSTRIAL TECHNOCRATIC INDICATORS: THREE DIMENSIONS OF TECHNOCRATIC COUNSEL

Postindustrial society is supposedly characterized by the growing importance of expertise and experts. Is this indeed so? What roles do experts play? What values could we expect experts to hold in the postindustrial future? Will they be significantly different from the roles and values of experts in industrial societies? To probe these questions (though clear-cut answers to these questions are certainly not available) this section attempts to point to three technocratic indicators that should be considered in macro-analyses of societal change. Unlike much of the work of the social indicators movement that focuses almost entirely on indicators of performance, this section suggests that one fruitful way to pose the question about alternative postindustrial futures seriously is to focus on *indicators of structural change*. Hopefully, this is a modest effort in that direction. To restrict the discussion, three "exploratory" indicators that bear on the relationship between technocratic counsel and societal guidance are mentioned: (1) institutional indicators that support technocratic counsel; (2) multiple roles of technocratic counsel; and (3) the alleged transformation from industrial to postindustrial technocratic values.

Critics of the inflated claims often made by systems experts ask one basic question: What effect did all these experts have on public policy? If one were to be kind to the specialists, the answer would have to be rather little. Much more critical appraisals have been reached, of course.[63] The halo surrounding PPB had already vanished by 1969. For some, the demise of PPB is now complete.[64] The "new economics" tends to linger in those "governments in exile" such as The Brookings Institution and the Departments of Economics at Harvard and MIT. Still, appearances are deceiving and this certainly relates to technocratic counsel. Some of the symbolic aspects of technocratic politics, especially its initial dynamism during the "crusades" of the 1960s, have tended to diminish.

It would be premature, however, to proclaim "the death of technocracy," as Alvin Toffler does in the last chapter of *Future Shock*.[65] On the contrary, a description of some institutional indicators might show some of the structural components that support the proliferation of technocratic counsel.

The Institutional Dimension

One visible sign of the growth of expertise is found in the employment patterns of the federal government. As table 5.1 indicates, the decade of the 1960s witnessed a 49 percent increase in the number of scientific personnel employed by the federal government. For social science personnel, the increase between 1960 and 1970 was 52 percent. These changes, as table 5.1 suggests, cannot simply be explained by the

Table 5.1. Selected Employment Trends in the Federal Government, 1960–70

	1960	1970	% Increase
Total federal government[a]	788,818	1,028,019	.30
Scientific, professional, technical personnel	153,363	208,257	.26
Scientific only	53,264	79,390	.49
Social science personnel only	4,672	7,113	.52

SOURCE: Adapted from U.S. Department of Commerce, *Statistical Abstract of the United States 1972* (Washington, D.C.: Government Printing Office, 1972), pp. 400, 525.

[a]Excludes Department of Defense and Post Office personnel.

"normal" growth in the federal government. Nor can these increases be explained merely by the growth of "professionalization," which is a vague, catchall term that often obscures qualitative changes. Besides, the growth of professional and technical personnel is primarily explained by the overall increase in federal government personnel. (This should not be construed as evidence that a purposive effort to "technicize" the federal government has been under way. In fact, one might still make the case that, in some respects, the federal government still has not fully adjusted its employment patterns to the overall increase in the highly educated portion of the labor force. While the federal government's employment of scientists increased by 49 percent in the ten-year period, the output of doctorates in the United States increased by 185 percent.[66])

The data lend some support to the proposition that a technical infrastructure seems to be emerging within the federal government. The continuation of this trend would mean that one prerequisite for guidance—an adequate supply of technical manpower in guidance areas—will have been achieved.

The changing nature of this infrastructure is not the only institutional indicator that has some relevance for postindustrial futures. Earlier studies of the top positions in the executive branch of government have shown two trends that bear on the present argument. First, the educational level of those studied (assistant secretaries, deputy secretaries, directors, etc.) has risen over time. This is hardly startling; the same trend is true of the population as a whole. Second, the number of appointees that can be characterized as specialists or experts has also increased over time. As a rule, these individuals tend to have little or no full-time government experience prior to appointment. Typically, these specialists have Ph.D.s in economics or physics. Some have advanced degrees in systems engineering. Many worked for some of the largest corporations such as Eastman Kodak or Litton Industries; some of the economists were employed by the major financial institutions in the United States. One even finds a smattering of former associate professors among this group.[67] In a study of assistant secretaries from the Truman, Eisenhower and Kennedy administrations, Dean Mann found that education levels "indicate greater emphasis in later years on more advanced training for management positions, especially those involving complex technical problems."[68] Singling out the Department of the Treasury he added: "Appointments made by George Humphrey and Douglas Dillon at the beginning of the Eisenhower and Kennedy administrations show clearly the present tendency to recruit men of high technical ability with appropriate financial backgrounds."[69] Similar recruitment policies were followed by both Presidents Johnson and Nixon.

Recruitment trends from 1961 to the present suggest that a new type of "in-and-outer" has emerged.[70] The Wall Street law firm–assistant secretary–Wall Street route is still operative; however, a second kind of mobility (Rand Corporation–assistant secretary–Litton Industries) has become increasingly common. It is the mobility of the technocrat, a facet of postindustrial society.

The structural manifestation of this trend in the federal government is found in persons who occupy the "planning and evaluation" posts in the executive branch. Of sixteen such positions examined for the Nixon administration, eight were occupied by individuals with Ph.D.s in either economics or physics; two had advanced specialized degrees. Only one of these individuals had substantial governmental experience.[71] Recruitment trends for executive departments show this gradual emergence of the "new men," particularly in the Departments of Defense, Health, Education, and Welfare, and Treasury. (The Office of Management and Budget, contrary to the image some have of it as a haven for Rand dropouts, does not fit this pattern. Biographical data that were available for nineteen of the top officials of OMB during the Nixon administration showed that only three individuals fit the above description of mobile technocrats. Most were career civil servants.) Mobility was one of the hallmarks of the systems analysts during the 1960s; they were primarily responsible for bringing program budgeting to the civilian agencies of the federal government. In a caustic critique of this situation Ida Hoos has written:

> [T]he techniques spawned in the Pentagon by RAND economists became transferred to the war on poverty and to many other battles on the home front through the subsequent movement, in the perpetual game of musical highchairs, of the former Department of Defense Whiz Kids into civilian agencies. Now similarly rationalized as economic matters because they, too, require allocation and use of resources, non-military affairs of all kinds became the target for the "powerful tools of technology."[72]

The dispersal of these new "in-and-outers" did not abate under the Nixon administration. In some areas, the concern for management coordination, as exemplified by some of Nixon's appointments, has grown in recent years.[73]

The White House network provides an environment within which technocratic counsel may flourish. The use of experts, noticeable in FDR's administrations, grew during the 1960s. Despite the Nixon administration's antiintellectual, antiacademic image, a few key posts in the central guidance cluster were held by former academics.

What do the data in table 5.2 show? Comparing 1972 to the "base" year (1960), the institutions of technocratic counsel—the CEA, NSC, and OST—have grown, but hardly in a monotonic pattern. More important, however, is the increase in the White House Office and the Office

Table 5.2. Employment Trends in the Executive Office of the President, 1960–72

	1960	1965	1968	1969	1970	1971	1972
White House Office	446	333	273	344	311	600	584
Office of Management and Budget	434	524	594	582	633	727	710
Council of Economic Advisers	32	46	78	53	59	59	63
National Security Council	65	38	35	46	75	83	78
Office of Science and Technology	—	70	83	74	89	68	72
Total	977	1011	1063	1099	1167	1537	1507

SOURCE: Adapted from *Statistical Abstract of the United States 1972* (Washington, D.C.: Government Printing Office), p. 400.

of Management and Budget in 1971. At this point the issue of political power, raised at the beginning of the paper, must be addressed, if only partially. The growth in the White House Office and OMB invariably were related to President Nixon's attempts to establish tightened management and coordination. Surely his proposed reorganization plans should be seen in this perspective. Aggregate increases or decreases in technocratic counsel become secondary within this broader context. Moreover, it is within this structural setting that the essentially subservient role of the expert becomes most apparent. Those who see the dominance or tyranny of experts as a problem of postindustrial society should take pause by trying to separate more quantitative changes in the number of experts in a given area from qualitative shifts—the White House attempts at management and coordination being a prime example—that may have wider and, perhaps, long-range significance.

The institutional setting within which technocratic counsel finds itself does not necessarily provide a conflictless atmosphere for the flowering of expertise. While seemingly an obvious point, much of the literature on postindustrial society tends to minimize this issue. The political precariousness of technocratic counsel is best illustrated by the Nixon administration's deflation of its interest in social indicators which was highlighted by the abrupt dismantling of the National Goals Research Staff. One could only surmise that such projects were out of character with the White House coordination plans. On the other hand, one should not overlook the wider political ramifications that may be behind the limited inauguration of new guidance areas.

Technology assessment is a case in point. In an article entitled, "Teddy Kennedy's 'Shadow Government,'" Jude Wanniski, a member of the *Wall Street Journal's* editorial staff wrote:

> Technology assessment sounds innocent enough, but the White House is worried. Partly because it has just finished a general housecleaning of administration "science experts" who were really nothing more than political operatives for the Nixon opposition. This collection of academicians will no doubt rise from the ashes to work for OTA [Office of Technology Assessment] and Sen. Kennedy.[74]

The point here, of course, is that technology assessment, like social indicators, program budgeting, macro-economic growthmanship, and futures research, will in all probability become embroiled in political conflict. All this suggests that students of postindustrial futures should be constantly aware of the fact that the acquisition of information is rarely an end in itself.

Alternative Roles: Guidance, Legitimation, or Both?

What types of role patterns should be expected of experts as the capacities for societal guidance grow and the corresponding need for more specialized information increases in postindustrial society? The current literature is particularly obscure on this issue. A dichotomy is found between those who view the role of experts as one of guidance and those who see experts as legitimators and ratifiers of policies and decisions made by others.

Most of the arguments that attempt the notion that postindustrial society will witness the flow of power from politicians to experts seem to be derived from the "axiom" that knowledge and information are scarce resources. From this, the following propositions are developed:

PROPOSITION 1. *Knowledge in advanced industrial systems is an instrument of political power.*

1.1. *Societal complexity and rapid rates of change have the effect of making existing forms of knowledge and information obsolete. This increases the demand for new knowledge and information.*

1.2. *The problems of advanced industrial society require specialized knowledge and information. This establishes the primary social role of experts.*

1.3. *The problems of industrial society are increasingly amenable to solution through the application of existing knowledge and information.*

1.4. *Because of the technical complexity of most policy decisions, ex-*

perts are increasingly brought into the decision-making process to supply specialized information and advice.

1.5. *The political power of experts increases due to this social rule. Politicians, because they are dependent on experts for knowledge and specialized information, witness an erosion of political power.*

Variants of these propositions can be found in the writings of such diverse theorists of industrial and postindustrial society as Daniel Bell, Zbigniew Brzezinski, Jean Meynaud, Alain Touraine, J. K. Galbraith, Raymond Aron, and most obviously, Jacques Ellul.[75] Some see a developmental process in which the social role of the "men of knowledge" leads to a shift in power. Thus, Raymond Aron could write, "beyond a certain stage in its development industrial society itself seems to me to widen the range of problems referable to scientific examination and calling for the skill of the social engineer."[76] Similarly, Amitai Etzioni has argued, "to know is to have power, and social knowledge is a source of power over society. The more malleable society becomes, and the more valid and comprehensive the social sciences become, the greater will be their potential power. It is for this reason that an active orientation among social scientists assumes increasing importance."[77] This point of view was held by some of the early advocates of social indicators who felt that improved knowledge and information (which, of course, they would supply) would lead to more "rational" policy.[78] In another area, Walter Heller, a leading spokesman for the "new economics," described part of his role as one of making the doctrine palatable for political consumption, thereby facilitating policy guidance.[79]

The above description of the social role of the expert in advanced industrial political systems tends to see the specialist as an agent of change, responsible for societal steering or guidance. Policy formulation is dominated by experts who, it is argued, increasingly monopolize the difficult technical choices that are inherent in contemporary public policy.[80] In its most extreme form, the argument concludes by stating that policy *decisions* are, in reality, made by experts and merely ratified by those who hold only symbolic power, i.e., the politicians.[81]

An alternative explanation of the social role of experts focuses on the process of *legitimation.* Whereas the above description establishes the predominance of societal guidance as the fundamental role of experts in advanced industrial systems and, by extrapolation, postindustrial society as well, a contrary argument states that the social role of experts is limited to that of symbolic ratification.[82] Stated in propositional form, this alternative assessment states:

PROPOSITION 2. *The primary social role of experts is to* legitimize *policy decisions made by the real holders of power.*

2.1. *Major policy alternatives pose value choices that are inherently conflictual.*

2.2. *Value disparities reflect the balance of power within the political system.*

2.3. *Choice, therefore, symbolizes the "victory" of a particular structure of power.*

2.4. *After the decision is made, policy makers look for ways to legitimize their decisions. Technical explanations and justifications serve to diffuse conflict.*

2.5. *The image of the expert who is "above politics" is a useful legitimizing tool. Moreover, since they are expendable, experts serve as convenient scapegoats for policies that have failed.*

Both positions treat the policy maker–expert relationship as a zero-sum game; therefore, the permutation of social roles is limited in each set of propositions. However, the "central guidance cluster" of modern governments includes multiple roles, many of them played by technocratic actors, that are often in conflict with each other.[83] In the United States we have witnessed a proliferation of staff roles where experts have become quite commonplace. The relative influence of experts in these staff roles varies according to the particular area of expertise, its perceived capabilities, and the specific administration served. The Council of Economic Advisers, for example, has experienced varying degrees of influence. Some staff roles—the short-lived National Goals Research Staff is the best example—may be occasionally caught in bureaucratic crossfires. Under this condition experts would be most expendable.

Technocratic counsel could be expected to perform the dual roles of guidance and legitimation. The history of the "new economics" from 1961 to 1969 is a case in point. Technical guidance in the major macroeconomic policy area has consistently come from presidential economic advisers. According to Lawrence Pierce, "the council helps the president specify his own policy objectives. At the beginning of the year, the council translates the president's general economic objectives into a set of moving targets, toward which policy actions during the year can be aimed. . . . It tries to restate the president's implicitly stated goals in economic language that can be used to direct policy choices."[84]

The political zenith for the advocates of the "new economics" accompanied the "Keynesian celebration," to use Jesse Burkhead's apt phrase, following the 1964 tax cut.[85] It would be rather simplistic, however, to suggest that, because the "new economics" was fundamental in policy guidance, the President's economic advisers were dominant in terms of the formulation of policy. On the contrary, additional evidence suggests that the economists' recommendations were sometimes bypassed. Often charges of "political inertia" or the "lack of political will" are disguised complaints by experts who feel that their advice is being ignored. This, at least, seemed to be the view of some economists, including the CEA, who called for a tax increase in late 1965 to stem the rate of inflation caused, in part, by the Vietnam war.[86] Similarly, Arthur Okun, in evaluating President Nixon's decision in 1969 to request an ending of the 7 percent investment credit, said in a *New York Times* interview:

> Nearly all, if not all, of the President's principal economic and financial advisers were on record as saying they wanted to stick with the credit. Maybe they had a change of heart, but at least it does raise the question of who is giving the advice to the President and on what basis he is making his decisions if he does not come out on the side of his principal economic advisers.[87]

This ignores the fact that, under certain conditions, policy advice may be politically unacceptable. The rejection of a tax increase in 1966 is a case in point. Besides, economic advisers, as Okun probably knows quite well, have been called upon to justify and legitimize administration policy.[88] These should also be included in the analysis of the multiple roles of technocratic counsel.

Technocratic Values: Resiliency or Evaluation?

The two previous technocratic indicators—institutional support for technocratic counsel and their multiple social roles—lend some evidence to the hypothesis that technocratic politics and societal guidance appear to be "correlates" of the emerging postindustrial society. A third indicator—what may be called the *evolution of technocratic values*—is now discussed in an effort to both identify some of the principal technocratic values and the degree to which they may be undergoing change.

The notion of "technocratic ideology" has been of central concern for those interested in the influence of experts in advanced industrial systems. Yet the description of the various elements that supposedly contribute to such an ideology is one-dimensional and, in fact, rather redundant. With slight variations, one finds the following themes in the critical literature concerned with technocracy:[89]

1. Efficiency and functional rationality are behavioral norms that are widely held by experts.

2. A belief in inevitable progress is part of a developmental view of history.

3. A view of society that tends to minimize conflict. Conflict is seen as a corollary of ignorance; therefore, the application of knowledge will reduce conflict.

4. Depoliticization is held as both a desirable and inevitable process. Politics and rationality are considered antithetical to each other. The developmental process is characterized by the replacement of politics with technology.

While expressions of these technocratic values are rarely stated in such an integrated and comprehensive fashion by technocratic counsel, there is certainly no dearth of evidence to support the observation that a subtle "technocratic ideology" exists, to varying degrees, in contemporary advanced industrial systems. For example, what Daniel Bell calls the technocratic mode[90]—norms of efficiency, rationality, and output—have been frequently espoused by advocates of program budgeting. In this connection, former director of the Bureau of the Budget under President Johnson, Charles L. Schultze, wrote: "The PPB system provides the decision process with a new group of advocates. They are, in effect, 'partisan efficiency advocates'—the champions of analysis and efficiency."[91]

The uncritical faith in progress coupled with a deemphasis of the potential conflictual by-products of economic and technological change are evidenced in the growthmanship of the "new economics" of the 1960s.[92] Avoidance of politics exemplified by the depoliticization theme is also prevalent in much of the futures literature. A content analysis of the dominant theme of all the articles published in volumes 1 to 4 of the journal *Futures*, for example, revealed that 47 percent of the articles dealt with methodology, 22 percent focused on physical or technological futures, 15 percent concentrated on social change, 9 percent political futures, and 3 percent economic futures. A trenchant critique of depoliticization in futures research was made by John Goldthorpe:

> If a situation can be defined as a social problem then the question that tends automatically to follow is that of what can be done to remedy or alleviate it; that is a question of means of techniques ... the language of social problems can be used to discuss what are often in fact situations of social *conflict* in such a way as to politically "defuse" them—minimizing the apparent relevance or rival ideologies, while maximizing that of non-ideological, pragmatic, technico-administrative solutions. Politics then becomes reduced to little more than haggling over the respective merits of those "solutions" which the experts deem to be flexible.[93]

Unfortunately, examples of what Goldthorpe is referring to abound. This engineering approach to societal change which envelops the various elements of technocratic ideology can be found in the government-sponsored reports that have called for more use of applied social science to "solve" various social problems.[94]

More serious than the actual ideology, however, is the charge that it lends support for established interests. In other words, technocratic ideology is said to be inherently conservative since it contributes to the maintenance of existing forms of stratification and dominance.[95] This view, though perhaps overstated, should not be dismissed out of hand. In discussing the role of experts, Clark Kerr wrote: "The experts help settle the inevitable conflicts of interest on the basis of facts and analysis, and also with an eye to preservation of the existing system, rather than on principle except for a general attachment to the concept of a reasonable and a balanced society."[96]

A survey of futures research also indicates this tacit acceptance of present structures along with an implicit equilibrium model of society. More important, support for present concentrations of power is reflected in the research that has been done and is under progress.[97] In the case of social indicators, the scarcity of research concerned with *indicators of institutional change* reveals a basic acceptance of current structures of power. Of the twenty-two research projects funded by the National Science Foundation in 1971 only one appeared to be concerned with an issue (the distribution of wealth) that may be construed as controversial. The grant also happened to be the smallest of the twenty-two projects listed. Projects that received the most financial assistance tended to focus on the "measurement of social change," values, and value change. Much less attention was given to the theme of the "quality of life" that was so central to the first phase of the social indicators movement's history. Of the twenty-one research projects funded in 1972, two appear to be directly concerned with structural indicators of political change. The macro-managerial utility of much of the current positivist efforts of research on social indicators and alternative futures suggests that creative technocratic innovations are not incompatible with established structures of power.[98]

The roots of technocratic values are to be found in the industrial order. For Daniel Bell and Jean Meynaud, technocracy as a mode of thought began with Saint-Simon.[99] Theodore Geiger traced the origins of technocratic values to what he calls "redemptive activism" from which one derives the norms of efficiency and rationality as well as a fundamental belief in progress. These values began, according to Geiger, with the rise of Western civilization.[100] In one sweeping sentence, Theodore Roszak tries to establish the link between centuries of technocratic thought: "Certainly the pure technocratic system that Francis Bacon heralded in his *New Atlantis* and which Saint-Simon, Auguste Comte, and Thorstein Veblen were later to champion, is best regarded as no more than an ideal type of what Saint-Simon called the 'administrative state'—the society beyond politics to which social engineers like Simon Ramo might aspire."[101] Are these technocratic values undergoing change?

It is increasingly argued that the underpinnings of technocratic values, so firmly entrenched in industrial society, are now being undermined by vicissitudes of postindustrial futures. Ronald Inglehart provides evidence to illustrate that "post-bourgeois" values, which are not attached to either the economics of scarcity or the politics of industrial society, are emerging in Western Europe.[102] The past three presidents of the American Political Science Association have all, to varying degrees, reflected on the implication of value change for a positive, committed—and by inference—applied political science.[103] In a more popular, though no less serious vein, Alvin Toffler has pronounced the end of technocracy: "What we are witnessing is the beginning of the final breakup of industrialism and, with it, the collapse of technocratic planning."[104] What is its replacement? For Toffler it is "the strategy of social futurism."[105] David Easton describes a "post-behavioral" revolution in the social sciences.[106] Heinz Eulau envisions a "consultative commonwealth."[107] Still others look for a panacea in the "policy sciences."[108] How valid are these various claims of new posttechnocratic values?

What we are witnessing is not the death of technocracy, as some would have it, but, rather its "perfuming"—"technocracy with a human face"—with its blending of superficial humanism and traditional technocratic values that are alive and well. A few recent illustrations of this are in order. Gross national product, never felt to be an adequate and accurate all-purpose measure of welfare to thoughtful social scientists, is now undergoing some renovation by economists who, by making some adjustments to the national income accounts, are designing a new measure of economic welfare—appropriately called NEW.[109] Despite the new concerns for welfare and consumption rather than output aggregates, this recent effort still stems from the assumption that the construction of a single measure, even if made up of noncommensurables, is a useful exercise. Functional rationality and output criteria are still prevalent. In another area we find the "tech-fix" mentality, with its sole emphasis on means and little or no expression of social goals, operative among some social scientists.[110] This view finds its latest and fullest expression in a recent article by Herbert Simon where he laments the fact that although technology has been used successfully in solving physical and ecological problems, man's "human insatiability"—exemplified by "aspiration values" that become transformed into zero-sum games—poses the greatest challenge to date. According to Simon, "Our hope lies in knowledge, in understanding ourselves. Here as with the other problems, we are going to need more and better technology, not less."[111]

The tendency to minimize conflict, to assume that it is an aberration rather than a fundamental part of the human condition that is not always amenable to quick, and certainly not complete, solutions, is indicative of this new perfumed technocratic tendency to allude to a particular humanist theme and submerge it beneath a sea of standard calculational values. It is in this sense that the upsurge of concern for "social costs," "negative externalities," and the "social responsibility" of corporations are not inherently incompatible with the technocratic mode. On the contrary, they represent the latest, and perhaps most creative, union between a perfumed humanism and the technocratic mode. What we might well witness in the near, post-Watergate future, is the "greening of technocracy"—"technocracy with a human face"—the intimations of which are already apparent in the present. Divorced from fundamental structural change that would reduce concentrations of power and hierarchy, such envisioned value changes implicit in the revitalized social concerns and the higher levels of rationality implied by such concepts as "postbehavioralism," "policy analysis," and "systems synthesis" that supposedly alter the attitudes and behavioral patterns of experts become self-righteous proclamations separated from the real world of politics.

THE NORMATIVE DILEMMA

It seems evident, if the above analysis is essentially correct, that a major dimension of postindustrialism is the institutionalization of societal guidance in the structure and process of public policy. The use of information, especially applied social science, will most likely increase. One "correlate" of this probable tendency, it has been suggested, is the growth of technocratic counsel. In this respect, societal guidance and technocratic counsel, though salient features of postindustrial society, have their roots in the industrial order. Some of the ramifications of these phenomena were explored in the discussions of three indicators of technocratic politics. A few notes on the normative implications of these probable developments should be made.

A subtle ambivalence concerning the roles of experts and specialized knowledge pervades much of the literature on postindustrialism. While a great deal of consensus exists on the theoretical and empirical magnitude of the issue, the normative stance taken by the various writers has been quite diverse. It would not be unfair to note that Daniel Bell, despite his conclusion that postindustrial society will experience conflict between technocratic and political decision making, essentially views the growing influence of experts in a favorable light. Zbigniew Brzezinski is less unequivocal: "Deliberate management of the American future will become widespread, with the planner eventually replacing the lawyer as the key social legislator and manipulator."[112]

On the other hand, no dearth of negative interpretations of the societal ramifications that flow from the influence of experts exists in the current literature. Herbert Marcuse has argued: "Scientific-technical rationality and manipulation are welded together into new forms of social control."[113] Similarly, Theodore Geiger has written that "by virtue of the crucial role assigned to the scientifically trained, self-selecting elite positivists tend toward a presumed benevolent authoritarianism which, in the more democratic societies of North America and northern Europe, is usually implicit rather than overt."[114] The normative implications of planning, particularly as they relate to the difficulty in reconciling expertise with popular control, has been recognized by Andrew Shonfield: "The worst danger to democratic institutions would be if it were pretended that there was nothing whatsoever to worry about—because a standing committee of the nation's major interest groups working in collaboration with a team of high-powered economic experts had succeeded in taking the issue right out of politics."[115] The dilemma has been well put by Giovanni Sartori: "We shall have to surrender, in the long run, to the need for proceeding swiftly in the direction of a democracy which, without being governed by experts, relies openly on their advice."[116] Those who view the present and the emerging postindustrial society in less than idyllic terms must address themselves to this central issue.

Proposals for reform might profitably begin by reevaluating the implications of the three postindustrial technocratic indicators outlined above. For example, technocratic values, though seemingly resistant to change, might be transformed. In this connection, Bertram Gross has suggested that the positivist value-free posture, so prevalent among technocratic counsel, be scrapped in favor of "*value-creating decision-making.*"[117] This does not suggest a retreat from technology and, more specifically, guidance. Rather, it calls for the expansion of presently restrictive conceptions of rationality that tend to be held by guidance actors. The multidimensional character of an expanded rationality has been described by Hans Peter Dreitzel:

> *[T]he display of rational behavior on each level presupposes that such behavior is also based on the lower levels of rationality*—provided our present level of technology and organization is to be preserved. There is no political rationality which does not encompass the level of rationality a society has historically reached.[118]

Nevertheless, as Dreitzel argues, the political and moral implications of technological choice must become preeminent to technocratic counsel.[119] The prevailing tendency among technocratic counsel is to superficially recognize value and political choices and then dismiss them as "outside their department."

The issue is brought out rather clearly in two opposing positions about the utility of economics in determining the relative "value" of values in policy making. According to Charles Schultze, former director of the Bureau of the Budget in the Johnson administration, "Personal tax cuts that increase society's consumption of beer and whitewall tires hold equal status with increased public expenditures for education."[120] Such a choice is labeled a "value judgment" which is outside the competence of economists. Dubbing such a noninterventionist position the "Immaculate Conception of the Indifference Curve,"[121] Kenneth Boulding has suggested that economics could be utilized so as to elucidate moral choices. Needless to say, within the economics profession, the former view has prevailed.

Inherent in a multidimensional concept of rationality is the realization that the expert has a social obligation[122] that goes beyond mere service to societal elites. In particular, the *distributive effects of information use* might serve as an operational beginning for both the expansion of rationality as a value and as a normative prelude to changes in technocratic behavior. This puts the issue of the *ends of guidance* at the center of what appears to be the dilemma of the role of technocratic counsel in postindustrial society. One proposal along these lines is found in a recent article by David Apter in which he suggests that a new style of planning ought to include "marginality as social cost."[123] In any case, it seems appropriate that the recurring question, first asked by Robert Lynd: "Knowledge for what?" could be paraphrased and expanded to: "Guidance for what and for whom?" This brings us to a final note on the possible ramifications of value and role transformations for postindustrial evolution.

As noted earlier, much of the thrust toward societal guidance and technocratic counsel has been directed toward the maintenance of present structures of power. However, it is conceivable, though admittedly difficult from an operational perspective, to envisage system-transforming reforms emanating from rejuvenated guidance areas with experts that recognize both the valuations of guidance and the social obligations of the expert. In the case of social indicators, information and new conceptualization is needed on crime, population, health, education, the content and flow of media information, and civil liberties. New information that is being collected on unemployment may challenge official statistics, directly confront the "conventional wisdom" concerning the acceptable level of unemployment, and most important, provide alternative concepts to the "labor force" and the quality of work. The use of some form of the corporate social audit—presently a tool of executive management—might conceivably become a system-transforming reform if done externally on both private and public corporations. When combined with such concepts as the "quality of life" and workers participation, it could become a powerful tool for the construction of a "societal calculus"—a broad total system approach to societal planning.[124] Such a vision naturally assumes the need for new information, more expertise, and planning that is not only qualitatively improved but normatively explicit.

It would be naive to assume that such system-transforming reforms are probable. The thrust of this inquiry suggests that the future of societal guidance and technocratic counsel will most likely continue to serve present structures of power. To the extent that these reforms may be plausible, it is nevertheless important to caution against any immediate restructuring of hierarchy and concentrated power. Any such changes would take several decades. In the search for alternatives— solutions to the dilemma posed by Sartori—the reconciliation of expertise and popular control—must be found. Nothing less than the future of democracy is at stake.

NOTES

1. The theoretical and empirical underpinnings of "postindustrial" society are still in their embryonic stages. This chapter uses the term in a "literary" sense to identify political systems that are highly industrialized—without entering into the debate whether "supraindustrialism," "advanced industrialism," or "postindustrialism" is the best analytical concept. The issues raised, it is suggested, could have theoretical, empirical, and normative importance for the past, present, and future of highly industrialized political systems. If this is true, then "postindustrial" society is adequate for the purposes of identification.

    Technocracy is a government ruled by experts. However, this is rarely the definition currently employed in the contemporary critical literature. Rather, it is preferable to speak of degrees, tendencies, and dimensions of *technocratic counsel*—the roles and influence of experts in the guidance of public policy.

2. On Henri Saint-Simon see Frank Manuel, *The New World of Henri Saint-Simon* (Cambridge, Mass.: Harvard University Press, 1956); and Emile Durkheim, *Socialism and Saint-Simon*, trans. Charlotte Sattler (Yellow Springs: Antioch Press, 1958). Few persons would consider Marxism in a history of technocratic thought. Nevertheless, behind his trenchant criticism of capitalist industrialism, one finds an optimistic view of the benefits of technology and a deterministic analysis of managerialism as an inevitable feature of industrial society. This is even more pronounced in Engel's famous interpretation of the "withering away" of the state. See Thorstein Veblen, *The Engineers and the Price System* (New York: Sentry Press, 1921), p. 166; Auguste Comte, *System of Positive Polity* (New York: B. Franklin, 1968); James Burnham, *The Managerial Revolution* (Bloomington: Indiana University Press, 1960); Raymond Aron, *The Industrial Society* (New York: Praeger, 1967).

3. Aspects of this argument are found in Jean Meynaud, *Technocracy*, trans. Paul Barnes (New York: Free Press, 1960); John K. Galbraith, *The New Industrial State* (New York: Signet, 1967); Zbigniew Brzezinski, *Between Two Ages* (New York: Viking Press, 1970); Jacques Ellul, *The Technological Society*, trans. John Wilkinson (New York: Vintage Books, 1964).

4. See Norman Birnbaum, *The Crisis of Industrial Society* (New York: Oxford University Press, 1969), pp. 81–83; Alain Touraine, *The Post-Industrial Society*, trans. Leonard Mayhew (New York: Random House, 1971), pp. 158–60; Andre Gorz, *Strategy for Labour*, trans. Martin Nicolaus and Victoria Ortiz (Boston: Beacon Press, 1967), pp. 122–27; Frederic Bon and Michel-Antoine Burnier, *Les Nouveaux Intellectuals* (Paris: Seuil, 1970).

5. Niccolo Machiavelli, *The Prince* (New York: New American Library, 1952), p. 114.

6. Samuelson's remarks were made at a speech given at the New School for Social Research in March 1971. The quotation can be found in Paul M. Sweezy, "On the Theory of Monopoly Capitalism," *Monthly Review* 23 (April 1972): 10.

7. Thomas R. Dye, Eugene R. DeClercq, and John W. Pickering, "Concentration, Specialization, and Interlocking Among Institutional Elites," *Social Science Quarterly* 54 (June 1973): 16–20.

8. Dean Mann, *The Assistant Secretaries* (Washington, D.C.: Brookings Institution, 1965); and David Stanley, *Men Who Govern* (Washington, D.C.: Brookings Institution, 1967).

9. Richard J. Barnet, "The National Security Managers and the National Interest," *Politics and Society* 1 (February 1961): 260; Gabriel Kolko, *The Roots of American Foreign Policy* (Boston: Beacon Press, 1969), p. 19.

10. Daniel Bell, "The Measurement of Knowledge and Technology," in *Indicators of Social Change*, ed. Eleanor B. Sheldon and Wilbert E. Moore (New York: Russell Sage Foundation, 1968), pp. 145–246. See also Bertram M. Gross, "Planning in an Era of Social Revolution," *Public Administration Review* 21 (May/June 1971): 259–96.

11. Fritz Machlup, *The Production and Distribution of Knowledge in the United States* (Princeton, N.J.: Princeton University Press, 1962).

12. Aggregate data support Daniel Bell's extrapolation of this new social class. His normative assessment of the meaning of this trend, however, is debatable. See Bell, "Measurement of Knowledge," pp. 153–55.

13. For examples of the use of the concept of societal guidance see Amitai Etzioni: *The Active Society* (New York: Free Press); Etzioni, "Indicators of the Capacities for Societal Guidance," *The Annals* 338 (March 1970): 25–34; John Friedmann, *Retracking America* (Garden City, N.Y.: Anchor Books, 1973), pp. 18–21.

14. The concept of "consumer intensivity" has been developed by Alan Gartner and Frank Riessman as a way of looking at some of the emerging production relations in a "service" or "consumer" society. The examples they use are drawn primarily from education and health. The concept may prove quite useful in exploring some of the issues of political economy in a future "consumer" society. Nevertheless, it is important to remember that the issue of power is not absent in areas that may be consumer intensive. In this connection, Gartner and Riessman have examined the conflicts that may evolve under conditions of consumer intensivity. In the case of the relationship between princes and their counsel, we have an area that is consumer intensive and oligopsonic. This is another way of repeating the story by Daniel Bell of the social scientists of the 1960s saying, "I have a solution, who has a problem?" The work by Gartner and Riessman is found in *The Service Society and the Consumer Vanguard* (New York: Harper & Row, 1974).

15. The idea of "technocratic counsel" attempts to avoid the quicksand of the sterile debate concerning the "amount" of power experts have. Power, as political scientists are uncomfortably aware, is rarely "measured" precisely.

16. The selection of areas of expertise is not intended to be comprehensive. The influence of physical scientists has been considered elsewhere. The same is true of lawyers and accountants. The selection of these four groups bears theoretical and empirical relevance to the theme of "postindustrial" change.

17. Reprinted in *A Modern Design for Defense Decision*, ed. Samuel Tucker (Washington, D.C.: Industrial College of the Armed Forces, 1966), p. 214.

18. Peter Drucker, *The Age of Discontinuity* (London: Pan Books, 1971), p. 447.

19. Daniel Bell, *The Coming of Post-Industrial Society* (New York: Basic Books, 1973), pp. 364–65.

20. This is the point made by Herbert Stein in *The Fiscal Revolution in America* (Chicago: University of Chicago Press, 1969), pp. 380–81.

21. Edward Flash, Jr., *Economic Advice and Presidential Leadership* (New York: Columbia University Press, 1965), p. 276.

22. Tucker, *A Modern Design for Defense Decision*, pp. 34–35.

23. Daniel Bell, "Technocracy and Politics," *Survey* 16 (Winter 1971): 17.

24. Alice Rivlin, "The Planning, Programming, and Budgeting System in the Department of Health, Education, and Welfare: Some Lessons from Experience," in U.S. Congress, Joint Economic Committee, *The Analysis and Evaluation of Public Expenditures: The PPB System*, 91st Cong., 1st sess., 1969, p. 911.

25. The effect of PPB on the centralization of power has been one aspect in the debate on the overall effects of PPB. See Alain Enthoven, "The Planning, Programming and Budgeting System in the Department of Defense: Some Lessons from Experience," in ibid., pp. 901–8.

26. See Allen Schick, "A Death in the Bureaucracy: The Demise of Federal PPB," *Public Administration Review* 33 (March/April 1973): 148.

27. This section is based on Bertram M. Gross and Jeffrey D. Straussman, "The Social Indicators Movement," *Social Policy* 5 (September/October 1974): 43–54.

28. This is illustrated by the social indicators publication which was prepared by the Statistical Policy Division of the Office of Management and Budget. For a criticism see Albert Biderman, "Social Indicators—Whence and Wither" (Paper presented at the first annual Social Indicators Conference, American Marketing Association, 17–18 February 1972, Washington, D.C.), pp. 2–3.

29. Michael Springer, "Social Indicators, Reports and Accounts: Toward the Management of Society," *The Annals* 338 (March 1970): 1–13.

30. This segment within social indicators is found in the current "National Goals Accounting" study being done at the National Planning Association, Washington, D.C.

31. See statement by Gerhard Colm, in U.S. Congress, Senate *Committee on Government Operations, Hearings*, before a subcommittee on Government Research, on S. 843, 1st sess., 1967, pp. 36–37.

32. The concept of the "central guidance cluster" was developed by Bertram M. Gross in his analysis of national economic planning in the United States. See Bertram M. Gross, "The Managers of National Economic Change," in *Public Administration and Democracy*, ed. Roscoe Martin (Syracuse: Syracuse University Press, 1965), pp. 101–27.

33. Daniel Bell, "The Idea of a Social Report," *Public Interest* (Spring 1969): 84.

34. See statement by Dwight A. Ink, in U.S. Congress, Senate, *Committee on Labor and Public Welfare, Hearings*, before a subcommittee on Evaluation and Planning of Social Programs, on S. 5, 1st sess., 1971, pp. 36–39.

35. Eli Goldston, *The Quantification of Concern* (New York: Columbia University Press, 1972), passim. See also David Rockefeller, "The Essential Quest for the Middle Way," *New York Times*, 23 March 1973, p. 37.

36. Paul Samuelson, *Economics* (9th ed.; New York: McGraw-Hill, 1973), pp. 195–97.

37. Springer, "Social Indicators," p. 13.

38. This overly optimistic view of the societal uses of knowledge pervades Bell's picture of "postindustrial" society. The same is true of Brzezinski, *Between Two Ages*, p. 12.

39. Jay Forrester, "Counter Intuitive Behavior of Social Systems," *Theory and Decision* 2 (1971): 109–40.

40. Herman Kahn and Anthony Weiner, *The Year 2000* (New York: Macmillan, 1967), p. 193.

41. *Report to the Members 1972* (Croton-on-Hudson, N.Y.: Hudson Institute, July 1972), p. 5.

42. President's Task Force on Science Policy, *Science and Technology: Tools For Progress* (Washington, D.C.: Government Printing Office, 1970).

43. Paul Dickson, *Think Tanks* (New York: Atheneum, 1971), pp. 310–12.

44. *Report to the Members*, pp. 11–12.

45. Theodore Geiger, *The Fortunes of the West* (Bloomington: Indiana University Press, 1973), p. 270.

46. Ida Hoos, *Systems Analysis in Public Policy* (Berkeley: University of California Press, 1972), p. 243.

47. Bell, *Coming of Post-Industrial Society*, p. 263.

48. U.S. Department of Commerce, *Statistical Abstract of the United States*, 1972 (Washington, D.C.: Government Printing Office, 1972), p. 522.

49. Ibid.

50. Ibid., p. 525.

51. U.S. Department of Commerce, *Statistical Abstract of the United States*, *1969* (Washington, D.C.: Government Printing Office, 1969), p. 531.

52. This use of modernization is found in Erwin Hargrove, *Professional Roles in Society and Government: The English Case* (Beverly Hills: Sage Publications, 1972), p. 71.

53. This is one of the major points made by Alice Rivlin in *Systematic Thinking for Social Action* (Washington, D.C.: Brookings Institution, 1971), pp. 56–60.

54. Wilbur Cohen, former secretary of Health, Education, and Welfare, held this view. See "Social Indicators: Statistics for Public Policy," *American Statistician* 22 (October 1968): 14–16.

55. Mancur Olson, "The Plan and Purpose of a Social Report," *Public Interest* (Spring 1960): 93.

56. W. Williams, *Social Policy Research and Analysis* (New York: American Elsevier, 1971).

57. Robert Anthony, "Closing the Loop Between Planning and Performance," *Public Administration Review* 31 (May/June 1971): 390.

58. Bell, "Technocracy and Politics," pp. 6–7.

59. Brzezinski, *Between Two Ages*, pp. 202–3.

60. For a description of strategic decisions see Bertram Gross, "Management Strategy for Economic and Social Development, Part II," *Policy Sciences* 3 (March 1972): 5–20.

61. Mancur Olson, "Social Reporting and Policy Analysis," *The Annals* 338 (March 1970): 115.

62. The inattention given to changes in the corporate environment by proponents of the "postindustrial" thesis is quite remarkable. Only by ignoring the structures of economic power can one give undue weight to intellectual institutions as the dominant institutions of the "new society."

63. Hoos, *Systems Analysis in Public Policy*, passim.

64. Schick, "A Death in the Bureaucracy," p. 146.

65. Alvin Toffler, *Future Shock* (New York: Bantam, 1970), p. 447.

66. *Statistical Abstract of the United States, 1972*, p. 530.

67. Mann, *The Assistant Secretaries*; and Stanley, *Men Who Govern*.

68. Mann, *The Assistant Secretaries*, p. 20.

69. Ibid., p. 38.

70. The term "in-and-outer" was coined by Richard Neustadt to describe the role of lawyers in the political process. See "White House and Whitehall," *Public Interest* 2 (Winter 1966): 55–69.

71. Biographical data for Nixon appointees were gathered from *Who's Who in Government 1972/73*.

72. Hoos, *Systems Analysis in Public Policy*, p. 47.

73. Examples would include James Schlesinger, former Secretary of Defense and Clay Whitehead, former director of the Office of Telecommunications, both considered to be specialists in systems analysis.

74. Jude Wanniski, "Teddy Kennedy's 'Shadow Government'" *Wall Street Journal*, 27 March 1973, p. 20.

75. Bell, "Technocracy and Politics," pp. 1–26; Meynaud, *Technocracy*, p. 13; Brzezinski, *Between Two Ages*, p. 12; Galbraith, *New Industrial State*, p. 178; Aron, *Industrial Society*, pp. 148–49; Ellul, *Technological Society*, pp. 259–267.

76. Aron, *Industrial Society*, pp. 164–65.

77. Etzioni, *The Active Society*, pp. 15–16.

78. See Raymond Bauer, ed., *Social Indicators* (Cambridge, Mass.: MIT Press, 1966), passim.

79. Walter Heller, *New Dimensions of Political Economy* (New York: Norton, 1967), passim.

80. Fiscal policy is said to be a good example of this trend. See Lawrence Pierce, *The Politics of Fiscal Policy Formation* (Pacific Palisades, Calif: Goodyear Publishing, 1971), pp. 106–7.

81. Ellul, *Technological Society*, p. 259.

82. This alternative view is found in Guy Beneviste, *The Politics of Expertise* (Berkeley: Glendessary Press, 1972), pp. 44–45. See also I. L. Horowitz,

Foundations of Political Sociology (New York: Harper & Row, 1972), pp. 414–18.

83. Gross, "Managers of National Economic Change," passim. See also Pierce, *Politics of Fiscal Policy Formation*, pp. 88–106.

84. Pierce, *Politics of Fiscal Policy Formation*, pp. 114–15.

85. Burkhead, "Fiscal Planning—Conservative Keynesianism," *Public Administration Review* 31 (May/June 1971): 335–45.

86. Heller, *New Dimensions of Political Economy*, pp. 94–98.

87. Pierce, *Politics of Fiscal Policy Formation*, p. 123.

88. See Robert Eisner, "War and Taxes: The Role of the Economist in Politics," *Bulletin of the Atomic Scientists* (June 1968): 13–18.

89. These themes are found in Meynaud, *Technocracy*, pp. 207–92; Touraine, *Post-Industrial Society*, p. 59–76; Dreitzel, "Sociology and the Problem of Rationality: Notes on the Sociology of Technocrats," *Politics and Society* 2 (Winter 1972): 165–82.

90. Bell, *Coming of Post-Industrial Society*, p. 354.

91. Charles Schultze, *The Politics and Economics of Public Spending* (Washington, D.C.: Brookings Institution, 1968), p. 96.

92. The theme of growthmanship is found in James Tobin, *National Economic Policy* (New Haven: Yale University Press, 1960); Heller, *New Dimensions of Political Economy;* Arthur Okun, *The Political Economy of Prosperity* (New York: W. W. Norton, 1970).

93. John Goldthorpe, "Theories of Industrial Society: Reflections on the Recrudescence of Historicism and the Future of Futurology," *European Journal of Sociology* 12 (1971): 284.

94. See National Academy of Sciences, *The Behavioral and Social Sciences: Outlook and Needs* (Englewood Cliffs, N.J.: Prentice-Hall, 1969); also President's Task Force on Science Policy, *Science and Technology: Tools for Progress* (Washington, D.C.: Government Printing Office, 1970).

95. Full explanations of this argument are found in Gorz, *Strategy for Labour*, p. 122; Herbert Marcuse, *One-Dimensional Man* (Boston: Beacon Press, 1964), pp. 1–18; Touraine, *Post-Industrial Society*, p. 3.

96. Clark Kerr, *Marshall, Marx and Modern Times* (Cambridge, Mass.: Cambridge University Press, 1969), p. 205.

97. Michael Marien, "Herman Kahn's 'Things to Come,'" *Futurist* 7 (February 1973): 7–15.

98. A more elaborate critique of these aspects of social indicators is found in Gross and Straussman, "The Social Indicators Movement."

99. Bell, "Post-Industrial Society," pp. 102–3; Meynaud, *Technocracy*, p. 195.

100. Theodore Geiger, *The Fortunes of the West* (Bloomington: Indiana University Press, 1973), pp. 14–57.

101. Theodore Roszak, *Where the Wasteland Ends* (Garden City, N.Y.: Anchor Books, 1973), pp. 34–35.

102. Ronald Inglehart, "The Silent Revolution in Europe: Intergenerational Change in Post-Industrial Societies," *American Political Science Review* 65 (December 1971): 991–1017.

103. Karl Deutsch, "On Politial Theory and Political Action," *APSR* 65 (March 1971): 11–27; Robert Lane, "To Nurture a Discipline," *APSR* 66 (March 1972):

164–82; Heinz Eulau, "Skill Revolution and Consultative Commonwealth," *APSR* 67 (March 1973): 168–91.

104. Alvin Toffler, *Future Shock*, pp. 446–87.

105. Ibid.

106. David Easton, "The New Revolution in Political Science," *American Political Science Review* 63 (December 1969): 1059–60.

107. Eulau, "Skill Revolution and Consultative Commonwealth," p. 168.

108. See Yehezkel Dror, *Ventures in Policy Sciences* (New York: American Elsevier, 1971), passim, as an example.

109. William Nordhaus and James Tobin, "Is Growth Obsolete?" *Fiftieth Anniversary Colloquium* (New York: National Bureau of Economic Research, Columbia University Press, 1972), 5:4–5.

110. See Amitai Etzioni and Richard Remp, "Technological 'Shortcuts' to Social Change," *Science* 175 (7 January 1972): 31–37.

111. Herbert Simon, "Technology and Environment," *Management Science* 19 (June 1973): 1121.

112. Brzezinski, *Between Two Ages*, p. 260.

113. Marcuse, *One-Dimensional Man*, p. 146.

114. Geiger, *Fortunes of the West*, pp. 33–34.

115. Andrew Shonfield, *Modern Capitalism* (New York: Oxford University Press, 1965), p. 236.

116. Giovanni Sartori, *Democratic Theory* (Detroit: Wayne State University Press, 1962), p. 404.

117. Gross, "Planning in an Era of Social Revolution," p. 291.

118. Dreitzel, "Sociology and the Problem of Rationality," p. 175.

119. Ibid.

120. Charles L. Schultze, "Is Economics Obsolete? No, Underemployed," *Saturday Review* (May 1972): 57.

121. Kenneth E. Boulding, "Economics As A Moral Science," *American Economics Review, Papers and Proceedings* (May 1969): 2.

122. Dankwart A. Rustow, "Relevance in Social Science, or the Proper Study of Mankind," *American Scholar* 40 (Summer 1971): 487–96.

123. David Apter, "The Premise of Parliamentary Planning," *Government and Opposition* 8 (Winter 1973): 6.

124. See Gross and Straussman, "The Social Indicators Movement," for an extended discussion of these points.

ELITE IMAGES AND SYSTEM CHANGE IN SWEDEN*

M. DONALD HANCOCK

Assessments of postindustrial change in specific nation-states as well as the international system depend in large degree on the analyst's choice of subject and his underlying metatheoretical assumptions.[1] Studies emphasizing the depletion of energy resources and ecological decay differ in kind in their substantive conclusions from studies based on projections about the potential capacity of technology to ameliorate the human condition.[2] Correspondingly, Herbert Marcuse's vision of equality under humanitarian socialism contrasts radically with Edward Banfield's pessimistic view that class inequality and urban decay will resist reform efforts.[3] While diversity in emphasis and prescriptive judgments have yielded the undeniable benefits of spirited public debate on policy requirements, they have also obscured causal relations among multiple factors of change in the modern world.

This study attempts to clarify such relations by integrating a theoretical view of volitional change with empirical evidence on the probable

*Research for this chapter was conducted during my appointment as an International Affairs Fellow in Stockholm. I am grateful to the Council on Foreign Relations, Inc., for its financial support and to colleagues and students at the Universities of Stockholm, Uppsala, Mannheim, and Texas (Austin) for their intellectual stimulation, advice, and helpful criticism. Among those to whom a special note of gratitude is due are my wife, Kay, Gideon Sjoberg, Nils Elvander, Leon Lindberg, Uwe Schleth, and Ulf Himmelstrand.

167

course of future change in Sweden, one of the world's most advanced economic and sociopolitical systems. Following an introductory discussion of political choice and system change, I consider alternative patterns of future domestic Swedish politics. These alternatives are then evaluated on the basis of elite views toward significant sociopolitical issues which I compiled on the basis of interviews with sixty of the nation's leading political, administrative, interest-group, and media officials. In my conclusion I suggest some implications of the Swedish case for comparative study.

My basic assumption is that elite images of the present and the future will to a significant degree determine policy choice and hence the direction, scope, and quality of system change.[4] For appraising the prospects of national and global transformation in the postindustrial era, elite attitudes toward system change therefore comprise a crucial predictive index.

SYSTEM CHANGE AND LEADERSHIP CHOICE

Much of the present disparity in basic conceptions of change and views of the future of advanced society begins with the unit of analysis. Among the principal indexes of system change are material, technological, and sociopolitical factors, each of which has served as the central focus of national and global studies. The results vary according to the particular index chosen for emphasis.

Through its concentration on the mounting pressure of human demands on finite supplies of material resources, the proliferate literature on the energy crisis, environmental problems, and the population explosion has tended to depict a bleak future of physical destitution. In contrast, social scientists who have emphasized technological or sociopolitical indexes of change are neither as uniformly deterministic in their projections nor as pessimistic about man's capacity to survive with dignity in tomorrow's world. Zbigniew Brzezinski, for instance, argues that technetronic innovation can enhance the quality of individual life, just as Marcuse celebrates the potentially liberating effects of automation.[5]

For both substantive and methodological reasons, selective analysis has tended to obscure understanding of the interdependence of material, technological, and sociopolitical variables of change. In the former case, publicity and intellectual fads have raised some issues more than others to the level of public consciousness. For example, the public debate on ecological decay—as salutory and necessary as that debate may be for improving the prospects of physical survival—has overshadowed parallel efforts to explore alternative patterns of social and political change in advanced societies. Simultaneously, the prevailing tendency to project material and technological trends into the future has distracted attention from volitional aspects of sociopolitical behavior. While it is appropriate to chart linear projections from the present in predicting the depletion of natural resources in the future, lineality does not constitute a convincing metaphor for assessing the capacity of men and women to alter the physical and social terms of their existence in accordance with qualitative models of a better world.[6]

A promising approach for achieving greater clarity about relations among physical and sociopolitical change variables is to explore the quality of elite choice as a principal determinant of system change. To define basic terms, I mean by system change processes of enhanced or lessened control by persons over their physical, social, and individual environments.[7] I have suggested in other contexts that system change may involve the loss of previously attained levels of control over humans' environments (*regressive change*), the persistence of prevailing economic and sociopolitical characteristics (*maintaining change*), or the attainment of new control capabilities (*transforming* or *active change*). Each form of change may characterize any nation at any point along the preindustrial-postindustrial continuum of modernization; each may involve the loss, persistence, or attainment of new physical and sociopolitical control capabilities; and each illustrates the importance of elite behavior as both a cause and a necessary condition of change.[8]

Elites encompass those persons who possess the authority, power, and superior access to communication flows to make and enforce binding decisions on the members of a given society (or subsystems thereof). Established elites by no means enjoy complete autonomy of action, even in ostensibly totalitarian regimes. A number of factors may limit their range of choice in making decisions—including their basic value assumptions about the person and society, the material and social resources at their disposal, the preferences and behavior of nonelites, and their nation's relative degree of independence/dependence in the international system.[9] Nevertheless, the power and higher status normally accorded national and subsystem leaders (including economic elites) assures them a pivotal role in determining short-term policy and hence longer-term change outcomes. Accordingly, the "quality of elite choice" refers to elite decisions or nondecisions that either directly affect the intensity and direction of system change—such as the modernizing initiatives of many leaders in the third world—or indirectly sanction through inaction change that is initiated by nonelites (such as the commercial activity of economic entrepreneurs during capitalist development).[10]

Elite commitment to the preservation of an established system is likely to yield maintaining change, at least in the short run (for example, in Haiti), whereas elite sponsorship of an ideological blueprint of rapid industrialization and social mobilization can promote active system change (as in the Soviet Union). Either kind of outcome becomes more likely in proportion to the degree of elite agreement on the desirability of system maintenance or transformation, respectively. When, in contrast, elites are only minimally attached to established economic and sociopolitical patterns or they are deeply divided over policy goals, some processes may atrophy (such as state services or economic productivity) and/or the system may become vulnerable to the ideological attacks of antielites who seek to displace the system altogether. In the latter two cases, the short-term result is likely to be regression.[11]

An important caveat is in order. In any given instance, elite preferences may prove the necessary condition for a particular pattern of system change but not its immediate cause. Just as domestic and/or international constraints may force leaders in a particular society to forgo proclaimed policy priorities, unexpected events in either arena can prompt sudden departures in policy and change outcomes. A contemporary example is the indeterminate domestic effect of the energy shortage in the advanced industrial states. Thus, any assessment of the quality of leadership choice as a determinant of system change must take into account impending events—such as emerging policy contradictions or international crises—that may compel leaders to act in a particular manner when they might otherwise prefer passivity or to decide on a different course of action.

Regressive, maintaining, and active forms of change have characterized both preindustrial and industrial societies in the past, with each pattern potentially inherent in the contemporary transition to postindustrial society in the advanced nations of Western Europe, North America, and Asia. Characterizing these countries are increased affluence, the preponderance of white-collar employees over blue-collar workers, and a corresponding growth of service industries, technetronic innovations, pressing environmental problems, and renewed ideological controversies over relations between the individual and the various collectivities that dominate his life. Given both the interdependence of physical and sociopolitical factors of change and the qualitative variable of leadership choice in determining change outcomes, no uniform model of postindustrial society is likely to emerge in the decades ahead. Changing material and technological resources will expand or contract the scope of policy decisions just as policy decisions can determine the allocation of economic and social resources. Accordingly, alternative models which take into account elite attitudes toward system change will serve as a more useful "prediction" of the future than unilinear projections from existing economic and sociopolitical characteristics of any given nation.[12] The remainder of this chapter comprises such an undertaking.

THE SWEDISH CASE: THE RANGE OF FUTURE ALTERNATIVES

As one of the world's most industrialized, affluent, and politically modernized nations, Sweden offers suggestive case data for exploring the prospects of alternative domestic futures. In comparison with other countries in Western Europe and North America undergoing aspects of postindustrial change, Sweden is larger than Holland, England, and West Germany but smaller than the United States; more affluent than all but the United States; and socially the most homogeneous. Moreover, Sweden is highly bureaucratized with one of the world's most extensive networks of social welfare services, and manifests a degree of elite unity on basic constitutional principles and decision processes that may exceed even that of Britain. Unlike the United States but like other highly developed nations in Western Europe, Sweden is dependent on international trade for a third or more of its gross national product. Similar to Holland, Sweden has a multiparty system but claims a longer record of stable one-party rule (under Social Democratic aegis) than any Western democracy.[13] Finally, like all highly advanced nations, Sweden has experienced in recent years a steady increase in the number of white-collar workers, increased public sensitivity to environmental issues, and an extensive domestic debate over authority relations and the participatory rights of individual citizens.

In light of dominant economic and sociopolitical trends in the early 1970s, five patterns of change appear conceivable in Sweden into the 1980s and beyond. All but the last constitute a logical alternative to prevailing indexes of modernity, with each representing a different resolution of the tensions generated by multiple forces of postindustrial change. The five patterns may be briefly summarized as follows:[14]

1. *Regressive change caused by a decline in economic productivity.* Such a pattern could result either from a general decline in international trade (due in part to the shortage of oil and other energy resources) and/or hesitation by Swedish economic leaders to expand investments in the face of domestic sociopolitical uncertainty. Both factors contributed to a leveling in the rate of increase in national productivity and a rise of unemployment after 1970.[15] An exacerbation of such trends would prompt discernible regression in the material conditions of modernity in the years ahead.

2. *Regressive change caused by intensified sociopolitical antagonism.* Either parallel with potential losses of economic capabilities or as a separate phenomenon, the intensification of group conflict could significantly disrupt social and political cohesion. Since the 1930s Sweden has achieved a striking record of relative labor-market tranquility due in large measure to widespread elite-mass acceptance of the principle of

group solidarity. Established patterns of social cohesion became strained, however, when workers at the state-owned LKAB iron mine in northern Sweden began a massive wildcat strike against union orders in December 1969 and high-level salaried employees walked off their jobs in February 1971—the latter to protest Social Democratic efforts to reduce national wage discrepancies.[16] If such demonstrations against established group authority and the solidarity principle prove forerunners of a continuing trend in domestic relations, the result would be temporary regression on the sociopolitical plane of modernity.

3. *Transforming collectivist change.* As a policy response to either of the preceding patterns of regressive change or in a series of independent initiatives, national leaders could expand centralized administrative control over Sweden's physical and social resources. Such a pattern would be consistent with the ideological commitment of the majority Social Democrats and their allies in the Federation of Trade Unions (LO) to achieve collective conditions of mass security and equality. Collectivist change would take the form of more direct state supervision of economic processes, decreed rather than negotiated wage settlements on the labor market, and a further concentration of decision-making authority in the Royal Chancery and ministerial departments.[17] Local and regional government structures and the traditionally autonomous administrative boards would suffer a corresponding diminution in their authority.

4. *Transforming libertarian change.* Under conditions of renewed economic growth and a decline in the intensity of social conflict, an alternative model of transforming change is conceivable that would maximize individual choice and participatory opportunities. This pattern of transformation would encompass increased participation by industrial and salaried employees in decisions affecting the quality of their work environment, increased emphasis on internal democracy within political parties and interest groups, and political decentralization to restore authority to local and regional government organs.[18]

5. *Ad hoc maintaining change.* In some respects a description of national policy throughout the early 1970s, this pattern would combine elements of economic and sociopolitical regression (such as rising unemployment) and fragmented political initiatives to restore equilibrium through recourse to legislated coercion or partial reforms along the lines suggested in the alternative models of transforming change. The likelihood of such a pattern would increase in direct proportion to the parliamentary weakness of the party or parties holding cabinet office and elite dissensus on national policy priorities.[19]

Although each of the five models of domestic Swedish politics demands far greater elaboration than is possible in the present context, the summary sketch suffices to provide a framework for analyzing elite attitudes toward system change. In 1972 the potential existed for any one of the alternative patterns to become dominant in the intermediate future. Economic growth was at a virtual standstill, unemployment was at its highest point since the end of World War II, and the nation had witnessed an unprecedented move in 1971 by the Swedish parliament to legislate an end to the white-collar strike. In the major urban centers of Stockholm, Göteborg, and Malmö, various ad hoc groups challenged established authority patterns through public criticism and direct action protesting the deterioration of the physical and urban environments. Vocal New Left and radical liberal critics of persisting economic and social inequalities had prompted the governing Social Democrats to adopt a new economic program in 1968 that envisioned a significant extension of social controls over private enterprise, but following their loss of an absolute parliamentary majority in the September 1970 election the Socialists were restrained in their capacity to implement it. At the same time various royal commissions, which are appointed by cabinet officials to gather expert information and consider policy alternatives before formal government bills are drafted, were considering changes in legislation affecting labor-market relations and the environment of the workplace which could ultimately encourage features of both collectivist and libertarian transformation.[20] Opposing a perceived concentration of political and indirect economic controls in the hands of the executive-administrative apparatus, leaders of the nonsocialist opposition parties responded with various policy proposals to decentralize certain government functions and economic activities. Together the Social Democrats and spokesmen of the nonsocialist bloc engaged in an extended partisan controversy over regional policy—including optimal means to discourage further concentration of industry and urbanization in the southern third of the country, ensure a more rational allocation of Sweden's natural resources, and mitigate environmental problems.

The quality of leadership choice will prove decisive in determining how these multiple forces of change and policy proposals will coalesce in a discernible pattern of system change during the remainder of the decade and beyond. Swedish political and economic leaders cannot directly influence trends in international trade, but they may choose between activist or passive policy measures that will filter the effects of such trends on the domestic economy. National elites cannot arbitrarily decide to reverse or even stop the growth in the number of salaried employees, but leaders of the LO and the white-collar unions can seek through conciliatory measures to lessen the risk of conflict between their organizations. Depending on the composition of the national executive and working relations between the parliamentary majority and the opposition, political elites can act on either a rigidly partisan or a compromise formula in encouraging processes of collectivist and libertarian change, respectively. Sweden's future, in short, is by no means closed to deliberate policy choice.

LEADERSHIP ATTITUDES TOWARD SYSTEM CHANGE

To anticipate the possible outcome of conflicting pressures of system change in Sweden, I interviewed sixty leading officials in the Social Democratic and the three nonsocialist political parties; the Departments of Finance, Industry, Commerce, and Foreign Affairs; the LO, the two largest white-collar unions, the Swedish Federation of Industries, the nation's two largest private banks, and the National Association of Farmers; and key policy makers and/or editorialists in the public radio-television corporation (*Sveriges Radio*), the liberal newspaper, *Dagens Nyheter*, and the Social Democratic newspaper, *Aftonbladet*. Given the underlying assumption of this analysis that elite attitudes constitute an independent variable of system change, the sample of respondents was chosen among those persons who, because of their official position and/or reputation of significant influence within their particular organization, are likely directly to affect patterns of change in the foreseeable future. The sixty respondents were selected in approximate proportion to their group's or department's or indirect media participation in national decision processes.[21] They included 29 Social Democrats and top officials in the LO and the departments cited above; 27 national spokesmen of the nonsocialist parties, interest groups, and private banks; and 4 media representatives.

The interviews were conducted in Swedish on the basis of a 21-item questionnaire, with most of the questions (14) dealing with foreign-policy issues which are analyzed in a separate article.[22] Seven questions concerned elite perceptions of domestic affairs, and were designed to assess elite attitudes toward change in light of the five patterns of Sweden's future outlined in the preceding section. Explicitly, they called for the leaders' views of domestic change, relations between blue-collar and white-collar workers, the past and probable future effects of protest-group activity as an impetus for system change, future patterns of mass political participation, and the prospects of centralization-decentralization in the political system. All of the questions were open-ended; the responses were subsequently coded and collapsed in the tables that follow. To facilitate comparison of attitudes among the various elite groups, the total frequencies of their responses are broken down into executive-administrative, nonsocialist, and media-representative categories.[23]

In a deliberate attempt to permit the respondents to define their own view of pressing domestic issues and policy priorities the first two questions elicited (1) elite *projections* of probable domestic change during the next five to ten years and (2) elite *preferences* for change during the same period. The theoretical distinction between these questions is important, for the responses indicate not only "realistic" or pragmatic prognoses of the immediate future but also utopian visions of more distant transformation. Depending on which groups are able to contribute the most direct influence on policy formation through their control of or access to authoritative decision structures, data on such visions can provide useful clues for anticipating future elite behavior.

The elites' predictions and preferences clearly reflect the substantive questions that have dominated the domestic Swedish debate in recent years. As indicated in table 6.1, the most commonly anticipated change is the increased influence of employees at their place of work over company or administrative policy and the quality of their work environment. Beyond the cautious expectation that no significant changes will take place, which occupies second rank in part because of overt cynicism about the future among the media representatives, Swedish leaders anticipate in decreasing order an intensified debate on the rationalization of domestic resources (including the introduction of environmental controls and regional policies to discourage further urbanization and industrialization in the southern part of the country), a change of government, and a declining rate of economic growth. Cited with equal frequency at the bottom of the list were political reforms to promote further democ-

Table 6.1. Elite Predictions of Most Likely Domestic Changes During the 1970s
(responses with frequency of five and above)

Change	Total Frequency	Subtotals by Party and/or Occupational Position		
		Socialists, High-level Administrators	Nonsocialists	Media Spokesmen
Increased influence of employees (including industrial democracy and improved environment of workplace)	20	12	8	0
No significant changes	13	6	4	3
Intensified debate on planning of total resources (including environment)	12	8	4	0
Change of government	12	3	9	0
Decline in economic growth	6	3	3	0
Broadened democracy	5	1	4	0
Continued implementation of equality policies	5	5	0	0
Decline in growth of public sector	5	2	3	0
Uncertain; depends on which party or parties control cabinet office	5	0	4	1

ratization, the continued implementation of equality policies, a decline in the growth of the public sector, and simple uncertainty on the eve of the September 1973 national election.

While Social Democratic and high administrative elites differ in their ranking of predictions from nonsocialist political and interest-group leaders, both groups concur on the relative probability of two features of potential system transformation: the increased influence of employees and greater attention to the rational use of Sweden's physical and social resources. They differ in their predictions, as underscored in table 6.2, on obviously partisan issues. Articulating a pious hope that

Table 6.2. Rankings of Elite Predictions of Change During the 1970s by Party and/or Occupational Position
(responses with frequency of four and above)

Predictions by Social Democrats and High-level Administrators	
Predicted Changes	**Frequency**
Increased influence of employees (including industrial democracy and improved environment of the workplace)	12
Intensified debate on total planning (including environment control)	8
No significant changes	6
Continued implementation of equality policies	5

Predictions by Nonsocialist Party and Interest-group Officials	
Predicted Changes	**Frequency**
Change of government	9
Increased influence of employees (including industrial democracy and improved environment of the workplace)	8
Broadened democracy	4
Intensified debate on total planning (including environment controls)	4
No significant changes	4
Uncertain; depends on which party or parties control cabinet office	4

was empirically grounded on opinion polls throughout 1972 indicating majority support for the three bourgeois parties among Swedish voters,[24] nonsocialist elites predicted a change of government in 1973 with far greater frequency than their socialist and administrative colleagues. Also, they anticipated further democratization of the political system in accordance with their own ideological emphasis on libertarian principles. In contrast, executive-administrative spokesmen ranked higher continued progress toward the Social Democrats' proclaimed objective of greater economic and social equality.

A broadly similar pattern of consensus and cleavage is apparent in the elites' ranking of preferred domestic changes during the remainder of the decade. The aggregate frequencies, which are presented in table 6.3, reveal an even stronger advocacy of increased employee influence and improved planning of total domestic resources than the predictions of actual change in table 6.1. Partisan cleavages are discernible through

Table 6.3. Elite Preferences for Domestic Change During the 1970s
(responses with frequency of five and above)

Preference	Total Frequency	Socialists, High-level Administrators	Nonsocialists	Media Spokesmen
Increased influence of employees (including industrial democracy and improved environment of workplace)	29	17	8	4
Improved planning of total resource (including environment controls)	20	11	9	0
Continued implementation of equality policies	10	8	2	0
Broadened democracy	9	3	6	0
Decentralized society	9	1	8	0
Stimulation of private enterprise	9	2	7	0
Change of government	9	2	7	0
Less emphasis on economic growth, more emphasis on creating a better society in which to live	6	1	5	0
Tax reduction, tax reform	6	1	5	0
Full employment	6	4	2	0
Educational reform	5	1	4	0

Table 6.4. **Rankings of Elite Preferences for Domestic Change by Party and/or Occupational Position**
(responses with frequency of four and above)

Preferences of Social Democrats and High-level Administrators	
Preferences	**Frequency**
Increased influence of emloyees (including industrial democracy and improved environment of the workplace)	17
Improved planning of total resources (including environment controls)	11
Continued implementation of equality policies	8
Full employment	4

Preferences of Nonsocialist Party and Interest-group Officials	
Preferences	**Frequency**
Improved planning of total resources (including environment controls)	9
Decentralized society	8
Change of government	7
Stimulation of private enterprise	7
Broadened democracy	5
Less emphasis on economic growth and greater emphasis on creating a better society in which to live	5
Tax reduction, tax reform	5
Educational reform	4

the remainder of the list, however, and in the ranking of socialist-administrative and nonsocialist preferences in table 6.4. Social Democrats and administrators would accord greater priority to economic and social issues, including equality measures and full employment, whereas nonsocialists emphasize the desirability of political reforms and qualitative changes such as political decentralization, a change in the composition of the national cabinet, and greater concern with the "quality of life." But Socialists do not claim a monopoly of socioeconomic issues. Ranking third as a desirable change advocated by nonsocialist spokesmen were government measures to stimulate private enterprise as a means to ensure economic recovery and future expansion.

Although approximately one-fifth of the sixty respondents predict no significant domestic changes in the discernible future and one-tenth expected continued economic decline (see table 6.1), the overwhelming majority of the elite sample thus anticipate continued system transformation (albeit competitive visions thereof) in the future. Relative optimism also characterizes leadership attitudes toward specific features of postindustrial change, even though executive-administrative and nonsocialist elites diverge in their assessments of future relations between the state and individual citizens.

In the first instance, a question about relations between industrial and salaried employees—which was prompted by the white-collar strike in 1971 that some observers had interpreted as a harbinger of social disintegration[25]—elicited the plurality response that the risk of social conflict among both groups will diminish in the future. (See table 6.5.) Rather than being an expression of "class warfare" or assertive group

Table 6.5. Elite Predictions of Future Relations Between Industrial and Salaried Employees
(in absolute numbers)

Prediction	Total Frequency	Socialists, High-level Administrators	Nonsocialists	Media Spokesmen
		Subtotals by Party and/or Occupational Position		
Considerable risk of social conflict	3	1	2	0
Marginal risk of social conflict	15	8	7	0
No change in present relations	1	0	1	0
Declined risk of conflict as socioeconomic differences disappear	24	11	12	1
As traditional socioeconomic differences disappear, new tensions will arise such as bias against foreign workers and conflicts between rich and poor	4	0	1	3
No opinion	1	1	0	0
Question not asked	12	8	4	0
Total	60	29	27	4

egoism, the 1971 strike and retaliatory lockout were interpreted by most respondents as a consequence of a breakdown of communication between interest-group officials and their negotiating partners in the government. Of those who had an opportunity to answer the question, one-half (24 persons) maintained that growing affluence, the successive leveling of differences in personal income, and new educational opportunities promised by the reform of the secondary school system during the 1960s would significantly lessen the prospect of serious antagonism between blue-collar and white-collar workers. In contrast, 15 of those questioned anticipated a marginal possibility of antagonism among diverse occupational groups and 3 emphasized that such a risk was considerable. Four respondents (3 of them spokesmen for the media) observed that new forms of social conflict are likely to arise despite the disappearance of traditional socioeconomic cleavages. The examples they cited included incipient hostility toward foreign-born workers and their families and possible conflict between persons at the extremes of income distribution.

Three additional questions pertaining to specific facets of post-industrial change concerned the past effects of various protest groups on domestic society and politics, the probable future role of protest movements, and the prospects of individual political participation. The responses, which are presented in tables 6.6 through 6.8, indicate a general mood of elite receptivity to the legitimacy of extraparliamentary activity against perceived shortcomings of the domestic system combined with ambivalence toward broadened participatory opportunities.

Table 6.6. Elite Appraisals of Past Protest-group Activity
(in absolute numbers)

Appraisal	Total Frequency	Socialists, High-level Administrators	Nonsocialists	Media Spokesmen
No effect on domestic affairs	1	0	1	0
Marginal effect; for example, they prevented trees from being cut down in one of Stockholm's parks	21	10	9	2
Positive effect on domestic and/or foreign policy	36	18	16	2
No opinion	0	0	0	0
Question not asked	2	1	1	0
Total	60	29	27	4

The columns "Socialists, High-level Administrators", "Nonsocialists", and "Media Spokesmen" fall under the spanning header "Subtotals by Party and/or Occupational Position".

Inspired by New Left and radical liberal attacks on class inequalities and American intervention in Southeast Asia which began in the mid-1960s, grass-roots political protests had proliferated by 1972 to encompass well-publicized criticism of urban planning and environmental problems. New protest groups included associations such as "Environment Center" and "Alternative City" and numerous community-action groups (*byalagen*) which seek to exert pressure on government officials to ameliorate local grievances. As indicated in table 6.6, more than half of the elite respondents positively evaluated such activity, with an additional one-fourth conceding (if sometimes only cynically) marginal effectiveness to protest groups operating outside established party and government structures.

Whether grass-roots protests will continue to play a significant role in future domestic relations is more problematic in the opinion of present leaders. (See table 6.7.) Although 27 respondents anticipate that such activity can assume from somewhat to significantly greater importance in the domestic sociopolitical debate, somewhat more (36) predict no change in present patterns or the decreased importance of ad hoc groups.

Table 6.7. Elite Predictions of Future Protest-group Activity
(in absolute numbers)

Prediction	Total Frequency	Subtotals by Party and/or Occupational Postion		
		Socialists, High-level Administrators	Nonsocialists	Media Spokesmen
Decreasing importance; the various protest groups of the 1960s and early 1970s are only a temporary phenomenon	15	7	5	3
No change from present scope of activity	11	5	6	0
Can have somewhat greater significance for the domestic political debate	24	11	12	1
Significantly greater role than at present	3	2	1	0
Risk that ad hoc protest groups can become undemocratic or reactionary	2	2	0	0
No opinion	3	1	2	0
Question not asked	2	1	1	0
Total	60	29	27	4

Ambivalence similarly characterizes the distribution of replies to a question about possible changes in participatory opportunities for individual citizens. As noted in table 6.8, 15 persons (10 of whom were nonsocialists) were convinced that participatory rights will be expanded in the present decade, but 9 (most of them Social Democrats and high-level administrators) were equally certain that participation will become more restricted. Between these poles, one-sixth of the persons interviewed pointed to the dual potential for participatory opportunities to expand or contract, and nearly one-third were rhetorically hopeful that they would increase.

Partisan cleavages are apparent in replies to a final item on the prospects of centralization versus decentralization of the political system. An issue largely monopolized by nonsocialist critics of the consolidation of local government structures into larger communes and a discernible tendency for officials in the Royal Chancery to assume more control over administrative processes, "decentralization" suggests an alternative formula to the Social Democratic emphasis on collectivist change.[26] Accordingly, partisan differences are predictable in the distribution of elite attitudes on whether system change will require further

Table 6.8. Elite Predictions of Future Opportunities for Mass Political Participation
(in absolute numbers)

Prediction	Total Frequency	Socialists, High-level Administrators	Nonsocialists	Media Spokesmen
Fewer opportunities than at present	9	5	2	2
No change from present	1	1	0	0
Potential exists for both fewer and increased opportunities	10	3	6	1
Marginally increased opportunities	1	1	0	0
Hopeful expectation of increased opportunities	18	9	8	1
Certain expectation of increased opportunities	15	5	10	0
No opinion	2	2	0	0
Question not asked	4	3	1	0
Total	60	29	27	4

Table 6.9. Prescriptive Elite Attitudes Toward Centralization-Decentralization of Swedish Political System
(in absolute numbers)

Prescriptive View of the Future	Total Frequency	Subtotals by Party and/or Occupational Position		
		Socialists, High-level Administrators	Nonsocialists	Media Spokesmen
Increased centralization is desirable and/or necessary	19	17	0	2
Centralization and decentralization are compatible	18	7	9	2
Decentralization is a desirable imperative	14	0	14	0
No opinion	1	1	0	0
Question not asked	8	4	4	0
Total	60	29	27	4

centralization or is compatible with the decentralization of state functions. (See table 6.9.) Of the 19 persons who argued that centralization is desirable and/or necessary, 17 were members of the executive-administrative elite; all those who view decentralization as a policy imperative were nonsocialists. In the middle of the spectrum, on the other hand, an approximately equal number of Socialists-administrators and nonsocialists believe that the further centralization of some political functions (such as the planning of general environmental control guidelines) is congruent with the decentralization of others (such as decisions of detail concerning policy implementation).

PROSPECTS FOR SWEDEN'S FUTURE

In action and word, Swedish elites demonstrated through the early 1970s a determination to mitigate regressive changes caused by economic stagnation and incipient sociopolitical antagonism. Domestically, cabinet officials acted to stimulate productivity by expanding subsidies to industry for employing young persons, women, and the handicapped; increasing the Labor Market Board's resources for public works; and raising childhood and family welfare allowances.[27] In a policy departure from reliance on multinational corporations for petroleum imports, government officials simultaneously approached Iran and several Arabian countries directly in an effort to ensure uninterrupted supplies of oil in the wake of the Middle East conflict in October 1973.[28] With respect to relations on the labor market, leaders of the LO and the three white-collar unions opened informal consultations prior to the 1973–74 nationwide round of wage negotiations on means to prevent a repetition of the disruption of labor solidarity in 1971. Although officials in the organization that had initiated the 1971 strike (the Swedish Confederation of Professional Associates or SACO) were initially rebuffed in their attempts to coordinate negotiating strategy in the public sector with the other major white-collar union (the Central Organization of Salaried Employees or TCO), SACO and TCO leaders reached agreement in February 1973 on cooperation on the communal level.[29]

Underscoring these overt efforts to shore up the established system are the elites' predictions compiled for this study. Only a minority of respondents projected the relatively sluggish economic trends of the early 1970s into the future, indicating a basic optimism among Swedish leaders that the domestic economy would enter a new phase of recovery and growth. On the sociopolitical plane of Swedish modernity, the fact that those persons who determine interest-group policy and working relations on the labor market anticipate a decline in social antagonism suggests that they will seek to avoid conflict in their own behavior. Hence their prediction may become a self-fulfilling prophecy.

Beyond the immediate issue of whether national policies to minimize the prospects of either pattern of regressive change can succeed, the decisive question for Sweden's more distant future is whether system maintenance or one of the competitive visions of collectivist versus libertarian transformation will prevail. The answer presumably lies in a combination of (1) economic and political factors that will structure particular policy choices and (2) attitudinal preferences among national elites. Under present conditions of economic uncertainty (exacerbated by the international energy crisis) and the absence of a cohesive parliamentary majority,[30] the intermediate prospect is that of a continuing pattern of system maintenance. Once (and if) economic and political restrictions on leadership choice are eased, however—for example, through economic recovery and the formation of a stable Social Democratic or nonsocialist government—the prospects of active change will by definition improve. Under such circumstances the elites' visions of the future articulated in this study will provide guidelines for the direction and quality of system change.

At a minimum, system transformation in Sweden will involve socioeconomic and political movement toward the twin goals ranked highest by leadership incumbents: the increased influence of employees over decisions affecting their work environment and the rationalization of Sweden's physical and social resources.[31] That is, regardless of the composition of the national executive, active change will be accompanied by a continuing expansion in the government's economic and social roles. But whether this expansion will serve ideologically defined goals of greater collective security and equality or enhanced individual freedom will depend on whether Social Democratic or nonsocialist elites dominate decision processes. As the interview data indicate, Social Democratic leaders and their administrative colleagues would favor the further equalization of socioeconomic opportunities and a necessary centralization of the political system. In contrast, officials in the nonsocialist parties and interest groups would accord partisan priority to political decentralization, indirect government stimulation of private enterprise, quality of life issues, and tax and educational reform. Moreover, nonsocialist elites express relatively greater optimism that opportunities for mass political participation will expand in the future.

This cleavage in partisan preferences is as old as the Enlightenment and the French Revolution, and has animated group conflict in Sweden throughout the transition to today's advanced industrialwelfare society. Economic and social reforms seeking to maximize collective conditions of cumulative security and equality characterized system change during the four decades of Social Democratic preeminence and will presumably provide the principal impetus for domestic policy initiatives under future Socialist cabinets. Acting to constrain exclusively partisan policy formation and implementation, nonsocialist leaders have promoted individual rights and greater freedom of choice within the national and other collectivities emphasized by the Social Democratics. Libertarian values would inspire some differences of nuance in political initiatives under a bourgeois coalition government—for instance, efforts to delegate greater administrative discretion to local and regional government units—but not at the cost of dismantling the various collectivities themselves. Elite unity in Sweden, on both constitutional principles and the central policy objectives noted in this study, is too pervasive to warrant expectations of dramatic shifts of policy outcomes as might occur with elite displacement in various other advanced nations.

Hence, given the finely tuned balance of political and social forces that has characterized group relations in Sweden since the early 1930s, future transformation is unlikely to involve the unequivocal dominance of one set of partisan principles over another. Assuming that national elites will continue to act in concert in mitigating the international and domestic causes of regression, the competitive emphasis on security, equality, and liberty will yield instead a synthesis of collectivist and libertarian change in the Swedish postindustrial state.

Proceeding on the assumption that human beings are an important variable in an ongoing process of system change in the advanced nations, this study indicates that in the case of Sweden leadership attitudes and behavior are likely to result in a synthetical pattern of collectivist-libertarian transformation rather than the theoretical alternatives of regression and system maintenance. Undeniably, political and group leaders are more predisposed toward optimism in their assessments of the future than their colleagues in the media (and social science) professions. But even if one cannot assume a direct causal relation between subjective elite preferences and actual change in the decades ahead, it is empirically apparent that Swedish leaders are emotionally committed to programs of action rather than complacency or counsels of despair. If modern men and women can, in fact, consciously modify their physical, social, and individual environments in accordance with utopian visions of change, this basic characteristic of leadership attitudes provides a necessary condition of active future change in the Swedish system.

In the global context of postindustrial transition, Sweden is, of course, only a single case study. The probability of transforming change in one instance does not provide a universal precedent. Sweden's high degree of social homogeneity and elite unity, for example, contrasts with the prevalence of sociopolitical cleavages in most advanced nations— suggesting that transformation as opposed to regression or maintenance may be the exception in tomorrow's world. And the failure of leaders in the industrialized states to manage environmental problems, material shortages, and their relations with the Third World would negate the prospects of postindustrial transformation even in countries where conditions otherwise favor such a pattern.

Accordingly, the analysis of the emerging postindustrial order would seem to require more extensive cross-national attention to the quality of leadership choice in determining physical and sociopolitical outcomes than has hitherto been the case. In the face of alternative potentials for regression, maintenance, and transformation, systematic knowledge of elite attitudes toward change in a variety of national settings can provide more reliable knowledge of the future than naive faith in deterministic ideologies or epistemologies.

NOTES

1. By metatheoretical assumption I mean, with K. B. Madsen, the philosophical level of scientific theory that determines the analyst's choice of methodology, data language, and mode of explanation. K. B. Madsen, "The Languages of Science," *Theory and Decision. An International Journal for Philosophy and Methodology of the Social Sciences*, 1 (1970–71): 138–54.

2. A good review of fourteen recent publications on the environment, ecology, and pollution is Charles O. Jones, "From Gold to Garbage: A Bibliographical Essay on Politics and the Environment," *American Political Science Review* 66, no. 2 (June 1972): 588–95. Emphasizing the depletion of natural resources is Donella H. Meadows, Dennis L. Meadows, Jorgen Randers, and William

Behrens, *The Limits to Growth* (New York: Universe Books, 1972). A Swedish variant on the same theme is Gösta Ehrensvärd, *Före—efter. En diagnos* (Stockholm: Bonniers, 1972). Among numerous optimistic projections concerning the future role of technology are Herman Kahn and Anthony J. Wiener, *The Year 2000: A Framework for Speculation on the Next Thirty-Three Years* (New York: Macmillan, 1967); Emmanuel G. Mestehene, "How Technology Will Shape the Future," *Science* 161 (12 July 1968): 135–43; and The Atlantic Institute, *The Technology Gap: U.S. and Europe* (New York: Praeger, 1970). More pessimistic views of technology are presented in Jacques Ellul, *The Technological Society* (New York: Knopf, 1964); and Karl-Henrik Pettersson, *Det herrelösa industrisamhället* (Stockholm: Forum, 1973). The latter author, who is an adviser in the Department of Industry in Sweden, advocates stringent social controls on research to halt the continuation of what he perceives is uncontrolled technological development.

3. Herbert Marcuse, *One-Dimensional Man* (Boston: Beacon Press, 1964); Edward C. Banfield, *The Unheavenly City* (Boston: Little, Brown, 1970).

4. On the importance of images of the future as a determinant of present policy choice affecting system change, see Wendell Bell and James A. Mau, *The Sociology of the Future* (New York: Russell Sage Foundation, 1971).

5. Zbigniew Brzezinski, *Between Two Ages. America's Role in the Technetronic Era* (New York: Viking Press, 1970); and Marcuse, *One-Dimensional Man.*

6. The projective fallacy of modern positivism and behavioralism is criticized in the "Epilogue" of M. Donald Hancock and Gideon Sjoberg, eds., *Politics in the Post-Welfare State: Responses to the New Individualism* (New York: Columbia University Press, 1972).

7. This definition of system change is derived from the complementary definitions of modernization in Dankwart A. Rustow, *A World of Nations* (Washington, D.C.: Brookings Institution, 1967); and C. E. Black, *The Dynamics of Modernization* (New York: Harper and Row, 1966).

8. M. Donald Hancock, *Sweden: The Politics of Postindustrial Change* (Hinsdale, Ill.: Dryden Press, 1972); and Hancock, *The Bundeswehr and the National People's Army: A Comparative Study of German Civil-Military Policy* (Denver: University of Denver, Monograph Series in World Affairs, 1973).

9. I have elaborated these constraints in a paper on "Convergence and Diversity: Contradictory Patterns of International-Domestic Change," presented at the Council for European Studies' conference on Patterns of Change in Advanced Industrial Society held in Monterosso al mare, Italy, on 7–11 November 1973.

10. In contrast to recent efforts to tabulate elite attitudes toward specific policies— for example, Allen H. Barton, "The Limits of Consensus among American Leaders" (Preliminary report of the American Leadership Study conducted under the auspices of the Bureau of Applied Social Research at Columbia University), a "quality of leadership choice" orientation emphasizes the active role that elites play in determining patterns of system change over time.

11. The adjective "short-term" needs special emphasis. Regression would prevail under conditions of conflict between established elites and antielites over control of authoritative decision structures if such conflict seriously impaired the day-to-day functions of the political system—but would not necessarily characterize the quality of system change that might be initiated by a given antielite once it succeeds in displacing the former rulers.

12. Such alternative models can be abstractly conceived as countersystems which Gideon Sjoberg has defined as logical counterparts (i.e., alternative structures, values, and/or policies)to an existing pattern. Through their juxtaposition and comparative analysis, countersystems can usefully serve to indicate how con-

tradictory structures, values, and policies might be reconciled in a new synthesis. See Sjoberg and Leonard D. Cain, "Negative Values, Countersystem Models, and the Analysis of Social Systems," in *Institutions and Social Exchange: The Sociologies of Talcott Parsons and George C. Homans*, ed. Herman Turk and Richard Simpson (Indianapolis, Ind.: Bobbs-Merrill, 1971).

13. Except for a three-month interruption in 1936, the Social Democrats have controlled executive office either alone or as senior coalition partner since 1932.

14. These patterns are an elaboration of the future alternatives I sketched in the conclusion to Hancock, *Sweden: The Politics of Postindustrial Change*. In the present analysis, theoretical elegance is compromised for the sake of anticipating "realistic" prospects of change in the Swedish system. For instance, there is no theoretical symmetry between the two models of regressive change and transforming change—except that the former represent loss of control over domestic environments and the latter indicate means of enhanced control. Also, it should be noted that the choice of models of active change is essentially conservative; no revolutionary alternative is posited which corresponds to the utopian visions of radical liberal or left socialist critics of the established sociopolitical order. This omission is due to my personal conviction, based on the observation of prevailing patterns of elite-mass consensus on basic constitutional principles in Sweden, that the construction of logical "antisystems" is not warranted at the present time.

15. In January 1973 approximately 128,000 persons were unemployed, representing 3.3 percent of the labor force, compared to 74,000 and 1.9 percent in January 1970. Figures for 1973 are from *Dagens Nyheter*, 10 February 1973, p. 9; for 1970, from Statistiska centralbyrån, *Statistisk årsbok för Sverige* (Stockholm, 1970), p. 239.

16. The LKAB strike ended in February 1970 after union leaders agreed to form a joint delegation with members of the local strike committee to open negotiations with company officials on higher wages and improved conditions of work. An excellent survey of the strike's prelude, course, and outcome is Edmund Dahlström, Kjell Eriksson, Bertil Gardell, Olle Hammarström, and Rut Hammarström, *LKAP och demokratin* (Stockholm: Wahlström & Widstrand, 1971). In 1971 over 6000 salaried employees struck to demand a 22 percent increase in wages. The government responded with a selective national lockout and legislation to compel an end to the conflict. A useful documentary compilation on the strike is Alf Nordqvist, *Land i lockout* (Lund: Fax-Böckerna, 1971).

17. Olof Ruin explores briefly the trend toward a concentration of authority in the hands of cabinet officials, administrative departments, and planning commissions in "Participation, Corporativization and Politicization. Trends in Present-day Sweden" (Paper delivered at the Sixty-second annual meeting of the Society for the Advancement of Scandinavian Study in New York on 5–6 May 1972).

18. These illustrations of libertarian change are drawn from both Social Democratic and nonsocialist proposals to improve the work environment, party efforts (especially among Liberals and Social Democrats) to encourage rank-and-file discussions of pending policy issues, and the nonsocialist emphasis on political decentralization. An example of the latter is Gustaf Jonnergård, *Decentraliserat samhälle* (Stockholm: LTs Förlag, 1972).

19. A contributing cause of the drift in national politics after 1970 was the fact that the Social Democratic cabinet was technically a minority government, dependent on indirect communist and occasional nonsocialist support to maintain itself in office.

20. The commissions included one to consider the possible suspension of Paragraph 32 of the statutes of the Federation of Swedish Employers, which grants

employers the right to assign labor, that is due to submit its policy recommendations in late 1973; a second on the work environment (*Bättre arbetsmiljö*, SOU 1972: 86), which published its recommendations in late 1972; and a third on employee security (*Trygghet i anställningen*, SOU 1973: 7), which submitted its proposals in early 1973. Whereas the first change would increase social (collective) control over private enterprise, the recommendations of the latter two commissions are intended to enhance the status of individual workers.

21. In choosing the sample I relied on my own knowledge of decision processes in the Swedish system and the advice of well-informed observers in the government, the media, and academia. Out of 74 persons who were invited to participate, 64 agreed to be interviewed. Four persons were asked questions dealing only with foreign policy; hence their responses were not utilized for this study. Since the respondents include two members of the cabinet, a leading personal adviser to the prime minister, three party chairmen, six vice-chairmen, and five national chairmen of organized interest groups, the interview results may be interpreted with some confidence as reflecting dominant attitudes within "establishment Sweden." Nevertheless, I do not wish to imply that the 60 respondents comprise "the" political elite in Sweden. Accordingly, I shall refer to them in the text as "leaders" or "elites."

22. M. Donald Hancock, "Swedish Elites and the EEC: Models of the Future," *Cooperation and Conflict* (Oslo: Universitetsforlaget, 1974), no. 4, pp. 225–42.

23. In addition to their common functional status as members of the executive-administrative apparatus, the Social Democrats and most high-level administrators who were interviewed for this study share party identity: at least 8 of the 12 administrators were members of or identified with the Social Democratic party.

24. For example, a November 1972 public opinion survey conducted by the Central Office of Statistics indicated that the nonsocialist parties would receive 49.6 to 52.4 percent of the national vote compared to 45.4 to 47.2 percent for the Social Democrats and Communists. *Dagens Nyheter*, 15 December 1972, pp. 1 and 12.

25. See "White Collar Strike Forces Swedes to Question Welfare State's Future," *New York Times*, 26 February 1971, p. 3.

26. Through consolidation of local communes, the number of primary municipalities decreased from over 3000 in the late 1940s to 905 by 1968. The projected goal is 282 "communal blocs" by the end of the present decade.

27. By early 1973 over 36,000 persons were employed under government-guaranteed provisions for so-called protected labor (*skyddarbete*). Parliament approved 1.6 billion crowns for use by the Labor Market Board in 1974 to stimulate employment; in February 1973 the board requested an additional 250 million crowns. At the beginning of the fall session of the Riksdag in October 1973, the cabinet presented a "stimulation package" envisaging expenditures of 2.5 billion crowns to "increase social services, stimulate private consumption, and raise employment especially among women, young people, and the handicapped." A special provision called for increasing annual state support for children from 1320 crowns to 1500 per child. *Nyheter från Sverige* (New York: Swedish Information Service, no. 43, 26 October 1973), p. 1.

28. Longer-term prospects for guaranteed petroleum imports will presumably depend on the ability of the European Community nations and their free trade associates (which include Sweden) to devise an adequate European energy policy. One component could conceivably be a special Nordic agreement whereby Sweden, Denmark, and Finland will be able to purchase oil from Norwegian fields in the North Sea.

29. *Dagens Nyheter*, 4 February 1973, pp. 1 and 2.

30. The September 1973 election reaffirmed the Social Democrats' minority status in parliament. The governing party received 43.6 percent of the popular vote compared to 5.3 for the Left Party-Communists, 25.1 for the Center, 9.4 for the Liberals, and 14.3 for the Moderate Unity (conservative) party. These percentages translated into a parliamentary deadlock: 175 seats for the Social Democrats and Communists, 175 seats for the three nonsocialist parties. Because the nonsocialist opposition was unable to unseat the Social Democrats with a vote of no-confidence, Prime Minister Palme declared his intention to retain cabinet office on behalf of his party.

31. Apart from the expressions of elite priorities recorded in this study, the royal commission reports noted in note 20 above and a new regional policy endorsed by parliament on 16 December 1972, will provide substantive impulses for both changes. The latter legislation is intended to help maintain the present level of population in each of Sweden's twenty-two provinces by providing for service guarantees for smaller communes and the transfer of some state functions from present urban areas to various "primary centers" throughout the nation, each with its own differentiated labor market. In addition, the regional policy bill calls for more stringent conservation measures and more rational planning in the use of land and water. The leading conservative newspaper in Sweden terms it "the most important reform" since the introduction of supplementary pensions in the 1950s. *Svenska Dagbladet*, 15 December 1972, p. 10.

7

PUBLIC POLICY AND THE COMPLEX ORGANIZATION: THE PROBLEM OF GOVERNANCE AND THE FURTHER EVOLUTION OF ADVANCED INDUSTRIAL SOCIETY

CHARLES W. ANDERSON

Eugene Skolnikoff's phrase "the governance of complexity" well defines the problem of politics associated with the further evolution of advanced industrial society.[1] The problem of government can no longer be discussed only with regard to the institutions of the state. The political order of industrial civilization includes not only what Charles Hyneman calls "legal government," but the corporation, the trade union, and other complex organizations as well. All of these share in the making of authoritative allocations of values and resources for the society, and in defining the rules by which members of the society will live. The distinctive polity of industrial civilization is defined not only by the various capacities of such institutions and the state as sources of authoritative decision and of law, but also by the intricate and interdependent web of relationships among them.

This complex political system is seen by many observers as both extremely powerful and highly vulnerable and fragile. It is powerful in that serious questions can be raised about the responsiveness of the system either to individual will or established mechanisms of public choice. Perhaps, as some have suggested, the industrial order has acquired a dynamic and momentum of its own, dictated by its internal norms of growth and profitability, which is impervious to conscious direction and control.[2] However, the system is also perceived as vulnerable. It may be liable to massive error, or it may produce unintended privation or disaster as the consequences of actions taken at one point in the system appear with cumulative and unforeseen impact at another. Many, including Lindberg, Vickers, La Porte, and Harold and Margaret Sprout,[3] question whether our knowledge of the dynamics of this complicated order is sufficient to assure that change works in benevolent or benign directions.

Furthermore, the fragility of the system may be reflected in its declining legitimacy. Many studies suggest that the trend line of support for critical political, economic, and social institutions is down. New forms of conflict and intergroup hostility appear. New groups enter the political process with unprecedented demands that cannot easily be assimilated to established patterns; and ancient cultural and ethnic rivalries are revived, on new terms, with new implications. Some see a growing cleavage between the values and assumptions of elites and mass publics over the desirable directions of change. The consensus on basic premises and beliefs which is fundamental to a workable political order seems threatened both by the emergence of subcultural solidarities and loyalties that set themselves apart and in opposition to existing political communities as well as by ideological dissensus among those whose arena of political action continues to center on the policies and affairs of the nation-state.

Such a picture may represent an extreme view. There are, of course, many forces making for continuity and normality that are also apparent in contemporary events. For the political analyst, the most difficult problem is whether to start from a posture of optimism or pessimism, whether to anticipate essential continuity or change. The present is, as I suggested, complex, and the future uncertain and unknowable; and there is an abundance of themes that can be woven together to create the scenario to which one is temperamentally disposed. Academic disputations on the "big questions" probably reveal more about the personalities of the participants than the issues themselves. Nonetheless, it is worth reflecting that such current and fashionable themes as "the limits to growth" and the "quality of life" have political as well as economic significance. Legitimacy, support, credibility, and a pattern of public policy that does not seem manifestly unjust or unfair are critical resources if we are to sustain the political viability of our civilization. If the "load" on the political system increases rapidly, if we cannot manage an increased volume and complexity of political choices with a certain measure of aplomb, we may begin to press against "limits" quite as real as those of natural resources, pollution, or arable land. Similarly, if the present and future appear more conflictual than the immediate past, our "quality of life" will be very much affected by our capacity to resolve public problems with a measure of civility and grace.

While much has been written about the political problems associated with the further transformation of advanced industrial society, far less has been said about potential responses to them. My proposal is to treat the "governance of complexity" as a problem of policy analysis—as concretely as is possible for such an abstract and global theme. The analytic problem will be to delineate alternatives and consider the implications of various approaches to the problem.

THE PROBLEM OF PRIVATE GOVERNMENT

The most direct and useful angle of attack would seem to be to consider the problem of "private government," of the relationship of the state to institutions other than itself. Advanced industrial society must be viewed as a total political order. The referent of such problems as participation, responsiveness, and democracy in contemporary social criticism is all complex institutions and the systems they define, and not the state alone. The sovereign decision on the distribution, character, and quality of the social product of industrial society is a shared one, and as private organizations accommodate themselves to decisions made by the public sector, so the state must accommodate itself to allocative judgments made by other institutions.

In at least two senses, private organizations are governments. First, through internal political processes and institutions, they make binding rules and commitments on behalf of their members which are enforced by sanctions. Second, they make authoritative allocations of resources and values, not only for their own members, but in the case of large-scale organizations, for society as a whole.

It is at least arguable that modern man is more intimately governed in those matters that affect his day-to-day life by private governments than by the state. I am sure that I adapt my behavior more to the rules of my university than to the laws of the United States in everyday life, and that my prospects are as strongly determined by the one as the other. Anthony Jay puts the matter as follows:

> For most of the employees of big corporations, the power of government to make them happy or miserable is very small: A rise in the bank rate may slightly affect the cost of a mortgage; over a long period, the establishment of a health service, the abolition of military service, the building of roads, the preservation of the countryside, and so on, may raise the general quality of their lives. . . . The power of the firm over their lives, however, is far greater. They can be told to go and live in another part of the country, or another part of the world, or to desert their wives and children for months or years; they can be publicly exalted . . . or publicly humiliated. . . . Of course, they are free to resign, just as the Neapolitan could go and live in Venice; but he might arrive with a record and a reputation,

> Venice might be no more congenial, and a man has to live somewhere. So the petro-chemical expert, the employee of an oil company, has not much alternative but to work for another oil company—and explain why he left the last one.[4]

And Philip Selznick remarks:

> In recent years, we have seen a transition from preoccupation with free-dom *of* association to a concern for freedom *in* associations. This renewed awareness stems from a realization that the private association can be more oppressive than the state. The loss of a job, or the right to pursue a profession, or the opportunity to continue one's education, may be far more hurtful than a jail term.[5]

To sharpen the focus, let us accept that the construction of a viable political order for the future will involve either the centralization of power in the hands of the state, or a restoration of trust and faith in the workability and equity of the pluralist order that presently characterizes Western industrial societies. If the latter is to be achieved, certain changes seem to be required in the system of private government that is the distinguishing feature of this order.

1. Complex organizations will have to become more responsive to individually and socially defined wants and needs. There must be relative coherence between the performance criteria of decision makers and those affected by decisions.

2. Assuming heightened, more diverse, and differentiated and sustained conflict over the role and performance of complex organizations, we will need to develop more effective and sophisticated conflict-resolving mechanisms within and between them.

3. Acknowledging complex organizations as a source of the operating rules for the system, we will have to develop institutions that will make such rule-making authority legitimate in our own eyes.

The analytic problem then becomes one of defining strategies of public action appropriate and plausible to meet these objectives. Two further conditions apply to a policy analysis problem constructed in this way. First, the language is addressed to *public* policy makers. We ignore changes that might occur autonomously within the political processes and institutions of corporations, unions, peak associations, and other complex organizations. The question is how public action can be contrived to effect institutional changes in "governments" other than the state. Second, the alternatives considered must be plausible in terms of the existing resources, capabilities, and operating rules of the political system.

THE ART OF THE POSSIBLE FOR THE LONG RUN

There is an abundance of proposals for total reform of the political order of advanced industrial society. However, the problem of policy making, the craft of government, is better understood as that of finding solutions to problems, or ways of coping with problems, within a given institutional order. If we were to experience a total transformation of values, if there were to be a revolutionary change of heart, our problem would, of course, be different. In the meantime, however, the problem is to perceive alternatives that follow from the operating rules of the going concern, to find areas of flexibility in what at first appears static and final, to see lines of evolution by which we might contrive a more desirable future situation out of the materials at hand.[6] To do this, of course, means that we must comprehend how the problem of private government is understood as an issue of public choice, and how that understanding emerged out of the assumptions, institutions, and values of the past.

Furthermore, when speaking to such large issues as the "future" of industrial society, we are dealing with public policy in very global terms, and for the long run. Any exercise in long-range planning or "futurology" must rest on postulated trends and continuities. The scenario of the future one constructs has much to do with the guiding variables and initial premises one selects. In dealing with public policy questions, moreover, one needs to be concerned with questions of feasibility. The issue is not only how we *might* perceive a public issue, or how we *ought* to perceive it, but how it is *apt* to be perceived in the process of public debate and decision.

For this reason, I would rather look to the possibilities contained in the going concern than to conjectural scenarios of the future or models of social criticism in defining alternatives for public choice. In recent years, we have been overwhelmed by the sheer proliferation of social theories of all kinds. As guides for public policy, none has been invested with much confidence or legitimacy. However, our dominant paradigms of public choice have had remarkable staying power.

In the Anglo-American world particularly, we continue to define public problems and to deliberate policy alternatives largely in terms of the conceptual apparatus of the common law, democratic theory, and a market-based political economy, and this despite the almost total transformation of these societies in the last two hundred years. Certainly, the content and character of these systems of thought has changed with time, but the basic logic and the essential standpoint for appraising public issues has been retained. In contrast, models of social explanation and criticism seem far more volatile and transient. Since the industrial revolution, for example, contractarianism, historicism, organicism, Darwinian evolutionary theory, pragmatism, positivism, and most recently, general systems theory, in many variations and combinations, have all been employed as basic metaphors for explaining the evolving industrial order. But given their durability and adaptability in the face of the societal transformations of the past two centuries, it seems reasonable to assume the persistence of our basic paradigms of public choice as we consider the further evolution of advanced industrial society.

We need such persistent and shared bodies of political principles and concepts if we are to come to agreement. In resolving conflict, disputes must be appealed to standards of evaluation that appear sufficiently disinterested and equitable to the adversaries to be accepted as decisive.[7] A paradigm of public choice specifies the grounds that are appropriate for making claims within a given political order. It tells us about the kinds of arguments that are apt to appear acceptable to political actors in arriving at policy conclusions. It defines the boundaries of the plausible, the range of reasons that will be taken as legitimate in political argument and public debate. The function of paradigms of public choice, such as the common law and the logic of political economy, is to provide criteria for the selection of definitive public commitments from among rival claims and possibilities and to justify decisions made on behalf of the community.

Paradigms of public choice may be contrasted with paradigms of explanation, which are designed to account for the way things are. They aim at understanding. Most social science theories are of this type.

Paradigms of social criticism are another category. They depend on what William E. Connolly has called a "contrast model,"[8] a plausible framework of values and assumptions that provide an alternative vantage point for appraising the social order. The object is normative reconsideration of the commonplace. Conjectural scenarios are imaginative interpretations of how extrapolated trends might appear as future social systems.

Any of these modes of analysis can be used in defining policy options for the future. My preference for working through paradigms of public choice is both analytic and normative. First, I think it is more reasonable to assume the persistence of established patterns of appraising public problems than to stipulate a particular change in public values. Second, I believe that conflict resolution and political civility rests on certain shared conceptions of equity and fairness that transcend the value differences in a society and that can be invoked in settling disputes. I think our established paradigms of public choice continue to be the best candidates for this job, despite their weaknesses and limitations, especially in comparison with the available alternatives.

Thus, while we can appraise the total political order of industrial society from a variety of standpoints, in defining our most plausible options for the future with regard to the problem of private government, the right questions are probably those we have been inclined to ask all along. With regard to the problem of the relation of the individual to the organization, the framework of debate in the Anglo-American world has remained remarkably stable since before the industrial revolution. We weigh the relative claims of private and public interest, of the right of voluntary association against the potential arbitrariness of private power. We consider the legitimate regulatory powers of the state in relation to the desirability of a pluralist policy, and we consider the impact of private actions on third-party rights.

The first step then, in looking for ways of reforming the going concern, is to look for possibilities contained in the logic and institutions of the going concern itself. In considering the "governance of complexity" we move next to the question of how this problem has historically been regarded in Western, and particularly Anglo-American societies.

THE FRAMEWORK OF THE GOING CONCERN

Three general approaches to the problem of private government are contained in the liberal paradigm of public choice. These are the law of associations, the law of the corporation, and the law of industrial relations, which is particularly interesting to us because of its treatment of the problem of "involuntarism" in private organizations, and imposition of democratic practice on the private association as a matter of public policy.

The Law of Associations

Especially in England and America, but in much of Europe as well, the problem of private government in the nineteenth century was fundamentally perceived by policy makers as having to do with the notion of contract. The objective of policy in these societies was, in Willard Hurst's words, "the release of human energies."[9] What was required was that the grip of particularistic and traditional obligations and commitments be broken, and that government provide a clean, open environment for the reconstitution of society on lines that would emerge from the process of individual choice. The perception of the problematic is well conveyed in Sir Henry Maine's idea of a societal movement from status to contract. The legal instrument of contract provided the critical means for giving order and form to a free society. As Wolfgang Friedmann observes, "The evolution from status to contract, from immobility to mobility, gradually pervaded all spheres of life, beyond the fields of commercial and labor contracts. It invaded family relations, and the law of succession. It becomes the basis of club and union membership."[10]

Contract unified the realms of politics and economics. As productive relationships might best be regulated by the voluntary commitments undertaken by buyers and sellers, employers and workers, so the state itself was to be construed as legitimated by consent; and the total polity, the political order, was to arise from the voluntary associations assented to as a matter of individual free choice. Certain assumptions about the architectonic role of the state, its task in providing order and coherence to the society as a whole, followed from the notion of contract, and particularly about the role of public policy in providing for the governance of institutions other than the state itself.

In the paradigm of public choice that has been dominant in Anglo-American society, the point of departure for political argument is the presumption that all associations other than the state are essentially voluntary in nature. They derive from the right of contract among free and equal parties. The state has neither the right nor the obligation to concern itself with their internal political order. Democratic structure and procedure is a problem that arises only in connection with involuntary associations, of which, presumptively, the only case is the state itself. Government must rest on consent, but in voluntary associations, the control of the individual over the authoritative decisions that affect him is secured in his right freely to contract into or to renounce affiliation.

From this initial position, its dilemmas and ambiguities, that which is apt to be perceived as politically problematic about the governance of the pluralist order arises. Private government becomes an issue of public policy when claims of the following kinds are put forward: (1) that the purposes or action of an organization are unlawful; (2) that the purposes or actions of an organization impose costs or unjust constraints on those who are not members of the organization; (3) that the actions of an organization harm members in ways that are unlawful or tortuous; (4) that there is a failure to fulfill the contractual obligations on which the organization is based; (5) that a party to the association was coerced, deceived, or was in some fundamental sense "unequal" in undertaking the contractual obligation; (6) that the association is in some significant sense involuntary; (7) when the state makes available a legal form (incorporation) as a utility or service for private association.

At base, the sense of Anglo-American law as it has evolved in the past century is that the state is generally indifferent to the internal form of governance of private associations so long as the requisites of free contract and legal probity are met. Mr. Justice Frankfurter's words, that courts have "a duty to enforce the rights of members in an association . . . according to the laws of that association. . . . Legislatures have no obligation to adjudicate and no such power . . ." seems to capture the Anglo-American view of the autonomy of the political systems of private associations.[11]

It should be apparent, however, that the implications of this framework of analysis are far from exhausted and that many of the questions of responsiveness of complex organizations can be asked within it. The logic of prescriptive indifference toward the governance of private organizations follows only under conditions that very much resemble the ideal model of perfect competition. Freedom of contract, the essential ground of public indifference to the conditions of private government, follows only when the parties may be presumed to be equal in relevant respects. Furthermore, the choice to leave the organization must be relatively "costless," which implies an institutional pluralism in which close substitutes exist in every field. When these conditions do not obtain, there is a case that can be made for public action to compensate for imperfections in the "pluralist marketplace." Furthermore, as an aspect of the law of tort, the problem of third-party rights, of the "negative externalities" of the performance of a complex organization are legitimate grounds for public concern.

Corporation Law

Unlike the law of association, the corporate form involves an act of public policy in defining the internal system of governance of the complex organization. Policy makers act as constitution makers. As Willard Hurst says: "A statutory charter had content beyond a mere license for private will: in its details it was more like a constitution, fixing the internal structure of the corporation."[12]

Historically, the terms of the corporate charter were a primary means of public control. The charter was a specific instrument, a particular grant of power. It was viewed primarily as a means of accomplishing public purposes through private action. In the mid-nineteenth century, however, the corporate instrument became less a special privilege and more a general utility, a means of general economic promotion rather than a technique for achieving specific public purposes. The British Companies Acts of 1844 and 1855, like a similar pattern in American law, provided standardized "packages" for corporate charter and status. By the early twentieth century, the power of the legislature to frame the corporate charter had diminished as a source of regulation. The political problem of the corporation came to be seen less as a matter of the specification of its internal political system, and more a matter of the control of its sphere of action. Special bodies of regulatory law, most prominently antitrust, developed outside the structure of the corporation itself.[13]

Nevertheless, the question of how the political form of the corporation should be regarded in public policy has never been completely closed. In the 1930s, there was a revival of concern for the rule-making functions of corporate enterprise and for business as a "system of power." In the United States, the Securities Act of 1933 and the Securities and Exchange

Act of 1934 were designed to impose some measure of "internal democracy" on the corporation, some greater degree of accountability to shareholders in a system in which ownership was increasingly divorced from management, through reporting and information requirements, the strengthening of voting rights, and the regulation of proxy voting. Certainly such measures were largely ineffective in "democratizing" the corporation, and they left many questions of corporate responsibility unanswered. Should the political constituency of the corporation be viewed as including only the shareholders, or is there a larger political community—including employees, suppliers, consumers and the public—whose interests should be accounted for in the political structure of the corporation?

To be sure, the predominant tendency has been to reassimilate the problem of the governance of the corporation to the liberal model of contractual association. In the United States particularly, the thrust of regulation applied to the corporation as a political system was designed to ensure that its voluntary, contractual character was sustained. The shareholder's more fundamental control was not that of his power in corporate policy information, but his ability to renounce affiliation—to sell his shares quickly in an open, active, and well-organized market.[14]

However, Ralph Nader's proposal for federal chartering of large corporations suggests that the question is not finally settled, that the logic of the corporate form in Anglo-American law may lead to new alternatives for the governance of complex institutions. The advocates of this approach speak of a new "social contract" which would create mechanisms within the corporation for more effective consumer and citizen participation in corporate decision making. Nader's vision appears to be one in which self-regulation would replace extensive governmental regulation.[15] Such an approach need not be confined to the question of restructuring the internal government of the corporation. A new "social contract" might also imply a redefinition of the rights and powers of corporations, the terms of their social responsibility, and in this sense, a return to the historic notion of public regulation through the terms of the charter rather than, or in addition to, regulation through statute law and regulatory commission.

Industrial Relations and Democratic Process

The third critical historic approach to the governance of complex organizations arises out of an enigma of the law of voluntary associations itself. When collective bargaining replaces individual contract for the worker, the trade union becomes, in a significant sense, an involuntary organization.[16] And in the liberal scheme of things, it is not the logic of contract, but of democratic theory that pertains to such bodies.

The workman is free, if he values his own bargaining position more than that of the group, to vote against representation; but the majority rules, and if it collectivizes the employment bargain, individual advantages or favors will generally in practice go in as a contribution to the collective result.[17]

The corollary was majoritarian, democratic theory applied, as a matter of public policy, not only to the decision to adopt collective bargaining, but to the internal political order of the union itself. The constitution of the trade union became a matter of public concern, and not only the law of contract and the logic of the labor market, but the entire paraphernalia of democratic theory and procedure as well came to apply as a realm of legitimate political debate on the evolution of this societal form. By the time of the Landrum-Griffin Act, most of the procedural safeguards associated with constitutional democracy, including periodic election, the secret ballot, free speech, the right of nomination and opposition, were imposed by public action on the political institutions of the trade union and enforced by public authority.[18]

Nevertheless, to make arguments from constitutional democracy appropriate to the governance of the trade union does not exhaust the chain of argument and policy that followed from this perception of the problem of pluralism as encountered in the field of industrial relations. A system of governance for the enterprise as a whole arises out of the collective bargaining relationship, aptly described by Selznick as a "constitutive contract."[19] American courts have supported the analogy, defining collective agreements as efforts to create a system of industrial self-government. A "common law" arises in the firm, whose existence and authoritative force is judicially acknowledged.[20] The process of labor contract becomes in effect a political institution of the enterprise, a legislative arena designed by public action and subjected to close and detailed surveillance by the state.

Needless to say, the particular inferences derived from the logic of liberal politics are unique to America. Other nations have seen the problem differently. Although Britain provides the closest parallel, the particular problem of the trade union and the collective bargain was not perceived as problematic in the same terms as in the United States, at least not until the Industrial Relations Act of 1971. Generally, and the rule applies to such matters as reporting and disclosure requirements in corporation law as well, private government has continued to enjoy more autonomy in Britain and the Commonwealth. Japan so far seems to have taken the basic liberal model and adapted it to an indigenous heritage in which the enterprise is far more powerful and compelling, while traditional, as a political order and form of political community. In Northern Europe, the national "peak" association (of enterprises, consumers, or labor) plays a role as a form of private government, acknowledged in public policy, that has a different logic and tradition than in the Anglo-American world. In Southern Europe, especially Spain and Portugal, a Catholic corporatist tradition simply proceeds on different assumptions than the liberal model concerning the role of the state as architect of the pluralist order. A full comparison of these various approaches to the problem of private government will not be attempted here. Rather, I will concentrate on the implications of the Anglo-American variant.

POLICY ALTERNATIVES AND PRIVATE GOVERNMENT

Complex organizations are in two senses private governments: they make binding decisions on behalf of those associated with them, and they make authoritative allocations of resources. These are different themes in public debate, and should be treated separately. Let us begin with the problem of possible lines of evolution in public policy toward the internal government of the complex private organization that follow from the logic of the liberal paradigm of public choice.

Democratic Process

The idea that complex organizations should become more "participatory" or "democratic" is an idea that has been recently revived. In a civilization in which the legitimacy of the public order rests on democratic norms and values, there is a strain toward consistency. If the legitimacy of the state rests on consent, how do we legitimate the rule-making authority of the corporation, the university, the association, and other forms of complex organization? The appraisal of private government from the point of view of democratic theory is found in much of the literature on the subject. It is a theme that is apparent in Sanford Lakoff's writings, in Seymour Lipset and Peter Bachrach, and something of the "guild socialist" tradition is an often unrecognized, but consistent idea in the work of Robert A. Dahl.[21]

However, the historic position of liberalism was that democracy was a problem of the legitimacy of the public order, but not of private government, which rests either on the notion of contract or the power of government to establish legal forms for private undertakings, as in the corporate charter. In the history of American public policy, the problem of democracy in private organization becomes a matter of public concern only as a matter of the reform of the corporate charter, in the case of the political party when the organization is deemed to be an integral part of the political system itself, or in the case of the trade union, when the association is in some significant sense involuntary. And only in the case of the trade union has the full paraphernalia of democratic practice been imposed on the private organization as a matter of public policy.

Nevertheless, it can be seriously contended that many of the characteristic organizations of advanced industrial society are involuntary in that the decision to leave them is far from costless to the individual. The order is not fully pluralist, for no alternative institutional outlet, no close substitutes exist. The argument could plausibly be applied to the public school system, professional guilds such as those that exist in law and medicine, and economic institutions of a monopolistic or oligopolistic kind.

In recent years, the complex organization, and particularly the corporation, has become the focus of a variety of political demands, emerging from a diverse assortment of groups including the antiwar movement, environmental-protection bodies, consumer-advocacy organizations, and others. Whether or not this form of political activity will become a permanent part of the political process of advanced industrial nations is still an open question, but it does raise the issue of the relevant constituency of the private organization, and of the creation of arenas for the confrontation of adversary interests, and for conflict resolution.

Some would argue that such adversary interests are more appropriately routed through political authorities—through regulatory agencies, legislatures, and the courts. Particularly in the 1960s, however, it became apparent that the governmental structure of the corporation, or the private association, would be increasingly the focus of new forms of political conflict.

The issue has been raised as to whether the "community" represented in the political structure of the corporation should be redefined to include representation of consumers, public-interest advocates, employees, and others affected by the decisions and actions of the enterprise. What is yet unclear is whether this conception of the changed constituency of the corporation is viewed in democratic or neo-corporatist terms. Consumer-action groups, such as Nader's "Operation GM" or Common Cause, perceive the issue as one of "representation" for consumer interests in the internal decision-making processes of the firm. From the point of view of democratic theory, however, the actual "representativeness" of such groups is open to serious question, and the problem of how an effectively democratic process of representation could be contrived for such interests within the system of corporate government seems difficult indeed. What the advocates of such reform seem more to have in mind is a form of adversary proceeding rather than democratic process within the complex organization, a confrontation of perspectives, issues, and information not normally taken into account in the process of corporate decision making. What is envisioned may have more to do with the kind of process usually associated with adjudication, or with neo-corporatist structures which aim at a harmonization of "natural interests," rather than the "democratization" of the complex organization itself.

"Worker participation" raises other issues about institutional change in the political structure of the enterprise. While codetermination has been institutionalized in Northern Europe and such nations as Yugoslavia, many trade unionists in the Anglo-American world and in other nations find that the "constitutive contract" arising out of the collective-bargaining relationship provides a satisfactory institutional model and are hesitant about the potential dilution of worker interests were labor to play a role in management decisions themselves. The difficulty in the European Economic Community in defining a common policy on company law, given the German dedication to *mitbestimmung* and the commitment of the English and French to collective bargaining, is illustrative of the difficulty.

Nonetheless, as Ralph Nader's idea of federal chartering of corporations and a "new social contract" illustrates, one theme for political argument and policy choice in the further evolution of advanced industrial society might concern the more comprehensive democratization of the polity by extending the values, norms, and operating principles of the democratic polity to other areas of the pluralist political order. The prospect is not all that radical or unconventional. Precedents exist in the National Labor Relations Act and related reforms of the government of corporations and political parties in the New Deal period. It is a possibility which has a certain propriety in terms of the ongoing commitments of the liberal polity.

Contractual Voluntarism

Democratization is not the only policy implication that may arise from the dilemmas of involuntarism in complex organizations. In his brilliant essay "Exit, Voice and Loyalty," Albert O. Hirschman observes that there are two general social processes that pertain to the capacity of the individual to cope with an unsatisfactory institutional relationship. Exit is the ability to leave the association, voice the power of participation in the policy making for the group.

> To resort to voice, rather than exit, is for the customer or member to make an attempt at changing the practices, policies and outputs of the firm from which one buys or of the organization to which one belongs. Voice is here defined as any attempt at all to change, rather than to escape from, an objectionable state of affairs.[22]

If the problem of the further evolution of the political order of industrial society is construed as one of contractual voluntarism, it is equally plausible to argue that the public responsibility is to restore the conditions of contractual freedom as it is to democratize involuntary organizations. This is the historic logic of antitrust as an alternative to industrial democracy or democratic socialism. The contemporary debate over shifting public educational funding from support for the school to support for the student is of the same type. A system of educational "vouchers" which parents or students could use to purchase education would result not only in more individual control over educational opportunities and more equality of access to education, it is argued, but would also create a more pluralistic, diversified, and responsive educational system.[23]

If this is the way the problem of private power is perceived, the charge falls on the public authorities to create market effects intentionally, to create, or establish conditions for the creation of, alternative institutions and organizations to those which have become culturally dominant. The argument can be broached in many ways, in many arenas. If the fact that the choice to leave one's present employment is not truly "costless" for the employee, it is equally pertinent to argue for industrial democracy or for full-employment policies, public support for relocation costs, labor exchanges, and retraining programs.

The ideal of contractual voluntarism also invokes the historic idea of pluralism, that associated with Gierke, Figgis, Maitland, Laski, and Cole—the conception of a society organized about a wide variety of effectively autonomous, voluntary associations. If, as has frequently been suggested, the emergence of postindustrial society is to be associated with the growth of subsystem solidarities, alternative life styles, new forms of community association and small-group endeavor, one problem of public policy will be to provide the legal, institutional, and political base for such a wider, more diversified associational life. Here the public problem is not one of providing alternatives for "exit," but regulating the institutional life of a more diversified society. The issues of private government concern not only the internal political order of unique and unprecedented associations, but devising means for the resolution of conflict in a more fragmentized, heterogeneous society.

Much in the legacy of the law of associations speaks to the problem. The episode of social experiment in America in the 1960s is perhaps significant. The community organization, the commune, the protest movement, new life styles and family patterns were controversial and a major source of public debate, but they created few actual dilemmas in the law of associations. The commune did result in a brief episode of controversy in California property law, concerning the dispositions of assets of defunct communities of this type. The more stable forms of communal living, fragmentary evidence from Wisconsin would seem to suggest, have found existing cooperative organization or standard business law satisfactory for purposes of their internal governance and legal form. More commonly, of course, for groups that had opted out of the larger society, the question of contractual obligation, of the rights of individuals and the nature of governance within such bodies, simply did not arise as a matter of public concern.

"Due Process" and the Private Government

In complex, modern society, our interactions with complex organizations are so frequent, numerous, and manifold that neither "exit" or "voice" may provide satisfactory resolution of the problem. For many purposes, the question of the potential arbitrariness of private power, of the relationship of the individual to the organization, is better defined in terms of "right" rather than "participation" or "choice." In many areas, the real interest of the consumer runs less to participation, or the operation of the market, and more to assurances of contractual performance and the expectation of fair treatment in his dealings with the organization when the transaction becomes complicated or things go wrong. For the employee, the more critical day-to-day issue is less apt to be that of sharing in management decision, or the possibility of going elsewhere, and more that of protection against discrimination at the point of hiring, whimsical or arbitrary authority on the job, and the rights he enjoys against layoff, transfer, or termination against his will.

A third possibility, then, in considering options for public policy with regard to the internal governance of private organizations, is to view their rule-making functions as an extension of the legal system. If we were to take up this question this way, our concern would be with the conformity of the operating rules of private bodies to general norms of procedural fairness, equality in the contractual relationship, and the rights and obligations that attach to the role structure and the performance of the organization. One acknowledges the rules of private organizations as a source and realm of law, and moves to make them consistent with the higher-order legal principles of society as a whole.

In American jurisprudence, considerable attention has been given recently to the problem of "due process of law" within private government. Courts have been willing to enforce norms of procedural fairness not only on public and quasi-public agencies, but also on such semi-monopolistic organizations as unions enjoying closed-shop agreements. They have stopped short in such cases as the expulsion of students without notice or hearing from private universities, where the autonomy of such institutions still seems to be the stronger claim.[24] However, an evolving body of judicial doctrine points toward the assimilation of private law to public law not only through the constitutional dictum of due process, but on grounds of general common law standards of procedural fairness.[25]

This concern for establishing a larger realm of legality is also apparent in the evolution of norms concerning the rights of entry into an organization and those governing the ultimate sanction of the private government, the power of expulsion. As public law increasingly regulates the power of private associations to select their own "citizens"— through antidiscrimination legislation and the like—so associational membership is increasingly viewed as a "valued possession" of the member, a source of livelihood perhaps, at least of status and self-esteem. While the law is far from definitive on this point, there is a growing sense that arbitrary power over individuals will be viewed as an issue of public policy.

The United States has moved further than Britain in assimilating the private government to general norms of legality. Even in the United Kingdom, however, where there is a historic disposition to view the acts of "domestic tribunals" as matters that are not of policy concern, a growing sense that an issue of private power exists is evident. The Donovan Commission on Trade Unions and Employers Associations of 1965[26] and the Industrial Relations Act of 1971 both point in this direction. There does seem to be a pattern of convergence between the Anglo-American model and that of other industrial societies, particularly those of continental Europe, where the state has been historically more assertive in defining the operating rules of private associations and organizations.

A Scenario for Future Public Debate

No clear evidence exists that the trend of public policy is apt to run more strongly toward increased participation, a larger pluralism, and more fulsome freedom of choice, or an extension of the domain of legality. There is little to suggest that we are heading toward the universalization of democracy, to a system in which mass participation and electoral competition will characterize the arenas of private government as well as those of public authority. It is perhaps somewhat more likely that we will adopt neo-corporatist forms of representation, including consumer, employee, and other interests in the decision making bodies of the firm. Nor is it plausible to envision the future in terms of an ultimate pluralist ideal of a society which is "an assembly of autonomous groups, living in harmony with one another, but offering individuals a wide variety of alternative opportunities for self-expression and self-fulfillment."[27] The process of incorporating the private government into the realm of law will probably continue, but carried to its ultimate conclusion, this suggests to me a kind of new medievalism, a comprehensive system of statuses, rights, and obligations, tying together all the institutions of society in an organic whole. Perhaps that is a plausible vision of the future, but the safest conjecture would seem to be that all three processes will be advanced at different times and places, in different sectors of the society; that as a total polity, advanced industrial society will remain a "mixed system" for the indefinite future.

The significant question raised by the three alternatives is not that of the projection of trends, but of normative choice. The three imply very different political values. They suggest an agenda for debate over what kinds of principles we want to realize as we consider the further political development of our civilization.

At critical points, the argument for increased participation, or for a richer pluralism—in the sense that this implies the essential autonomy of voluntary associations—conflicts with that of an expanded notion of individual rights, of an extension of the domain of legality. Community control of schools appears a fine ideal until the right of the individual student to a certain kind and quality of education arises. The more one refines one's notions of what the individual is entitled to expect from the performance of a complex organization, the less scope it has as an autonomous source of policy.

A recent controversy illustrates the conflict between individual right and the autonomy of pluralist association. The Supreme Court of Wisconsin was asked to rule on a case brought by the Amish community, a small, traditional religious sect, that it be exempt from compulsory public education laws. The Amish argued that the integrity and preservation of their distinctive religious culture depended on the insulation of their children from the secular values of public schools. The Wisconsin decision turned on the First Amendment question of religious freedom; the court ruled for the Amish, and the decision was subsequently upheld by the U.S. Supreme Court. The terms of the argument are more significant than the decision itself or the specific religious issue, for it stated, at a far from trivial level, the serious dilemma of pluralism and individual right that is locked into the heritage of liberal society. In a dissenting opinion in the Wisconsin case, Mr. Justice Heffernan argued:

> The state's interest and obligation runs to each and every child in the state.... Those young Amish who leave the group have received no education that equips them for modern American life. By not enforcing the school attendance law, the State of Wisconsin has consigned these young people to a future without any choice or goal except those of the traditional Amish life.[28]

The question of "shop-level" democracy provides an illustration of the conflict between the values of participation and individual right. To be sure, there are values to be realized in providing for a system in which hours, the organization and rhythms of work are determined by collective choice at the smallest level of organization. However, it is hard to see how the democratic autonomy of the shop could extend further. Beyond this, rights of other parties begin to appear. There are obligations of contract for the firm as a whole, and public regulations concerning price, quality, and the rights of consumers. The autonomy of the shop is restricted by the obligations that fall increasingly on the complex enterprise, for the character, quality, and dependability of its product. Furthermore, there are rights of individuals against the "government" of a shop organized as an exercise in participatory democracy. Since employment is a valuable association, sanctions that might be imposed by majority consent are subject to scrutiny for their fairness to the recalcitrant individual.

Family law provides a third illustration of the dilemma. There is a tendency in many modern societies to see the family, for purposes of public policy, more as an "autonomous association," less as the subject of public definition and regulation than was historically the case. Through changes in divorce and property law, we are coming to see the family as a more flexible social form, its formation, dissolution, character, and internal governance more a matter for determination by the parties concerned than a matter of public policy. Nonetheless, the dilemma persists between the claims for social experimentation, for a greater pluralist autonomy, at this small-scale level, and those of individual rights and responsibilities. Family law cannot ignore the rights of children or relationships that are manifestly unfair or hurtful to some party. The ground rules that a responsible society must apply to this form of contract will continue to be argued. The debate within the liberal paradigm is perennial.

THE REGULATION OF THE COMPLEX ORGANIZATION

The political legitimacy of the pluralist order of industrial society is not only a problem of the internal governance of the complex organization. What is also at issue is the performance, responsiveness, and control of the system defined by the intricate interdependence of such institutions. This brings us to the second side of the problem of private government—its role in making authoritative decisions that have general public consequences. In almost all modern nations, this has been the more apparent issue of public policy. The question of public decision has been less that of the internal representativeness of the organization and more that of the impact of its actions on society as a whole. The problem has been to find means of public regulation and guidance that were compatible with the liberal paradigm, with the norms of contractual voluntarism and associational autonomy. Always the search has been for mechanisms of control that did not override the self-correcting and self-regulating features of the market and of associational pluralism.

It is probably worth recognizing at the outset that the sphere of action of the complex organization has never been unencumbered. Despite the bias in liberalism in favor of self-regulating mechanisms, as John R. Commons long ago pointed out, even at the height of laissez faire, the "working rules" of the system, the law of contract, property, rent, wages, and the rest constituted a complex pattern of rights and duties, entitlements and restraints.[29] Similarly, the market never was a purely impersonal, automatic mechanism. The terms of its operation, its perfection and control, always has been a matter of public concern. As Karl Polanyi has noted, the road to liberalism was one of the most sustained and deliberately planned public efforts in history.[30]

The troublesome problem of the contemporary moment is that we are no longer sure that the regulatory techniques so carefully contrived over the past thirty to forty years still work. The three basic approaches to the public guidance of a complex pluralist polity that have characterized our time are neo-Keynesian economic management, "democratic" or "indicative" planning, and regulatory law. These three are in some sense parallels to the basic alternatives in the field of the internal governance of the private organization. Democratic planning pairs with "internal democratization," the one for decision making *among* complex organizations, the other for decision making *within* them. Neo-Keynesianism is the equivalent of "contractual voluntarism," in which the object of policy is to sustain and work through self-regulating processes of choice. Regulatory law, applied to the impact of the complex organization on society, is the same as extending the domain of legality to its internal rule making.

These three approaches have been critical to sustaining the legitimacy and viability of the pluralist polity. All three represent adaptations of the basic liberal paradigm to the conditions of the advanced industrial age. All three have become established and to a large extent legitimate parts of the policy repertoire of the modern nation, often after difficult and prolonged doctrinal and political struggles. Still, we are no longer certain that these techniques will continue to represent effective approaches to the governance of the pluralist industrial policy in the future.

Keynesianism

The story of Keynesianism is an elegant example of the discovery of adaptive alternatives from within the logic of liberalism. The idea of the market, of the decision-making autonomy of the firm is sustained. The system is compatible with the norms of contractual voluntarism. Public guidance and direction was provided not by direct control of the sphere of action of the organization, but by manipulating its total environment of choice and action.

It may be that the complex enterprise, and increasingly, too, the giant trade union, have grown in scale and autonomy in recent years in ways that make them increasingly impervious both to the neo-Keynesian measures of budgetary and fiscal management and the monetary policy solutions of the Friedman school. The sustained inflation experienced in all industrial nations may be symptomatic of a sea-change in the relationship of the public and private orders. The giant industrial firm, largely self-financing, whose investment cycle is substantially longer than that of public policy, which is increasingly multinational in its operations, may be simply less responsive to the instruments of budgetary policy, control of interest rates, or the money supply, than was its predecessor of even ten or twenty years ago. The presumably constructive conflict of industrial relations takes on new implications when, under conditions of industry-wide bargaining, no advantage accrues to the firm that resists labor demands if it can assume that its settlement will become "standard" for the industry, and that prices will inevitably be passed along.

The postulated relationships in Keynesian theory seem in some cases to be running counter to predictions. To contract aggregate demand and capital supply in a period of overheating may not have much impact on prices. The giant firm, technology dependent, with largely fixed labor costs, may in fact have to raise prices in the face of such policies to sustain liquidity. Its less efficient competitor must do the same to escape bankruptcy.

What has changed, in part, are the institutional objectives of the complex enterprise. The problem is, in fact, more one of private government than economics in the strict sense, for it concerns changing policies of firms, new norms, and operating rules of their internal political systems, institutional adaptation and development. The goal of the giant corporation becomes less that of production and sale of product, more that of organizational growth for the long run. This momentum cannot be as much affected by countercyclical policies. The carrying forward of plans for global expansion, technological innovation, merger and amalgamation is not much responsive to neo-Keynesian measures. In fact, the objectives of institutional growth may actually be aided by contractive policies, insofar as the objects of takeover are weakened. And this indirect incentive to expansion will itself put pressure on the price of capital.[31]

The market becomes less legitimate and plausible as a regulator of the pluralist polity under conditions of increased concentration in many economic sectors. Increasing interdependency and the growth of the multinational corporation implies that the critical market mechanisms may operate between polities rather than within them. To be sure, concentration is far from a novel problem of policy in capitalist societies. But the conception of a two-tiered economy, some sectors of which are responsive to market forces and others not, does seem to require a reformulation of our idea of policy, and of the nature of the pluralist polity itself. The consistent thrust of American policy has been to try to sustain the market (through measures like antitrust), to use regulation as a surrogate for the market where it did not apply and most recently, to guide the market toward certain general policy objectives—such as full employment and sustained growth. We may have to rethink this agenda. We may want to visualize the market more selectively as an alternative to regulation, pertinent in specific sectors and not in others. We are clearly in a quandary as to the further development of political economic theory, perhaps awaiting the arrival of a new Keynes.

Democratic Planning

Little more than a decade ago, planning became legitimate both as a symbol and a process in Western industrial society. As in the case of Keynesianism, it seemed possible to accommodate a measure of public guidance and control to the operation of a pluralist polity of complex organizations through processes and institutions that were compatible with the liberal ethos. In a mixed economy, middle-range objectives could be set, and coordination to meet those objectives achieved, through deliberative process, by means of bargaining, argument, and planned accommodation among the critical economic actors.

Of course, planning never did become as important in the Anglo-American world, with which we are principally concerned, as it did in specific nations of Western Europe, most particularly France. What is important for our purposes is that this alternative approach to the total governance of the pluralist order has produced its own conundrums. For the temper of the public debate on planning in contemporary France raises the question of how far democratic theory can be appropriately invoked as an alternative line of evolution in the future development of industrial society.

Despite the increasingly elaborate consultative apparatus of the *Comisariat du Plan* and its parallels in other nations, the idea of "democratic" planning has always been something of a euphemism. The French early admitted that their technique really only worked satisfactorily when 80 percent of the production was concentrated in 20 percent of the firms.[32] In most nations, trade unions have been at best reluctant and halfhearted partners in the planning enterprise. (The exception is Sweden, where national wage bargaining between the peak labor and employer's associations is actually a form of national economic planning.)

Throughout Europe, the question of "participation" in national-level economic decision making has become an increasingly lively issue. The various processes of pluralist planning that have been devised since World War II appear to many publics not as means of adjusting the complex organization to public purposes, but as a closed system of elite domination. The critique extends, of course, to the interest-group bargaining, regulatory policy, and "contract state" processes that substitute for formal planning mechanisms in the United States. Even in systems where the corporatist framework is most highly developed, as in Sweden, the peak associations are perceived increasingly as remote and unresponsive.

The question of the appropriate constituency of national planning, of who should participate and how participation should be organized, raises issues quite like those involved in the "democratization" of the complex organization itself. The French experiments in decentralized regional planning, the creation in America of institutions of "adversary planning" such as Common Cause, may be suggestive innovations. However, to incorporate a greater variety of groups into the process of interest-group bargaining in the United States, or to extend the framework of corporate-interest representation elsewhere, may not be the same thing as "enhanced democratic participation." The individual citizen may still feel quite remote from the processes of decision making that affect his life. The legitimacy of systems of coordination and control of the complex organizations that characterize modern industrial society is still an unresolved question. The issue of how planning can be reconciled with the democratic norms that are the foundation of the public order in such societies will require further imaginative search for areas of flexibility and innovation.

Regulatory Law

Law defines the rights and obligations of persons and organizations. It specifies spheres of unencumbered action, what an organization *may* do without hindrance or constraint. It also defines limits to autonomy of decision and action, what an organization *may not* do in recognition of a right of action by another party. It declares a realm of obligatory action, what the individual or institution *must* do—as in the obligation to honor contracts. It specifies a certain field of action where the party *can* expect public support for an undertaking (as in the right of legal recourse in cases of illegal competition) and it defines areas where the organization operates at its own risk, where it *cannot* expect public support if another hinders the course of action it has set upon.[33]

Regulatory law has been an active and lively area of change in the regime of complex organizations, particularly in the United States in recent years. In many areas, our conceptions of the rights and obligations of complex organizations, toward individuals, other institutions, and the public order, are changing. Claims arise for greater consistency with the basic norms of the liberal paradigm. In a regime where contractual equality is a basic promise of legitimacy, racial and sexual discrimination define issues for public action. In a system where outcomes are deemed appropriate if they rest on individual choice and action, disparities of income, status, initial disadvantage or cultural deprivation challenge the basic consistency of the order. Such issues of "equality of opportunity" impose new obligations on government, and on the complex organization itself, to fair employment practices, "affirmative action," programs of "corporate responsibility" and the like.

Environmental protection is another area where there is a strain toward redefining the legitimate sphere of action of the complex organization—its rights to autonomous choice and the obligations that fall upon it. How are the "negative externalities" of production to be paid for? Who is to absorb the burden of the costs that are byproducts of the operation of complex organization—including not only pollution, but also human displacement and a perceived reduction in the "quality of life?" Is pollution of the air as a means of disposing of industrial waste a policy that the corporation *may* undertake, without hindrance, or do "rights" of other parties appear which imply obligations and restraints?

Consumer protection is another area where a change in our conception of relevant rights and responsibilities is apparent. Developments in negligence and contract law have imposed new obligations on the manufacturer for the quality and safety of his products, for the terms of time payment, "truth in lending," and other forms of contract. Class actions suits in the United States represent a new dimension of producer liability. Such changes imply a shift in the burden of right and responsibility. The original liberal notion of *caveat emptor* implied that a burden of responsibility for investigation, careful and prudent purchase fell to the consumer. To the modern mind, this seems both undesirable and unnecessary. In exonerating the individual of such responsibility, we intend to extend his or her sphere of freedom of action, of "carefreeness," and to impose on the manufacturer a burden of "carefulness."

Our sharpened perception of the normative power of the liberal paradigm, of the implications of its ideals of "fairness" and equity for the relationship of the individual to the complex organization, contain enigmas for the legitimacy of the system as well. We have been more imaginative of late in defining new possibilities for a just and humane civilization from the materials provided by the basic premises and concepts of the common law. From our inherited ways of defining legitimate claims and plausible arguments, we have found a rather serviceable agenda of ideals to be realized. But as our expectations increase, and we become more sharply aware of the inconsistencies in the system, the pressure on the crucial institutions we expect to make good on such claims becomes more intense. Disillusionment follows from performance "lags." Cynicism is the consequence when the pluralist order, when government and the complex organization, do not respond to what is obviously equitable, just, and required of them.

The Normative Implications

As in the case of the internal governance of the complex organization, the issue of public choice with regard to the total order of the pluralist polity is not merely one of effective technique, but of the values we wish to realize. To define the issue of the coordination and control of the system of complex organizations as one of the further refinement of political economy, of democratic planning, or of an extension of regulatory law is to emphasize different values and principles, to create different expectations about the performance of the order of advanced industrial society.

During the course of this century, our conception of what was legitimate cause for concern about the performance of the complex organization has changed many times. Always our expectations have grown higher. At the beginning of the century, we were satisfied if some semblance of the market mechanism could be restored through trustbusting. We were not yet moved to action by such issues as wages and hours; industrial safety; social insurance; the right of collective bargaining; the health, purity, and safety of the product; the operation of the stock market; and so on. These conceptions of the "problematic" came but gradually.

With the depression and the Keynesian revolution, our expectations increased. A highly interdependent and complex system could be brought to a pitch of sustained high performance through the use of mechanisms of budgetary and monetary management. The burden on the state, to assure peak efficiency not only by dampening business cycles, but also by creating sustained growth and full employment with relative price stability increased enormously. Keynesianism introduced not only new techniques of economic management, but new criteria for the evaluation of the performance of the system as a whole. Our normative framework changed. We were promised that the system could be made to operate like a well-oiled machine, producing greater and greater abundance, guaranteeing work for all, outcompeting the centrally planned economies. We are impatient with adjustments in the market mechanism. If beef or oil come into short supply, we expect immediate corrective action and are not willing to wait on the postulated mechanisms of classical market forces.

Such expectations have increased the "load," not only of decision but also of legitimacy on the public order. What is less frequently recognized is that the burden of sustaining peak performance also fell on the complex organization. Where once business cycles and a certain "slack" in the system were not regarded as legitimate issues of public concern, now if the private sector cannot meet the expectations defined by the critical Keynesian variables of growth, full employment, price stability, security of supply, and the like, we insist on public action to prod the private sector into still higher performance.

In recent years, our ideals with regard to the system have become higher still. We would sustain the productive performance of the system, but we add to our charge a concern for pollution, resource depletion, safety, congestion, amenity and aesthetic values, for a greater supply of public goods, for a reduction in the frantic way of life, for an end to work that is meaningless or not satisfying.

In a period of rapid value change, different individuals and groups attach different importance to the worth of sustained and enhanced affluence, to the threats implied by the "limits to growth," or to positive values of well-being and welfare other than those associated with economic growth. Hence, we require more effective techniques of conflict resolution, both within and between organizations, responsive to and capable of reconciling the heterodox interests involved.

Simultaneously, we wish to become more scrupulous about matters of individual rights, about the capacity of individuals to protect their own domain and to define their purposes in life against exercises of authoritative power, whether vested in public or private institutions.

In the current period, critical questions can be asked about the viability of established institutions and mechanisms of political economy, democratic process, and the law. As our expectations have increased, new loads have been placed on all the institutions that are central to our conception of the governance of the total pluralist polity. The character of the future order of advanced industrial society depends to some extent on the relative emphasis we give to each of these areas in public choice, on the accident of where new "breakthroughs" of innovative theory of technique first appear, and on which institutional nexus becomes the focus of public support.

However, the normative order of the future may appear differently depending on which of these lines of potential political evolution receives the greatest emphasis. Political economy is associated with "performance" values. The organizations and institutions of industrial society are not primarily perceived as forms of community, realms of solidarity, arenas for participation and citizenship. Rather, they are part of a mechanism, a system, that delivers products, services, income, and savings. Democratic theory is concerned more with "participation" values. The organization is viewed less as mechanism, more as an arena of organized human relationships, in which decision making and collective action are crucial. Law is concerned with "rights," and particularly with the definition of consistent principles that define the legitimate relationships of individuals with the organizations and associations to which they belong, with which they come into contact, which affect their capacity for free action and the exercise of individual will.

Our choice among institutional mechanisms of control thus implies a decision about relevant values as well. Different aspects of the liberal paradigm are associated with each of our established approaches to the overall governance of complex industrial society. Our knowledge is similarly compartmentalized, as anyone who has been to a conference involving economists, political scientists, and lawyers is well aware. To some extent, each of these disciplines is the guardian of a facet of our legacy of principles and norms. Perhaps one of the tasks of the future is the reconstruction of liberal theory, a new perception of the critical relationships among guiding principles, so that we might better appreciate the implications of the alternatives available to us, and better search out possibilities yet undefined.

Conclusion

We tend to overlook the essential newness of advanced industrial society. To be sure, the scientific and industrial revolutions date back two centuries and the transformation in thought that gave rise to liberalism is older still. The process which development theory calls "modernization" seems basically a nineteenth-century phenomenon in Europe and America. But viewed as a civilization, "advanced" industrial society, as distinguished from industrialism in general, is a raw and recent creation. It did not acquire its distinctive character until well into the twentieth century.

If the complex organization, and the political system of the pluralist industrial polity, is the distinguishing characteristic of the advanced or mature industrial order, this pattern has existed, in relatively coherent form, for at best the past forty or fifty years. As Peter Drucker puts it:

> Only a lifetime ago, at the turn of the century, the social world of Western man might have been represented as a prairie on which man himself was the highest eminence. A small hill—government—rose on the horizon, but while it was larger than anything else there it was still qute low. Today, by contrast, man's social world, whether East or West, resembles the Himalayas. Man seems to be dwarfed by the giant mountains of large-scale

organization all around him. Here is the Mount Everest of modern government. Then come the towering cliffs of the large business corporations, and scarcely less high and forbidding, the peaks of the large powerful labor unions; then the huge universities, the big hospitals—all of them creatures of this century.[34]

Given the relative newness of this societal order, it seems very unlikely that it has reached its final form. Often, we see ourselves as the legatees of a mature, or at worst, a dying or decadent civilization. But it may be that what troubles us most about the order of modern society is a consequence not of its maturity but of its relatively recent origin—that in many respects, as a human culture, it is still unfinished and quite primitive. We have not yet defined the relationships between individuals and the critical institutions, or the functional relationships of these organizations one to another, to our satisfaction. We have not yet attached to them the values and conventions that would make them legitimate and comprehensible in our eyes. In this respect, perhaps, industrial "civilization" has not yet been created.

I have argued that the political scientist's interest in the future of industrial society is primarily as a problem of public choice, of the conscious direction of the evolution of a civilization. However, the political realm is not an area of complete freedom of will but is contingent on the arguments that arise out of the initiatives that individuals and groups take, the claims they advance, and the criteria that we are willing to invoke to distinguish an appropriate case and that we eventually employ to arrange a settlement. I have further argued that, in Anglo-American society particularly, the liberal paradigm is a persistent point of reference. Since it is in large measure persuasive in our societies as to what counts as an appropriate claim, it provides us with a basis for assessing what is most likely to be perceived as "at issue" in the further evolution of these societies, what we are most likely to be choosing between, in what ways we are likely to be able to fashion our long-term destiny.

Within this familiar context, much latitude exists for development. Liberalism is in essence paradoxical. Because its strongest premises and ideals are often contradictory, it is a source of argument. The problem of politics in a liberal society is, of course, to reduce conflict to argument, and out of conflicting claims, to define new possibilities.

I grant that the logic of political discourse is not the only determinant of the course of a civilization. But I submit that the persistence of systems of political evaluation is a far surer guide to the future than the tentative and fluctuating models we employ in an effort to fathom the critical trends and forces of societal development.

Further, I would argue that the persistence of an organized logic of public choice is essential to political coherence, legitimacy, and survival. We need some basis for determining what is at stake, what standards are appropriately invoked in coming to definitive commitments for society as a whole if our future is to make sense to us, if it is to appear in our own eyes as fair, just, and equitable. I do not argue that liberalism is necessarily the ideal state of public consciousness for the creation of a better polity, but rather that it is what we have got, that its implications are far from exhausted, and that in choosing from among the claims appropriate within it, we can fashion very different types of political order.

The political skill of "choosing" the future course of industrial society then consists not only in deciding what to do, but in finding good reasons for what we decide to do. Politics exists mainly in the mind, and it is as important that the individual feel "at home" in a modern society that he or she considers both just and comprehensible as that we cope with the manifest challenges and uncertainties of the future.

NOTES

1. Eugene B. Skolnikoff, "Growth: The Governability of Complexity" (Paper delivered to the Wingspread Conference on Sustained Growth, 3 October 1973). Mimeographed.

2. Wolfgang Friedmann, *Law in a Changing Society* (2nd ed.; Harmondsworth: Penguin Books, 1972), pp. 320-27.

3. Leon N. Lindberg, "A Research Perspective on the Future of Advanced Industrial Societies" (ms., August 1973), mimeographed; Sir Geoffrey Vickers, *Freedom in a Rocking Boat* (London: Allen Lane, 1970); Harold and Margaret Sprout, *The Ecological Perspective on Human Affairs* (Princeton, N.J.: Princeton University Press, 1965); Todd La Porte, ed., *Organized Social Complexity: Challenge for Politics and Policy* (Princeton, N.J.: Princeton University Press, 1975).

4. Anthony Jay, *Management and Machiavelli* (New York: Holt, Rinehart & Winston, 1967), p. 178.

5. Philip Selznick, *Law, Society, and Industrial Justice* (New York: Russell Sage Foundation, 1969), p. 38.

6. Albert O. Hirschman, *Journeys Toward Progress* (New York: Twentieth Century Fund, 1963), p. 6.

7. Skolnikoff, "Growth: The Governability of Complexity."

8. William E. Connolly, ed., *The Bias of Pluralism* (New York: Atherton, 1969), pp. 19-24.

9. James Willard Hurst, *Law and the Conditions of Freedom in the Nineteenth Century United States* (Madison: University of Wisconsin Press, 1967), pp. 3-32.

10. Friedmann, *Law in a Changing Society*, p. 120.

11. *Kedroff et al.*, v. *St. Nicholas Cathedral of Russian Orthodox Church in North America*, 344 U.S. 94 (1952) at 122. In England, as in the United States, the law

220 / CHARLES W. ANDERSON

of trust provided the basis for the law of association. In the *Free Church of Scotland Case* (*General Assembly of the Free Church of Scotland* v. *Lord Overtoun* 1904 AC 55) the Judicial Committee of the Privy Council endorsed the position of public neutrality toward the internal governance of a religious body. The issue involved a suit by a minority faction of the Free Church, opposing merger with the United Presbyterians, claiming that the majority had involved themselves in change of doctrine that invalidated their title to property held in trust for the Free Church. In deciding for a narrow and literal interpretation of the terms of trust, the law lords refused to adopt the principle, advocated by Figgis, of majorty rule imposed by public action as standard of conflict resolution in the internal government of private bodies. See Leicester C. Webb, "The Corporate Personality and Political Pluralism," in L. C. Webb, ed., *Legal Personality and Political Pluralism* (Melbourne: Melbourne University Press, 1958), pp. 48–51.

12. James Willard Hurst, *The Legitimacy of the Business Corporation in the Law of the United States 1780-1970* (Charlottesville: University of Virginia Press, 1970), pp. 15–16.

13. Ibid., pp. 3–4, 21.

14. Ibid., pp. 85–86.

15. David Vogel, "Contemporary Criticism of Business: The Publicization of the Corporation" (Paper delivered at the American Political Science Association, 4–8 September 1973). Mimeographed.

16. On the problem of compulsory membership in trade unions, see Mancur Olson, Jr., *The Logic of Collective Action* (New York: Schocken Books, 1968), pp. 68–91.

17. *J. I. Case Co.* v. *NLRB 321* U.S. 329 (1944) at 339.

18. This merely suggests a large and complex area. For a good overview, see Ronald A. Wykstra and Eleanour V. Stevens, *American Labor and Management Policy* (New York: Odyssey Press, 1970), pp. 87–100, 123–90.

19. Selznick, *Law, Society, and Industrial Justice*, p. 151.

20. *Steelworkers* v. *Warrior and Gulf 363* U.S. 574 at 578–79.

21. Sanford Lakoff, *Private Government*, pp. 218–42; Seymour Martin Lipset et al., *Union Democracy* (Glencoe: Free Press, 1956), and "The Law and Trade Union Democracy," *Virginia Law Review* 47 (January 1961): 1–47; Robert A. Dahl, *After the Revolution* (New Haven: Yale University Press, 1970), pp. 104–66; "Worker's Control of Industry and the British Labor Party," *American Political Science Review* 10, no. 1 (October 1947): 875–900; with C. E. Lindblom, *Politics, Economics and Welfare* (New York: Harper & Row, 1953), pp. 519–21. Peter Bachrach, *The Theory of Democratic Elitism* (Boston: Little, Brown, 1967).

22. Albert O. Hirschman, *Exit, Voice and Loyalty* (Cambridge, Mass.: Harvard University Press, 1970), p. 30.

23. Alice Rivlin, *Systematic Thinking for Social Action* (Washington: Brookings Institution, 1971), pp. 133–40; Ivan Illich, *Deschooling Society* (New York: Harper & Row, 1972); Milton Friedman, "The Role of Government in Education," in *Economics and the Public Interest*, ed. Robert A. Solo (New Brunswick: Rutgers University Press, 1955), pp. 118–35.

24. *Greene* v. *Howard University 271* F. Supp. 609 (1967).

25. Selznick, *Law, Society and Industrial Justice*, pp. 250–76.

26. *Report of the Royal Commission on Trade Unions and Employer's Associations, 1965-1968* (Cmnd. 3623, 1968).

27. Maurice Cranston and Sanford Lakoff, eds., *A Glossary of Political Ideas* (New York: Basic Books, 1969).

28. *Wisconsin* v. *Yoder* 49 Wis. 2nd. 430 at 451–52.

29. John R. Commons, *The Legal Foundations of Capitalism* (Madison: University of Wisconsin Press, 1968), pp. 10–11, 143–218.

30. Karl Polanyi, *The Great Transformation* (Boston: Beacon Press, 1944), pp. 139–40.

31. Charles Levinson, *Capital, Inflation and the Multinationals* (London: George Allen & Unwin, 1971), pp. 37–39.

32. Andrew Shonfield, *Modern Capitalism* (New York: Oxford University Press, 1965), p. 138.

33. Commons, *Legal Foundations of Capitalism*, p. 6.

34. Peter F. Drucker, *The Concept of the Corporation* (New York: New American Library, 1964), p. vii.

STRATEGIES AND PRIORITIES FOR COMPARATIVE RESEARCH

LEON N. LINDBERG

We can now attempt a systematic comparison of the approaches of our authors to a comparative politics of the contemporary dynamics and future prospects of advanced industrial societies. In so doing, I also try to relate their work to that of other theorists and researchers. What is apparent from this exercise is that assessments of where we are and where we are tending depend a lot on analytical perspective. The future of politics in our societies appears differently depending on whether one is asking where we stand in an unfolding developmental sequence, attempting to characterize the dynamics of the system as a whole, inquiring into changes in underlying values, or asking what options are open to us.

No academic orthodoxy is apparent here, hence our portrayal of our prospects has neither the satisfying coherence nor the confident assurance of expert doctrine. It is not merely that the authors look at different actors in a manifold and perplexing reality. It is also that they think that the problem of how to grapple intellectually with the "problem" of the future can be approached in different ways. Nonetheless, there are important areas of convergence and these are discussed in part 1. In order to facilitate a comparison and really juxtapose these papers as the basis of a discussion of strategies and priorities for future research and inquiry, we need to put them in the context of some over-all framework or model. Such a framework is offered in part 2; it should facilitate a more precise identification of divergences of conception and imputed causal dynamics as well as lacunae wherein conceptual and theoretical development and empirical research are required. In part 3 I indicate how I have tried to grapple with these issues in my own on-going research.

1. AREAS OF CONVERGENCE

There seem to be three areas of primary agreement among our authors.

1. Advanced industrial societies are beset by serious destabiliz-ing trends or forces that seem likely to cause fundamental strain on the capacity of their governments and dominant elites to assure either effec-tiveness and continuity in public policy or adequate levels of support, legitimacy, or mass quiescence.

2. These transformations and strains are sufficiently basic to hold the potential of fundamentally altering the policy and structural char-acteristics of these societies. This may warrant a new look at where these societies are in some overall process of "development," a reconceptu-alization in terms of a transition, crisis, or turning point in moderniza-tion. And it may imply that there are a number of possible sets of policy and coalition options implying substantially different future develop-mental paths.

3. Less unanimously, there is a sense of a promising focus of re-search in the study of how elites respond to public problems in the face of changes in the composition of demands made on them, the resources at their disposal, and the load of decision making they are called upon to undertake. That such study should be both comparative and over time seems apparent. Such a focus is especially important since one can argue that to a very great extent the meaning and significance of potentially destabilizing situations or environmental impacts are fully perceptible only in patterns of political response to them.

Policy Intractability, Strain, or Failure

Our authors all agree—although they arrive at this conclusion by different routes—that governments, political leaders, and/or dominant elites today confront particularly difficult or intractable problems of policy design and social control. The authors vary in their assessments of the origins, the seriousness, and the "direction" of the problem and in the analytical perspective taken with regard to it.

La Porte and Abrams, viewing the whole system from the perspective of a detached analyst, see an acceleration of adaptive and policy errors because the organizations and systems we have created and within which we live have become so complex that they transcend the cognitive capacities of our leaders to understand them and to develop viable policies. Inglehart, from a like perspective, argues that certain changes in the value priorities of citizens have the potential of undermining system support and legitimacy both because of new demands that run counter to establish hierarchies and authority relations, and because of a decline in the utility of national security issues and economic growthmanship for social control.

Tsurutani and Straussman view societal change and its political consequences from a less detached perspective. In a way, they seem to be responding to Goldthorpe's injunction against adopting a "social problems" approach that implicitly accepts system stability as the goal of social science seeking to be of service to benevolent political managers. Tsurutani, viewing the system from the perspective of a newly mobilized mass citizenry in Japan, sees the Japanese dominant classes and government elite as unwilling to recognize and incapable of coping with either the negative costs of past economic and social policy or with the legitimate demands for participation that are being spawned by advanced industrialism. He analyzes the resultant strains on existing structures of power and interest, looking forward to their replacement by more responsive and representative ones. Straussman, too, sees the future of the system at stake; but the system he worries about is democracy itself. Contrary to the other authors, he finds that the present structures of power, unwittingly aided and abetted by legions of willing experts, economists, futurists, and assorted other social scientists, have both the intent and the capability of maintaining the power and control of the existing system. The trend to worry about is the increased dominance of this coalition of narrow rationality, manipulative expertise, and technocratic counsel, with "the real holders of power" being the corporate-executive complex.

Hancock, on the other hand, is more concerned with the orientations of policy makers themselves toward public problems. For Hancock this seems to flow from a conviction that elite preferences are what count if you want to chart societal development. He sees Sweden beset by a variety of potentially destabilizing or worrying trends, similar to other societies, but finds that the governing Social Democratic elite with its overriding egalitarian consensus is sufficiently permeable, responsive, and open to new groups and ideas to be able to steer successfully between the shoals of economic decline and "bureaucratization at the expense of individual liberty."

For Anderson, the problem is not simply to state our crises and our problems, but to ask what we can—and are likely to—do about them, and what the implications of alternative modes of response might be in terms of fundamental values. Anderson seems to address the policy makers, and more generally, all who participate in the public debate. His argument seems to be that what counts when a society reaches a turning point is what is perceived as a "problem" and what remedies are apt to appear as acceptable and persuasive to the actors in the political drama. The major constant for Anderson is the "paradigm of public choice," which gives us both an empirical referent for projecting what choices we are apt to make, and a context for the deliberation of options. The problem for Anderson is then to assess whether and in what ways the existing elites and institutional and evaluative structures might innovate in order to maintain their legitimacy and credibility and at the same time produce a pattern of public policy that does not seem manifestly unjust or unfair. Although he agrees that the liberal, pluralist order is seriously strained, he seems more optimistic than many of our authors about its long-run viability.

As I noted in the first chapter, this preoccupation with political instability, the intractability of policy, the possibility of policy failure, and the potential or actual alienation of mass publics in advanced industrial societies stands in sharp contrast to the dominant optimism of only a few years ago.

The one characteristic of modern industrial society singled out by almost all theorists of modernization was that "modern man" had *greater control* over the natural and social environment, and was blessed with "a rapidly widening control over nature through close cooperation among men"[1]; the individual is not "passive and acquiescent" but "believes in both the possibility and the desirability of change, and has confidence in the ability of man to control change so as to accomplish his purposes."[2] The 1960s also saw the highwater mark of optimism among economists that they understood economic dynamics, that uncontrolled booms and busts were a thing of the past, and that economic management and "fine tuning" represented yet another triumph of modern deductive rationality.[3] Political scientists viewed the modern polity with satisfaction, for it displayed, among other things, "a high degree of integration," a "prevalence for rational and secular procedures," "high efficacy of its political and administrative decisions," "a widespread and effective sense of popular identification," "widespread popular interest and involvement in the political system."[4] And with the heralded decline of irrational and divisive ideologies and of Weltanschauung politics characteristic of earlier stages of development, and in line with the "logic of industrialism," came the promise of a "pluralistic society" characterized by a multiplicity of interests and a dispersion of economic and political power, and offering a maximum of "inner freedom" and "private space,"[5] a society which somehow represented the "final and 'highest' evolutionary universal."[6]

There were, of course, dissenting voices—notably among critics of technological society and from the radical and Marxist traditions.[7] But these were distinctly in the minority, enjoying a rehabilitation only in the late 1960s and early 1970s. By then the signs of distress and malfunction were difficult to ignore, though there was (and is) no agreement on what to make of them. One of the most penetrating analyses came from Sir Geoffrey Vickers in his *Freedom in a Rocking Boat*, first published in 1970. Vickers traced the "self-set trap" of modern society to a series of destabilizing changes inherent in the wealth-producing system made up of private capitalism, market economy, and technological innovation.

> The System they compose spews from one spout a huge abundance of natural and unnatural products and sprays from another spout the tokens with which to buy them. It has displaced, though not replaced, the natural world as the immediate environment of Western man. It has involved each individual in a system of proliferating, faceless power, exercised increasingly not through the agencies of government but through the uncontrolled workings of the System itself. For good or ill, this system is the primary source, directly or indirectly, of the accelerating changes which are overwhelming the regulative powers of political and social institutions.[8]

We will not escape this "trap," says Vickers, without "political, institutional and cultural change, deeply penetrating the minds of individual men and women"[9] and involving "a huge increase in the load to be borne by the process of political choice."[10] He sees no way "to conserve the planet's resources and to distribute its product acceptably between man and man, nation and nation, present and future,"[11] except by strengthening the machinery of government, placing "at its disposal a larger share of resources including human resources, and to support it with more confidence."[12] Political authority will have to be "exercised more and more frequently in unfamiliar issues of vital importance, at remote levels and on a widening scale of space and time."[13]

Yet everywhere, says Vickers, the authority, not only of government, but also of business, trade unions, and the university, is losing its legitimacy; and the mutual "appreciations of the situation" between and among the "doers" and the "done-by," which must undergird collective action, are in dissolution. Somehow these "bottomless divides" must be bridged. The shape of the "post-liberal" world is unknown, says Vickers, but it "will stem primarily from new, shared experiences."

> These will, I think, be experiences of increasingly dramatic disasters, foreign or domestic, international or national. It is to be hoped that they will not be irremediable. We are creatures ill equipped to respond, even

individually, to what is only anticipated. Some trigger is needed to convince the busy, cushioned, comfortable West of the instabilities which are visible enough to the destitute, the impotent, the disillusioned and the desperate, even in their own countries.

There will be no lack of triggers.[14]

Vickers' pessimism was recently echoed even more gloomily by Robert Heilbroner the *The Human Prospect*. Heilbroner's list of "external challenges" is now well known in the wake of the widespread debates set off by the "doomsday literature" of the early 1970s, notably the *Blueprint for Survival* and *The Limits to Growth*; namely, the "demographic outlook," shortages of food and fertilizer, the persistence of the threat of war, especially nuclear blackmail of the rich countries by the desperate poor, environmental disruption, resource constraints, thermal pollution and its implications for industrial growth.[15] But, says Heilbroner,

the gravity of the human prospect does not hinge alone, or even principally, on an estimate of the dangers of the knowable external challenges of the future. To a far greater extent it is shaped by our appraisal of our capacity to meet those challenges. It is the flexibility of social classes, the resilience of socio-economic orders, the behavior of nation-states, and ultimately the "nature" of human beings that together form the basis for our expectations of the human outlook. And for these critical elements in the human prospect there are very few empirical findings on which to rest our beliefs.[16]

Heilbroner goes on to offer an assessment of the likelihood that either capitalist or socialist countries of the developed world will mount an adequate response. He concludes for the great majority of capitalist societies,

I do not see how we can avoid the conclusion that the required transformation will be likely to exceed the capabilities of representative democracy. The disappointing failure of capitalist societies to create atmospheres of social harmony, even in expansive settings, does not bode well for their ability to foster far-reaching reorganizations of their economic structures and painful diminutions of privilege for their more prosperous citizens. The likelihood that there are obdurate limits to the reformist reach of democratic institutions within the class-bound body of capitalist society leads us to expect that the governments of these societies, faced with extreme internal strife or with potentially disastrous social polarization, would resort to severe authoritarian measures.[17]

Democratic socialism faces the same "Hobbesian struggle for goods" and "whereas an authoritarian socialism could certainly enforce some kind of solution, it seems likely that this would entail a degree of coercion that would make socialism virtually indistinguishable from capitalism."[18]

For Heilbroner it is industrialism as a system—its growth dynamic, its heat emissions, pollutions, and resource profligacies—that is called into question, and he does not see how *any society* can bring about the required adaptations "through the conscious intervention of men, rather than by convulsive changes forced upon men."[19]

Daniel Bell also sees the dramatic increase in the ubiquitousness of political control as "the decisive social change taking place in our time,"[20] though he does not view its consequences as cataclysmically as either Vickers or Heilbroner. The essence of the phenomenon for Bell is the "subordination of the economic function to the political order."

> The forms this will take will vary, and will emerge from the specific history of the different political societies—central state control, public corporations, decentralized enterprises and central policy directives, mixed public and private enterprises, and the like. Some will be democratic, some not. But the central fact is clear: the autonomy of the economic order (and the power of the men who run it) is coming to an end, and new and varied, but different, control systems are emerging.[21]

The critical question is then who manages the political order and for whose or what ends. And this, says Bell, is an open question. One thing does seem certain, and that is that "the politicization of decision-making—in the economy and the culture—invites more and more group conflict. The crucial problem for the communal society is whether there is a common frame of values that can guide the setting of political policy."[22]

Marxists would generally agree with Vickers, Heilbroner, and Bell that the legitimation of an ever-expanding political authority will be capitalism's primary problem, would echo Heilbroner's expectations that authoritarianism will be its preferred or most likely response (they generally do not consider socialism!), but would sharply deny Bell's assertion that the power (and autonomy) of those who control the economic order is coming to an end, or that the question of political control is in any real sense an open one. James O'Connor, for example, sets forth a basic Marxist premise about advanced capitalism, that there is an increasingly severe contradiction between the two basic functions of the capitalist state, i.e., making *profitable capital accumulation possible* and *maintaining legitimization* or creating the conditions for social harmony.

> A capitalist state that openly uses its coercive forces to help one class accumulate capital at the expense of other classes loses its legitimacy and hence undermines the basis of its loyalty and support. But a state that

ignores the necessity of assisting the process of capital accumulation risks drying up the sources of its own power, the economy's surplus production capacity and the taxes drawn from this surplus (and other forms of capital). . . . The state must involve itself in the accumulation process, but it must either mystify its policies by calling them something that they are not, or it must try to conceal them (e.g., by making them into administrative, not political, issues).[23]

The problem is that this balancing act is becoming increasingly difficult as the requirements for sustaining capital accumulation require more and more overt forms of state intervention. The enormous capital demands of a technology-intensive industry, the increased scale of both risks and externalities, the destabilizing consequences of an internationalized capitalist system, the built-in inflationary bias of the system, and the competing demands on the budget from the disadvantaged and the unemployed who must be kept quiescent inevitably push the capitalist state into more active manpower policies, wages and incomes policies, industrial policies involving huge transfers to business, not to mention competitive currency devaluations and monetary conflicts with other states. At the same time there is a relative decline of public services and of the welfare state generally: private pension and insurance schemes undermine public ones; education, housing, transportation, and medical services all encounter fiscal constraints.[24]

As a consequence of these two interrelated trends in state action, the neutrality of the state becomes more and more difficult to sustain, and the legitimacy of the system will be increasingly contested.[25] The least costly strategy for the dominant elite to pursue in response is to seek to maximize economic growth, but even where this is not counteracted by other obstacles (as in Britain throughout the postwar period), it tends to reinforce all the existing trends toward promoting private capital accumulation in order to offer investment inducements. Furthermore, such a policy is ecologically irrational because

> The dilemma facing modern capitalism is that the rapid rate of economic growth necessary to service large corporations and contain class conflict will ultimately involve an increasing degree of environmental destruction.[26]

Marxists are deeply ambivalent when it comes to the question of "what happens next?" Conservative authoritarianism or a vast popular, socialist movement? Or an intermediate, crisis-prone system that is sustained primarily by the internal contradictions within conceivable *alternative* coalitions? Nicos Poulantzas[27] argues that a Bonapartist semi-dictatorship is "the real religion of the modern bourgeoisie," the "constitutive theoretical characteristic of the very type of the capitalist state." Ralph Miliband, on the contrary, is critical of this view.

As the extreme inflation of executive power and the forcible demobiliza-
tion of all political forces in civil society, Bonapartism is not the religion
of the bourgeoisie at all—it is the last *resort* in conditions of political instability so great as to present a threat to the maintenance of the existing social
order, including, of course, the system of domination which is the central
part of that order.[28]

What is critical to investigate empirically, says Miliband, is "whether
there is a real difference in the manner of operation between different
forms of the capitalist state."[29] We must avoid "obliterating differences
between forms of the capitalist state which are of crucial importance, not
least for working class movements."[30]

Sooner or later, and despite all the immense obstacles on the way, the
working class and its allies in other classes will acquire that . . . faculty of
ruling the nation [which] will, for the first time in history, enable them to
bring into being an authentic democratic social order, a truly free society
of self-governing men and women, in which as Marx also put it, the state
will be converted "from an organ superimposed upon society into one
completely subordinated to it.[31]

But this day seems far away, notes P. A. Allum, even in Italy where the
contradictions seem multiple and overlapping.

For while it is true that the inefficiency of the present system represents a
decline in hegemony of the ruling class that controls it, it is equally true
that the decline has not, as yet, provoked the rise of the hegemony of an
alternative class or coalition of classes.[32]

Bertram M. Gross[33] makes a similar point in constructing his
most probable scenario for America of techno-urban or "friendly fascism," in which he incorporates many of the points made by Marxists
and other critics of capitalism. He does not deny the mounting conflicts
and contradictions, nor the likelihood of serious policy crises, but does
doubt that this implies an erosion of power, for "the feet" of "the far-
flung diverse power elites in the central guidance clusters" of the new
macro-systems "are not made of clay," but "expertly ride the waves of
change."[34] The society they will create will contain at the same time
"more sophisticated, long-range, resource-based planning than ever before" but also "a widely prevalent and growing sense of drift, disorder,
and breakdown of social guidance."[35]

To a large extent, the power of techno-urban fascism would be rooted in
a technocratic ideology that would buttress faith in the system and a culture of alienation that would undermine faith in the organization of any
viable alternative.[36]

It would combine "selective repression operating through and around the established constitutional system with such forms of indirect control as rationed welfare state benefits conditional on good behavior, accelerated consumerism, credentialized meritocracy, and market administration through incentive manipulation."[37]

Many scholars, working from both Marxist and non-Marxist perspectives, see the rapidly changing contemporary international and transnational context as the most potentially destabilizing element of all.[38] Processes of change at national and international levels are clearly linked. There seems to be an ever-accelerating interrelatedness among countries made up of military vulnerability, environmental and ecological factors, economic interdependency, unequal development, economic competition, psychic interpenetration, contagion, diffusion, emulation.

These patterns of interdependencies and interactions clearly imply a consequent interpenetration of policy arenas in such areas as environment, energy, food, control of technology, regulation of the multinational firm, etc. Vital issues, including the management of inflation, the maintenance of international trade and settlement, and of economic growth and employment, even physical and biological survival, may depend upon the development of adequate international policies, "regimes or quasi-regimes," and institutions. Ever increasing international involvement thus produces new vulnerabilities: dependence on foreign workers; economic nationalisms from declining sectors; penetration and domestic political interference by multinational firms; resource dependencies such as food, oil; and other commodities. These dependencies and the claims and counterclaims that can be expected to flow from them may well produce powerful reactions that could disrupt the international networks and transactions upon which the industrial system depends.

These references to other entries in the debate about the future of advanced industrial society should serve to locate our authors in a broad spectrum of efforts at political forecasting. It should be kept clear, however, that the emphasis so many of these authors place on crisis, transformation, and discontinuity is essentially "prescientific"; they are "hunches" or "hypotheses" based on partial extrapolation of trends, emphasizing some tendencies and neglecting others. They may say less about social and political change than about the mood or state of mind of scholars in a uniquely faddish time, or about individual psychological insecurity resulting from the decline of religion, or "the sour residue" of a lost "faith in 'automatic' linear economic progress,"[39] and in science and technology; and the reader ought not to suppose that the "pessimism" of the authors represented here fully captures the contemporary Zeitgeist. Indeed, there is a broad body of commentary (e.g., the sustained debate between neo-Keynesians," "Friedmanites," "Austrians," etc.) that considers the problems of modern society as readily manageable.[40]

That social scientists are not immune from the ebb and flow of "irrational" fits of optimism and pessimism should be clear from our references to past modernization theorists. If the development theory of the 1950s and 1960s saw change as progressive and irreversible and thus resembled an eighteenth- and nineteenth-century faith in progress and reason, today's millennialism resembles the mood of the overwhelmingly pessimistic theories of social evolution and social change which prevailed in the 1920s and 1930s. Writers such as Spengler, Pareto, Sorokin, and Toynbee emphasized.

> The breakup of human community, the attenuation of religious values, the drift into alienation and anomie, the terrifying emergence of a mass society: these were the products of secularization, urbanization, and democratization.[41]

Lasswell, Mannheim, Arendt, and others warned of a trend toward totalitarianism, in Lasswell's words an historical trend "*from* progress toward a world commonwealth of free men, *toward* a world order in which the garrison-prison state reintroduces caste-bound social systems."[42]

The fascist experiences of the 1930s and World War II seemed to many to confirm the validity of such theories, but the rapid postwar recovery, the boom in international trade and industrial growth, and the transformation of capitalism "from cataclysmic failure" to "the great engine of prosperity of the postwar Western World"[43] seemed to give them the lie and nurtured the optimism of the 1950s and 1960s.

Of course, the postwar period with its relative affluence and social peace may only have been a temporary interlude, and what we see around us today is then only what Michael Mann has termed "a reawakening of the repressive side of Western society."[44] Mann suggests that "rather than breaking up in the late 1960s, Western society was perhaps slowly returning to its normal mode of existence, and its normal mode of suppressing enemies." The "abnormally peaceful" postwar period was a result of the war, which was internally cohesive especially for the victors. In order to give substance to the propaganda of national solidarity, governments forced employers to negotiate with workers, rationing was introduced and had a leveling effect, the elite officer castes were opened up, social welfare legislation was enacted. This atmosphere continued after the war "in the only substantial bout of income redistribution ever experienced by most Western countries."[46] Marxists argue similarly. The welfare state, writes Claus Offe, "seems to be more of a transitional phase in the development of Western post-World War II societies than an ultimate, stable sociopolitical arrangement."[47]

> What appears in the welfare state are new elements *within* advanced capitalist societies, but no basic changes of these societies. That is, the wel-

fare state has not changed political and economic power relationships. . . . (D)efense and space industries, corporate agribusiness, the industrial users of government-guaranteed foreign loans and publicly financed research and development capture the lion's share of state "welfare." . . . (T)he services of the welfare state are not major social accomplishments . . . but, rather are meager compensations for the price of industrial development . . . stopgap mechanisms to offset the process of rapid and often permanent deterioration of social life. . . . On the other hand, no government can afford to expand welfare services beyond a certain limit without being punished by inflation, unemployment, or both.[48]

Samuel P. Huntington, in "Postindustrial Politics: How Benign Will It Be?", one of the first systematic efforts to analyze postindustrial politics, demonstrates our epistemological dilemma very strikingly. After concluding on the basis of a projection/deduction from Daniel Bell and other "postindustrial theorists" that political tensions, disruptions, struggles among rising and declining groups forebode a postindustrial politics that "is likely to be the darker side of post-industrial society and measurably less benign than industrial politics,"[49] he feels constrained to point out that "postindustrial politics may not emerge . . . trends could conceivably level off or even reverse themselves . . . the current transition may lead to a neoindustrialism . . . [whose] political traumas and conflicts will be less intense and more familiar."[50]

As noted in the introduction, and as this review of short-term fluctuations in mood serves to emphasize, "we have few, if any, scientific laws or even good theories in the realm of societal dynamics." What we have are the competition of what Vickers calls "mutually inconsistent 'orders.'"

Again, the focus of science on *discovering* order in the world—a world which includes our human selves—renders suspect that aspect of the ordering process which is contributed by men themselves and tends to weaken the confidence with which men address themselves to their most human function, the function of imposing order on their experience and thus helping to shape their own future.[51]

Without such laws we have little firm basis for selecting which trends to project, much less for managing discontinuities and threshold effects, and causal structures. How then do we proceed? How can we move from unverifiable hunches to a more rigorous style of analysis? This brings us to the second and third areas of convergence among our authors.

Transitions and Alternative Development Paths

The answer suggested by our authors to the above questions begins with their implicit agreement that *somehow* we find ourselves in a time of crisis or transition. There is little doubt that the concept of "crisis" is used loosely and overmuch, both in daily parlance and in supposedly more rigorous social science research. Sidney Verba has tried to provide a more specific definition that would distinguish between "routine" problems and "crises." Legitimately to be called a crisis, a problem or set of demands must require "governmental innovations and institutionalization if elites are not seriously to risk a loss of their position or if the society is to survive."[52] Such crises can arise out of "environmental change that increases the relevant population for political activity"[53] (social mobilizaton leading to new demands); out of imbalances in government performance; out of changes in elite goals leading to elite dissatisfaction and division. Crises involve not only the creation of new institutions, but also the development of new accepted systems of norms. "Thus, crises represent situations in which the society moves in a new direction. They are the major decisional points at which the society is redefined, and are therefore relevant to sequential changes."[54]

But, admits Verba, it is not easy to develop "rules for deciding when a crisis exists, which problem area it is related to, and what the nature of the solution is."[55] We are indeed back to the weakness of theory in this whole area of development and modernization studies. In view of this weakness we have seen flower a variety of development interpretations in terms of general societal crises and ordered sequences among crises, the dominant one being the Committee on Comparative Politics' crisis of identity, legitimacy, penetration, participation, and distribution.[56] Suggestive as these formulations are as post hoc interpretation, they leave something to be desired as a tool for research on contemporary change and crisis. As Huntington has pointed out, the problem of applying a turning point, crisis sequence, or transitional approach "to the emergence of post-industrial society is that the key characteristics of turning points to that form of society are rather hard to pin down."[57]

Nevertheless, (and Huntington would agree), the concepts of "crisis" and "development transitions" remain attractive as orienting metaphors, primarily because transitional process theories of past development are more persuasive than the alternatives of "level of development" or "starting point" theories.[58]

A principal reason for this is that they may admit of voluntarist as against determinist explanations of development. An attention to crises brings us to focus on the particular issues of public choice that emerged at particular points in time, on the policy options that were considered and chosen by governing and influential elites, and on the way in which the crucial resources of contending actors were affected. Researchers working in this tradition have argued, in a variety of ways and from a variety of normative standpoints, that elites in the process of reacting to changes or transformations that impinge upon them and their societies not only determine the specific policy actions that are or are not taken in particular cases, but they also play a central role in shaping the future political cleavage patterns of the society, which in turn may result in changes in—or perpetuation of—the relative power of different elites. Different patterns of elite response and of interelite coalition formation may also help determine the effective political structures, decision rules, kinds of policy outcomes, and hence the stability/instability patterns that will characterize a given society.[59]

As Gabriel Almond has recently observed of other (the system-functional and social-mobilizaton) approaches to development, they

> tend to be deterministic; that is the choice or decision aspect of developmental processes tends to be treated in aggregate terms—volume of demands, voting rates, incidence of collective violence, or of governmental repression. . . . [They] give us statistical associations, but not explanations. The individual acts or events that add up to aggregate measures or that by themselves have causal value, are acts of human decision and choice.
>
> These system and social-mobilization approaches to developmental explanation have a mechanistic or organismic bias. Human choice, exchanges, bargains, and the frequent intervention into developmental processes of outstanding leaders without whom historical outcomes of great importance cannot be satisfactorily explained, are hardly the central perspective of system functional and aggregate statistical analysis of social process and change.[60]

For these reasons, Almond and his associates have undertaken the ambitious task of integrating what they call "rational choice-coalition theory" and "leadership theory," along with "social-mobilization" and "system-functional" theories into an overall explanation of development causation, which they hope will "show the way toward a general theory of politics."[61] Their effort involved "taking the historical cure" and produced a detailed study of critical developmental crises or transitions guided by a relatively sophisticated conceptual scheme and set of operationalized measures. One critical concept of their "process model of crisis and change" is the concept of "dissynchronization" which is defined as "a state of latent instability."

> Systemic crisis is manifested in a direct challenge to the authority of the incumbent contenders, generally expressed through noncompliance to government directives, non-sanctioned terms of protest, physical violence or the threat thereof.[62]

Dissynchronization arises

> either from a sequence of domestic and international environmental changes that alter inputs and increases the load upon the political structure or by elite-initiated performance changes, both structural and allocative, that can produce an incongruence between the structures of demand and allocation....[63]

I suggested in chapter 1 that although it would in principle be desirable to "test" often contradictory assumptions, assertions, and hypotheses posited about trends in the development of industrial society, in the hope that "diverging ideas might become critical instances for each other," this may well be impossible. And this not only because of the epistemological state of the social sciences or the ideologies, whims, and changing moods of researchers, but because seemingly contradictory hypotheses or findings may actually describe an existing reality replete with contradictions and dialectical processes. In such a circumstance, it seems to me eminently reasonable to focus an empirical analysis precisely upon such crises or upon sequences of dissynchronization, and the concepts of loads and capabilities would seem especially appropriate in this kind of effort.[64]

Ample evidence suggests that contemporary trends are producing some substantially *distinct policy problems*, contradictions, or dilemmas that appear to challenge existing conceptions and assumptions about public policy as well as existing power structures and decision-making systems. We have recorded the substantial agreement in the literature that more and more areas of national and international life will come under purposive regulation by government, that international and national systems will interpenetrate each other with destabilizing consequences for both, that "the market" will be less and less effective as an allocative or regulatory mechanism, that there will be a massive increase in the load to be borne by political choice, that the trend is toward society-wide planning and "explicit definition of social policy priorities" with a consequent politicization of almost everything. Capitalist societies are now characterized by what Emery and Trist call "turbulent environments" resulting from the growth of linked sets of complex, large organizations, a deepening interdependence of economic and other systems, a growing government reliance on science and technology with the result that more and more decisions are taken by people not markets, and a radical increase in the speed and load of communications.

We have also briefly sampled the rich and suggestive Marxist tradition whose most signal contribution is perhaps its emphasis on "internal contradictions" as producers as well as consequences of dynamic change, or emergent problems of political management of ruling elites in late capitalism. But too often research in this tradition has been tinged with an historicist bias, which has in the past produced many predictions manquées of "implacable contradictions" and "inevitable collapse." Nevertheless, it seems likely that advanced industrial societies—or their capitalist elites—having apparently learned in the 1950s and 1960s how to manage the business cycle and sustain economic growth and "full" employment, and in the 1960s and early 1970s how to manage their security relations with the Soviet Union and China, may face even more serious challenges in the 1970s and 1980s as a consequence of interacting trends and transformations in both domestic and international systems. One need only note such emergent issues as inflation *plus* recession (slumpflation), energy and resource scarcities, environment and pollution, qualitative vs. quantitative growth, heightened levels of international conflict *and* interdependence (especially between developed and developing countries), and neo-mercantilist implications of government responses to the effects of interdependence and of integration processes more generally (including the internationalization of capital and the power of multinational companies).

But even as the level of conflict and the load on political choice go up, the literature shows a widespread concern that public choice processes are less and less capable of assuming the burden effectively. They are bogged down by the established interests, the political and economic power and limited vision of dominant elites, by conceptual barriers on the part of policy makers (Vickers speaks of the mythology of competition and the market, and of the disjunction between the "user-supported" and "public-supported" sectors), by the breakdown of "internal and external regulators," and by the declining effectiveness of "mutual appreciations of the situation."[65] Many theorists thus foresee a serious decline in the decisional capacities of public authorities, a "loss of steering capacity," a regression into "decentralized violence,"[66] an "escalation of adaptive or policy errors."[67] Of course, whether or not a choice process is "effective" is substantially a matter of one's political perspective. What is an increased load for the dominant capitalist elite may represent increased options and political resources for challenging elites or groups. Hence, it may be better to speak of important changes that may be occurring in the political process itself, partly as a consequence of this multiplication of definitions of the situation and the emergence of so-called postindustrial issues, and partly as a consequence of secular trends affecting the resources of groups, elites, and counterelites, and the structures and transformation processes by which these resources create further resources. Among such often contradictory trends are increased levels of education and their impact on forms and styles of political participation; changes in values and ideologies; increased importance and politicization of the media; monopolies of knowledge skills by professionalized groups; the rise of ad hoc, single-issue political movements; but also the growth of executive-bureaucratic power and control of policy by what Gross[68] calls "complexes" (automobile-highway-petroleum, banking-speculator-construction); growing alienation, "disaffiliation," and delegitimization of authority; rising importance of technocratic planning structures, or "central guidance clusters," and trends toward capitalist national planning; growth of international corporate empires; increasing trends for governments to use science and technology as tools to "manage" dissent and manipulate public opinion.

The extent to which such trends in loads and capabilities are actually emergent and unidirectional, and their impact on the relative power and influence of politically relevant groups, and on the bargaining-communications-dominance processes of policy making in particular cases over time and different national societies could then be made a primary focus of research. One way of going about this is proposed by Almond and his associates. They have worked out a still rudimentary set of operational measures of "composition and direction of environmental impacts" (military, economic, demonstration, social mobilization, and economic performance) and of "polarization and coalition propensities" (issue-distance, issue-coalition preferences, relative resource weights for decision areas and for contenders in given areas).[69] A comparative analysis along these lines of the contemporary period of crisis, transition, or dissynchronization in a number of different societies would be especially useful.

Elite Coalitions and Policy Response

Besides thus identifying and somehow seeking to measure the load and capability dynamics of the contemporary period, a second principal focus of research flows from the above argument, namely, comparative and over-time studies of sequences of elite response or problem solving in the face of changes in loads and capabilities. The basic epistemological position I have been taking throughout is that there are multiple future possibilities in a present replete with rapid change, uncertainty, and turbulence, contradictions and seemingly opposed dynamic forces or trends. Divergent theories of the future simply reflect this situation of flux and indeterminacy, indeed they are part of that competitive process of imposing meaning upon human events in a "situation in which no plausible theory has emerged."

This is not to say that our future is not in some sense *determined* by broad patterns of social or economic change such as those analyzed by a Daniel Bell, by "complexity theorists" like La Porte, or by any number of Marxists, but only that *we cannot know if it is or not.* It follows that the chief purpose of research into these matters should be to illuminate what the areas of choice are and how human beings in different societies act within these "zones of freedom." We should seek to explore the widely accepted premises of many futurists that "the future of the future is in the present"[70] or that "the future cannot be predicted, but futures can be invented."[71] This seems important, for only if we learn to manage constraints and increase choice will we have the possibility of consciously choosing the sort of future we want. Even if a substantial part of this perception-response process of historical development is "determined" and not subject to choice (and this could be discovered), the most relevant task of the social scientist still lies within that narrow remaining area of choice. In this sense, then, we consider that the future will be made less by what is "objectively true" than by what people take to be true, how they relate that to their goals, what they try to do about it, what they are able to do about it, and what difference these efforts make for the kind of society that they will thus create. Therefore, in any analysis of trends and their impact on elites, or strategies, etc., we will want to ask how or why contrary trends did not develop or how or why counter-elites failed to develop effective countervailing pressures.

The focus ought then to be on sequences of actions and decisions over time. We should ask how different elites, groups, and institutions in advanced industrial or capitalist societies perceive the problematique of contemporary change, its threats, challenges, and opportunities. What do they seek to do about it? What do they manage to do about it? How do they react to uncertainty, to the evidence of counterproductive ideologies, intellectual paradigms, or failed policies? How do they process information relative to "contradictions," to new demands and to new claimants to power? How do they seek to influence or communicate with each other and with the general public? In terms of what symbols, myths, and ethical justifications? What use is made of "scientific" or "technical" knowledge or advice? What are the implications, for example, of declining authoritativeness and self-confidence (if any) of economists as policy advisers? How do elites act to maintain (or challenge) the existing distribution of power and benefits in society? How are their perceptions, strategies, and relative power affected by secular changes in available resources and in transformation processes? What coalition strategies are chosen and what bargaining processes ensue? How is the definition of what constitutes a problem, the development and consideration of "available" options, the selection and attempts to legitimate and implement particular policies, influenced by the above?

If the ultimate political meaning and significance of destabilizing trends and environmental transformations is fully perceptible only in the patterns of political response to them, it would seem that we should take advantage of the quasi-laboratory setting provided by the advanced industrial or capitalist countries today. This would involve viewing disciplined cross-national and longitudinal comparisons of problem-solving behavior and policy-making sequences as "quasi-experiments,"[72] in which to observe systematically the differential impact of the various change processes postulated by the authors here reviewed, the patterns of political response thereto, and the structural and policy consequences that ensue. Research can be carried out at a number of different levels of analysis, a partial list might include the following.

1. The focus of observation can be upon elite policy and coalition strategies—what Almond and associates call "power-policy-packages"—across a broad sample of countries, trying to extract from the comparison some kind of inventory of political responses to similar problems, and an evaluation and explanation of their relative efficacy. This would, in Charles W. Anderson's words, constitute "the inductive counterpart of the formal, deductive models of political economy and public choice, of game theory and coalition theory, which attempt to define the conditions of political rationality under postulated abstract conditions."

2. Or we may focus upon *policy content* including the cognitive bases of policy formulation (policy paradigms) that determine how a problem is defined and what options are perceived as available in different societies.

3. We may try to observe and explain trends in *interpolicy* linkages, constraints, and tradeoffs in order to clarify choices for a particular polity or class of polities.

4. We can stress the transnational linkages in policy formulation and implementation to reflect the increasingly evident, and as yet little understood, patterns of internationalization, interdependence, and external penetration of any nation's policy space.

5. We may emphasize *policy dynamics*, how policies change through time, as a way of linking substantive and processive aspects of the analysis of public policy. Provocative metaphors here are those of policy learning or policy reprogramming.

6. We may attempt to chart developmental paths for particular polities.

7. Or developmental paths for classes of polities—capitalist, socialist, Anglo-Saxon, Scandinavian, social democratic, etc. Explorations of convergence theories.

8. We might explore the usefulness of such macro-analytic concepts as "societal" learning—public learning—adaptive or active societies.

To this point I have dealt with some general areas of *convergence* among our authors and the related literature and with general *research foci* that one can derive from them. If we are to go beyond these broad generalities and admonitions, we will have to move to a more specific level of analysis that will permit us to discuss different analytical and historical stages or sequences so as to identify critical lacunae and disagreements, as well as agreements, in the literature. In order to do this we will need a general framework or model, and this can be constructed largely out of the elements discussed above.

2. STRAINS ON CHOICE PROCESSES AND ALTERNATIVE FUTURE DEVELOPMENT PATHS

The analytical-historical sequence that underlies our investigations of the comparative politics of the future of industrial societies must contain at least the following elements:

1. some assumptions, postulates, and empirical findings about instabilities or contradictions inherent in past and contemporary trends or developments

2. an analysis of *how* these are producing or are likely to produce a dissynchronization of loads and capabilities in political systems

3. an evaluation of initial response propensities of policy-makers as the effects of dissynchronization are felt, e.g., the weight of dominant policy paradigms and of established policy and coalition preferences (vested interests)

4. the consequences of these initial responses as far as the efficacy and legitimacy of policy are concerned

5. a conceptualization of the processes of debate and search for new policy and coalition options that are presumed to follow from persistent policy failure or policy intractability

6. some probabilistic statements linking sequences of subsequent policy and coalition choices back to the postulated sources of system instability and to the load/capability dissynchronization

7. a conceptualization of a "decision-tree" in which initial choices are linked to subsequent sequences and choices and to developmental outcomes, and often implying "irreversibility"; i.e., choice of one branch may foreclose other options and not allow for backtracking.

Figure 8.1 offers a general "model" of how these elements are sequentially related. In the discussion that follows, we divide the model into two phases: an initial "stimulus phase" in which sequences of policy failure or intractability follow from instabilities or contradictions impinging upon routine, status-quo-maintaining choice behavior, and a subsequent "response phase," in which the efforts of elites to "resynchronize" the system are traced to subsequent development outcomes by means of one or another sequence of coalition and policy choices.

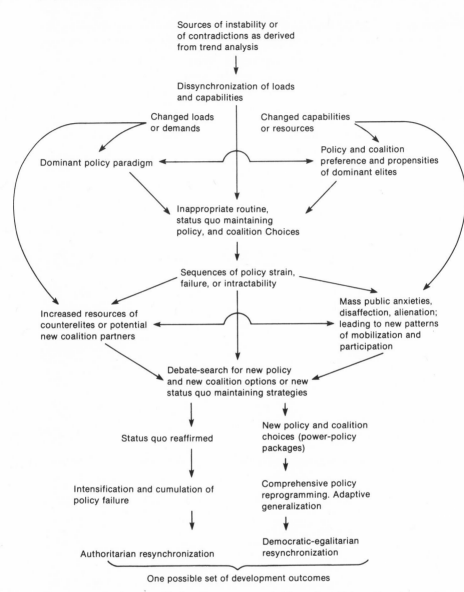

Figure 8.1. Strains on Choice Processes and Alternative Future Development Paths.

The nature and purposes of what is attempted in the following pages must be kept in mind. First, what I have sought to provide is an analytical model or framework within which to represent the arguments made by various authors. The general form of that model is based upon my own reading and interpretation of the literature on political modernization and development—notably that approach to such questions that stressed critical transitions or crises in order to "win back a bit of the autonomy of the political sphere" and to "rehabilitate the role of human choice and creativity in development problem-solving."[73] The model is not intended to be a representation of actual historical sequences in any country, but rather of some of the most salient aspects of the logic of thinking systematically about such sequences. Its chief purpose is heuristic—to clarify thought, to identify gaps and weaknesses in conceptual and theoretical development, and to suggest areas in which hypothesis formulation and empirical research would appear especially promising. Second, even then it is not possible within the space confines of this chapter either to take into account all the relevant variables and linkages or to give a full discussion of those that have been selected.[74] I can only offer a partial and preliminary survey of what is a vast, sprawling, and perhaps unmanageable topic. Third, and as has already been stressed, none of the authors represented in this volume, with the exception of La Porte and Abrams, have cast their analyses and speculations at such a macro-level. They are not responsible for, and may well feel uncomfortable with, the ways in which I have interpreted (or misinterpreted) the logic of their arguments. No scholar is ever entirely satisfied with the efforts of other scholars to "enfold" his work into their conceptual or analytical schemes. The things I have included in the model, and the ways they have been related to each other, very much reflect my way of looking at things; but it does, I hope, also do justice to each of our authors, while helping to indicate how and to what extent different formulations, findings, or hypotheses are complementary or in conflict.

The Nature and Sources of Policy Intractability, Strain, or Failure

Figure 8.2 represents the main elements and sequential relationships in what I have called the "stimulus phase." It seeks to identify the major sources or causes of the observed (or anticipated) policy intractability, strain, or failure which is said to characterize contemporary advanced industrial societies, and which drives them out of their normal mode of "dynamic conservatism."[75] The function of this part of the model is to make clear how the flux of contemporary change is thought to impinge upon the political sphere seen as a problem-solving, steering, or "hegemonic" system. Its conceptual debt to cybernetics and control theory is evident. Certain observed or postulated sources of instability or patterns of contradiction (a) are derived from some selection of trends empirically identifiable in the political, social, economic, ecological or cultural systems. Their political consequences are conceptualized as changes in the decision or demand load upon the state (b) and in the response capabilities of the state (c). That is, societal trends affect the

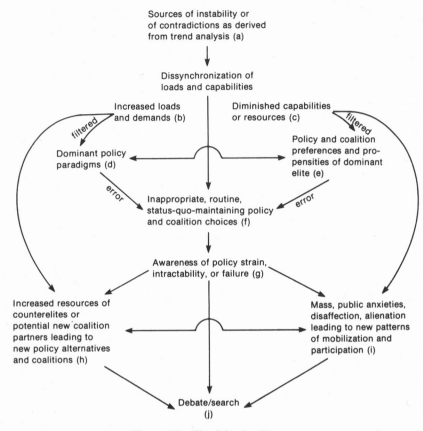

Figure 8.2. The Stimulus Phase.

steering or policy-making processes of the political system insofar as they substantially increase or alter the number, intensity, or nature of demands the state or dominant elite must confront, and insofar as they reduce or alter the response capabilities of such elites, i.e., the authority and legitimacy of authorities and regimes, the relative political resources of elites and counterelites, the availability of exchanges and acceptable coalition partners, the quality of shared understandings or "appreciations" in the society as to the role of the state, etc.

Because states tend to base new policies on past policies, because the parameters of choice and policy options are filtered or constrained by existing cause-effect beliefs and dominant policy paradigms (d), and by the policy and coalition preferences and propensities of those elites (e) that occupy decision-making roles in the state or have decisive access to these roles (and these factors interact and support each other), the initial response (f) is a routine, incremental, status-quo-maintaining one that does not require any reevaluation of policy or coalition preferences or propensities. Changes in loads and capabilities have, however, produced such a fundamental dissynchronization in the system that either or both dominant policy paradigms or cause-effect beliefs and policy and coalition preferences become sources of error. But perception and understanding of these new sources of policy error are lagged or delayed by selective perception, cognitive dissonance, administrative routine, inertia, selfishness, inattention, faulty information or information handling systems, lack of empathy, stupidity, etc. Hence, policy makers make increasingly inappropriate or self-defeating or manifestly inadequate decisions that fail either to meet the new load of demands or to restore or invent new capabilities.

Cumulative cycles of policy error gradually produce an awareness or realization of policy strain, intractability, or failure (g) that is shared by dominant elites, counterelites, and mass publics. Two further lagged aspects or consequences of the original dissynchronization of loads and capabilities are also visible in the model and are intensified by a general awareness of policy failure, namely, an increase in the relative resources of counterelites or of potential new coalition partners (h), and a heightened level of anxiety or dissatisfaction in the mass public (i). These may interact with each other in the form of new patterns of mobilization and participation and the active espousal of new policy and coalition options. Society is now in a "crisis," in that policy, institutional, and coalition innovations are necessary if the dominant elites are not to risk their positions, and the stage is set for a broad debate/search for new status quo maintaining strategies or for new policy and coalition options.

Now that we have the overall logic of the argument before us, we can not only locate and compare the positions taken by our authors and the evidence they adduce, but also evaluate the conceptual and epistemological underpinnings of the larger system of premises and hypotheses to which I have argued each author can in varying degrees be assimilated. Most importantly, we should be able to identify critical areas of research needed to test or elaborate each of the postulated elements and linkages. Taking advantage of the quasi-laboratory setting constituted by the near past and proximate future, to what extent can we empirically verify that these various things are in fact going on in advanced industrial nations? With what variations from country to country and from one problem area to another? What unanticipated variables or other linkages can be identified? Let us illustrate by taking up the major stages in the model's stimulus phase.

1. Sources of instability or contradiction as derived from an analysis of trends. Most models or theories of political change rely implicitly or explicitly upon some kind of underlying equilibrium-disequilibrium (in our case synchronization-dissynchronization) metaphor. Systems in equilibrium (synchronized) are neither necessarily or usually static or unchanging, nor without their sources of conflict. But these conflicts are under control, and the antecedent system is

> naturally viable, maintained by a *ruling* coalition. It may have been a highly responsive or coercive system, but whatever the case by responding to, manipulating, or effectively suppressing demands, the incumbent elites were able to maintain a relatively stable relationship between demands and allocations.[76]

A dissynchronization model thus needs to be "started" in order for the above stipulated sequence of steps to occur. The model begins to "run" when patterned changes within the political system, or its environment, alter inputs and performance and produce an incongruence between loads and capabilities, demands and allocations. The identification and analysis of trends as sources of such change is a critical element in any dissynchronization model, but, as our earlier discussions have emphasized, it is exactly here that analysts of past historical crises, turning points or transitional sequences in development, have experienced the greatest difficulty. Research along the lines of that reported in Almond et al. holds out substantial promise of future conceptual, empirical, and theoretical progress in this domain, as does a variety of other ongoing research projects.[77]

But, as has also been pointed out above, even if past developmental sequences come to be well understood, we shall have no assurance of the utility of such understanding for a postulated contemporary transitional phase. At any rate, our authors and others cited here now confront a situation in which any number of contradictory trends are visible at any point in time, we lack generally accepted criteria for distinguishing important ones from ephermeral ones, we do not know how they are related to each other, and in the absence of good theory we generally fall back on more or less sophisticated techniques of projecting one or more discrete sets of trends, a notoriously unreliable procedure.

And yet we must begin somewhere if we are to get our model to run and if we are to develop strategies of empirical investigation into the phenomena of contemporary change. Each theorist in effect makes his own selection, based on hunches, disciplinary biases, pretheories, ideological attachment, partial appreciations of the situation. Most of our authors do so in full recognition that these are no more than hypotheses for further investigation. The model as a whole can then be seen as an ordering device for the testing and elaboration of such hypotheses in the natural quasi-laboratory conditions available. It should be possible, first, to trace the logic associated with any set of supposed trends through the various steps in the stimulus phase (e.g., through the construction of more elaborate flow charts and various simulation exercises), and second, to design comparative, longitudinal research so as to observe the actual impact of the postulated or hypothesized trends upon different systems. An understanding of how various systemic and subsystemic factors affect the actual and perceived impact of one or another pattern of change is obviously of central importance. This would serve not only the goals of increasing our understanding of the contemporary period and clarifying future options, but also the tasks of constructing more general theories of social and political change.

Table 8.1 summarizes some of the major assertions made by the authors represented or reviewed in this volume about contemporary political instabilities as derived from their appreciation of environmental

Table 8.1. Sources of Political Instability, or of Contradictions as Derived from Trend Analysis

Organizational complexity and social interdependence	La Porte and Abrams
Growing power of private government over the individual and the state	Anderson
Postmaterialist vs. Materialist value priorities in mass publics	Inglehart
Costs of economic growth overtake benefits (pollution, resource depletion)	Tsurutani, No-growth or Steady-state theorists
Density of political regulation	Vickers
Demographic and ecological disasters	Heilbroner and many others
Internationalization of economies, diminished effectiveness of national policy instruments	Hancock and many others
Contradiction between state's functions of assuring accumulation and legitimization	Marxists
Expansion of political participation, declining and rising social forces, institutional cleavage, executive bureaucracy, and mass media	Huntington
Subordination of economic function to the political order and increasing ubiquitousness of political control	Bell
Growth of central guidance clusters and welfare, warfare—industrial—communications—police bureaucracies	Gross
The symbiosis of the "planning system" and the state	Galbraith
Increase in levels of international economic conflict	Heilbroner, many Marxists
Economic growth will slow down and increase distributional conflicts	Heilbroner, steady-state theorists, many Marxists

or political system trends. Each is in a sense searching for the functional equivalent(s) of the critical junctures and threshold issues identified by students of the past development of industrial nations. For example, Lipset and Rokkan identified four decisive *dimensions of cleavage* in Western politics, each associated with a critical historical juncture and with general policy issues that became salient in those periods[78]; and Rokkan, in another formulation, singled out four *basic processes* of societal development in Western European nation states.[79]

Lipset and Rokkan

Cleavage	Critical Juncture	Issues
Center-Periphery	Reformation–Counter-Reformation: 16th–17th centuries	National vs. supra-national religion
State-Church	National revolution: 1789 and after	Secular vs. religious control of mass education
Land-Industry	Industrial revolution: 19th century	Tariff levels for agricultural products; control vs. freedom for industrial enterprise
Owner-Worker	Russian revolution: 1917 and after	Integration into national policy vs. commitment to international revolutionary movement

Rokkan

Process	Issue
Penetration	State building
Standardization	Nation building
Participation	Development of political citizenship
Redistribution	Development of social citizenship

Table 8.1 is only a sampling of theses that abound in the literature. Of the factors listed many are contradictory, others are interdependent, and many different conceptual levels are represented. One way to sort them out might be to adopt Almond et al's strategy of conceptualization in terms of potentially destabilizing features and weak points in the "antecedent" or synchronized state of the system, and the environmental "triggers" that crystallize these potentialities into actual and overt challenge and propel the system toward a crisis. Table 8.2 gives a possible format for such an analysis.

Table 8.2. The Antecedent System

Destabilizing Features	Issues in Dispute	Environmental Triggers or Changes			
		International		Domestic	
		Military Economic Demonstration Effect	Social Mobilization	Economic Performance	

249

2. Do environmental factors in fact create a dissynchronization of loads and capabilities? Postulates, theories, hunches, projections of trends seem to guide the researcher where to look in the flux of events for the seeds of future change. In the analysis of ongoing change we must be alert to the possibility (probability) that the salient instabilities or triggers are the least evident and unanticipated, and hence this stage of the research process must be kept open. Yet, as we have repeatedly argued, in order to verify or falsify assertions at this level, or even to understand their implications, we have to develop ways of actually observing and crudely measuring or estimating the impact of such instabilities upon the political system. I have suggested a loads/capabilities imagery as one way of moving to this level of analysis. This is congruent with Almond et al.

> Changes in the international and domestic environments induce and stimu-
> late social and political mobilization, the processes of social and political
> mobilization generate new preferences and resources. The impact of new
> preferences on the existing distribution of preferences is to change the sub-
> stance of political issues, whereas the advent of new resources redis-
> tributes the balance of effective political resources. A new demand
> structure emerges from the confluence of these new preference and re-
> source distributions and becomes polarized when the distance between
> the contenders' issue preferences reaches extreme proportions and the re-
> sources that buttress these conflicting preferences become more nearly
> balanced.[80]

The initial task would seem to be to draw up profiles of the new demand structure and the associated resource/capability balance that is emerging in various industrial societies. Our authors offer a rich assortment of fragments (see table 8.3), some data-based, mostly hypothetical, but none has attempted an overall profile of the changing relationship between loads and capabilities, although La Porte and Abrams and Tsurutani perhaps come close. This is clearly an area in which conceptual development and the construction of at least crude aggregate operational measures is of the highest priority.

*3. How do dominant elites and decision makers in various coun-
tries respond as the initial effects of dissynchronization make their
appearance?* Are the model's expectations fulfilled, namely, that rou-
tine, incremental status-quo-maintaining choices are made? What is the differential effect of different structures of elite policy and coalition preferences and propensities? Of different decision-making and planning institutions and arrangements? How do the cognitive orientations of different policy makers structure what they perceive, determine what they consider problemmatic, and constrain the range of options perceived as available? Is the error-inducing effect of these "filters" markedly different from one issue area to another? From one country to another?

Table 8.3. Dissynchronization of Loads and Capabilities

Loads Are Increasing	Capabilities Are Decreasing
New policy problems requiring new instruments (Anderson)	Declining consensus on criteria for the evaluation of policy (La Porte, Vickers)
New policy tradeoffs: growth and environment, inflation vs. employment (Tsurutani, Heilbroner, Vickers, others)	More active state intervention highlights existence and influence of dominant elite (Marxists)
Increasingly polarized demands reflecting value differentiation (Inglehart, La Porte)	Decline in trust in government
	Decline in legitimacy of political institutions and in regime norms
Cross-stratal issues (Tsurutani)	Declining efficacy of standard instruments of macro-economic management
Higher expectations about government performance (La Porte, Anderson)	
	Ruling coalition loses cohesion
Problems requiring intergovernmental cooperation and joint policies	Changes in the relative distibution of resources among coalition partners and counterelites
Business requires more and more state subsidies (O'Connor)	Noncompliance and nonsanctioned protest increase
Sheer numbers and complexities of problems (La Porte and Abrams)	Decline in efficacy of international economic and political regimes and agreements

Several of the authors considered focus on this level of the model (Anderson, Hancock, La Porte and Abrams, Vickers), but generally without supporting empirical findings (except for Hancock).

There is general agreement that responses will be incremental, but sharp disagreement on the error-inducing consequences of such responses. Anderson stresses both the continuity and adaptive possibilities inherent in the liberal, free-market paradigm, whereas Vickers considers it disastrously "self-exciting."[81] Hancock is equally sanguine about Sweden. La Porte and Abrams stress the degree to which the underlying reality models, cause-effect beliefs, of policy makers in all highly industrialized, complex, and interdependent societies are likely to be profoundly inadequate. It would be particularly interesting to test their model of "the transition to unstable postindustria" in a country like Sweden, in which many of their indicators of technological growth, structure of the labor force and of occupations, organizational development, rational planning, and rapidly rising public expectations show a comparable development to that of California.[82]

4. What are the effects of policy failure at the level of the policy maker, dominant coalitions, contending elites, and mass public; and how do these interact? Many of the authors represented or described here clearly anticipate that incremental, status-quo-maintaining choices will be manifestly inadequate and that the dissynchronization or situation of latent crisis will persist and intensify as the consequences of inappropriate policy choices and the error-inducing effects of prevailing models of reality and the policy and coalition preferences of the dominant elite become more widespread.

La Porte and Abrams see two interacting sequences following upon increasing failure of government to deal with social problems: personal insecurity ⟶ personal malaise and alienation ⟶ new personal search for meaning; and political uncertainty ⟶ political dissent ⟶ new political ideologies. They foresee anxiety, uncertainty, new religions, social and political movements; but they do not suggest the ways in which these phenomena are likely to impinge on the policy maker and dominant elites or how they may serve to increase the resources of counter-elites or restructure mass or elite policy preferences. Tsurutani seems to see a more functional pattern of response in Japan, in which new patterns of mobilization and participation in response to policy malfunction is altering the shape of political competition, changing the locus or site of political action, and changing the balance of the relative political resources of the dominant elites and their challengers. He suggests a more general argument that Anderson might well make, namely, that crisis may produce a form of "pluralist adaptation," in the form of the creation of new associations and institutions in the private sector, or in the form of new symbiotic patterns linking associational interests to the state bureaucracy in certain sectors of economic policy. In any case, neither La Porte and Abrams nor Tsurutani ask about the impact of policy failure on the self-confidence or cohesion of the dominant elite, although theories of revolution would suggest that this is a critical variable.

When does dissynchronization and policy failure become in some sense intolerable? Can one measure, as Almond et al. have attempted to do, such variables as the polarization of demands, issue-distance, the increase in zero-sum expectations in political conflict, changes in the relative ability of contenders to accumulate resources, threats to the "incumbent constitution," the emergence or availability of alternative policy formulations or "ideas in good currency," and so forth? What sorts of issues or events (1973's candidate was energy, 1974's inflation and 1975's unemployment) seem to hold the potential of catalyzing such elements and forcing the system into a more fluid mode in which more innovative responses may be attempted?

Alternative Response or Development Paths

The response phase of the model sequence is signaled by the political system having been forced out of its normal incremental, dynamically conservative mode of problem solving into a more fluid situation in which innovations in policies, coalitions, and institutional forms are more and more actively debated within the dominant elite coalition, between them and alternative or contending elites on the one hand, and mass publics—or the "attentive public"—on the other. The model suggests that this debate or search process and the "fluidity" that makes it possible is the consequence of a further intensification of the dissynchronization of loads and capabilities brought about by the failure of routine modes of problem solving. (See figure 8.3.) The dominant elite itself becomes aware of the inadequacy of such responses, and perhaps loses cohesion and/or self-confidence (g). Alternative or contending elites continue to amass resources in various ways (h), including their ability to mobilize or threaten physical violence and active noncompliance, defections from the dominant coalition, increased votes in representative and policy-making institutions, cooptation offers from the dominant coalition, and the introduction of new policy ideas and options that receive a positive response from the public or from salient organized groups. Anxiety, disaffection, alienation, disaffiliation mount in the mass public (i); and new patterns of mobilization and participation emerge, shifting the resource balance between the dominant coalition and contending groups. The intensity and urgency of the debate and search may typically be accelerated by the emergence of certain catalytic

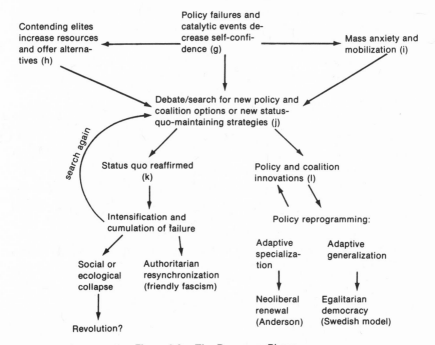

Figure 8.3. The Response Phase.

issues which "have the effect of precipitating a challenge to the political structures of accountability and authority."[83]

We can envisage a continuum of policy and coalition choices ("power policy packages") emerging from this debate and search process, ranging from status quo reaffirmation to what Hugh Heclo[84] calls a "comprehensive reprogramming" involving new policies and new coalition combinations. In the case of status quo reaffirmation (k) dominant elites choose to (are able to) reaffirm their initial policy and coalition preferences because they cannot imagine alternatives as viable or because the status, power, and economic reward cost are deemed too high. Their cohesion and self-confidence may be restored, but the load-capability dissynchronization persists, eventually pushing the system into some kind of breakdown phase (ecological disaster, decentralized domestic violence, revolution) and/or into some form of authoritarian resynchronization in which challenges from contending elites are repressed and public acquiescence managed or manipulated. The other polar development outcome follows from a debate and search process more attuned to the demands of publics and contenders, to an open analysis of the sources of policy failure, and to the tasks of active relegitimation of the system (1). In the ideal case this produces a truly "adaptive generalization" and a democratic resynchronization of the political system. Let us examine each of these stages more closely with a view to locating our authors and to clarifying some of the more important conceptual and research issues.

1. The debate or search for new policy and coalition options in nonroutine situations. The conceptualization of "crisis" or "nonroutine" problem solving presents us with special problems, and is surely one area in which progress needs to be made, for most of our models of public decision-making rationality, bargaining and exchange, incrementalism and economizing, assume normal or routine situations.[85] We have much less insight into how policy makers grapple with novel, perplexing, and unanticipated issues of public choice. But as Philippe Schmitter and Donald Schon have pointed out, it is precisely at these relatively rare junctures that one can inquire most deeply into the very essence of the decision-making capabilities of political systems—the alternatives that are considered; how conflicting public and private interests interact; how compromises, hierarchical authority, or coercive sanctions are mobilized. During a crisis, notes Schmitter,

> a decisional system considers or reconsiders the range of "acceptable" alternative courses of action it has to choose from and concretizes its priorities.... This is the level at which "the mobilization of bias"—the structural inability to listen to or consider certain strategies or solutions—becomes apparent; where "non-decisions" are made to reject public action on a given issue, either remanding it for private, i.e. "market," allocation

or ignoring it altogether; where "trade-offs" are forced to the surface between contradictory objectives and complementary ones stuggling for the same limited resources.[86]

Similarly, Donald Schon argues that the most important stage in public adaptation to rapid change is "that barely visible process through which issues come to awareness and ideas about them become powerful."[87] for this is where conflicts crystallize, issues are identified, solutions made available, sides defined and chosen. "These antecedent processes," says Schon, "are as crucial to the formation of policy as the processes of discovery in science are crucial to the formation of plausible hypotheses."[88] They are essential to change in public policy and thus a close analysis of these processes will yield basic insights into the vitality of a society's "capacity for public learning."

> A learning system must transform its ideas in good currency at a rate commensurate with its own changing situation. More broadly, the adequacy of a learning system is in part shown by how far its ideas in good currency are adequate to the situation actually confronting it.[89]

Despite the obvious importance of "crisis problem solving" at the societal level we have, as Hugh Heclo has pointed out, very few studies of "what kind of learning mechanisms governments in fact are."[90] Heclo's own pioneering *Modern Social Politics in Britain and Sweden* (a comparative study of the evolution of social policy conceptions "from relief to income maintenance" over an 80–90 year period) stands almost alone as an analysis of the dynamics of policy change, of adaptation to changing conditions and changing attitudes, and of its interaction with elections, parties, interest groups, and administrators. Heclo seeks to look at politics as "learning."

> Politics finds its sources not only in power but also in uncertainty—men collectively wondering what to do. Finding feasible courses of action includes, but is more than, locating which way the vectors of political pressure are pushing. Governments not only "power" ... they also puzzle. ... Policy-making is a form of collective puzzlement on society's behalf.[91]

He isolates three principal factors from his comparison of British and Swedish experience: the role of "individual agents of change,"[92] the "interactions of political institutions,"[93] and "the impact of previous policy."[94] He argues that political structures are best seen as "crannied hosts supporting individual agents of change"; these "middlemen at the interfaces of various groups" perform the function of injecting new ideas; and political institutions have served as "social assemblers, bunching activists into cohorts whose common exposure to outside stimuli evolves into rough bodies of shared interpretation."[95] But previous policy is the "most pervasive manifestation of policy learning."[96] Heclo is ambiguous in interpreting the import of this latter finding. On the one hand, he argues that the "momentum and experiences generated by established policy" are "more relevant than changes in the possession of political power"[97] in explaining the incremental progress of policy; on the other hand, he admits that "social policy has developed in the interstices *allowed to it* by "sound economic thinking."[98] The point is obviously important for several of our authors who argue that it is exactly past policies and the canons of "sound thinking" that are plunging our societies into crisis. For Marxists, of course, "sound economic thinking" is indistinguishable from "the bias of the capitalist system" (Miliband) or the "hegemony of the dominant class" (Gramsci).[99]

Perhaps Heclo is correct when he chastises those whose glib preoccupation with the revolutionary obscures change itself; "attention centers on the glittering pageant and dramatic incident rather than the elusive processes that evoke the incidents."[100] Perhaps the changes we seek to understand will inevitably be slow and incremental—even barely perceptible, owing more to continuity and incrementalism than to "paradigm shifts" or their public policy analogues. But, if a majority of our authors are correct, such will not suffice and either other forms of "learning" will be triggered in more dramatic fashion, or the crises of our time will deepen.

Heclo's study underscores the points made earlier about the normal propensities of systems and about the limits of our knowledge when it comes to more discontinuous kinds of policy changes, when the routine search for solutions "in the neighborhood of the problem"[101] produces unanticipated and undesired and costly consequences, and more innovative policy and coalition searches seem necessary. Heclo has more recently distinguished between "selective reprogramming" and "comprehensive reprogramming" and between "adaptive specialization" and "adaptive generalization" in describing policy accommodations to endogenous and exogenous circumstances.

Selective reprogramming is the norm in the bulk of government policy making.

> External information on current trials and internal information on previous experiences are combined into successive, selective adjustments of behavior.... Changes are likely to occur as adaptive specializations, that is, refinements introduced into an otherwise unmodified behavioral design. In identifying adaptive specialization it is not the size (increment) of the change that matters but its contribution to a more precise, more narrowly efficient responsiveness to specific conditions.[102]

Comprehensive reprogramming, on the other hand, involves "wholesale paradigm shifts."

> To study comprehensive reprogramming implies relatively greater attention to adaptive generalization. Rather than dealing more effectively with narrower, more specialized conditions, adaptive generalization means improving capacities to deal with a wider, more variable range of events. . . . [It] can only rarely be identified in the actions of one subsystem and its selective programs [but rather] appears in system-wide reinterpretations and accumulations.[103]

Karl Deutsch in his classic *The Nerves of Government* places learning capacity, creativity, and innovativeness at the center of his political analysis; but little systematic research has been attempted along the lines suggested by his formulations. For Deutsch, the learning capacity of a system is its ability to invent and carry out new policies: to combine items of information into new patterns, and to make uncommitted resources available to the system. Social learning is a function of the range of internally available recombinations of knowledge, manpower and facilities; the extent to which information processing and storing facilities can be subdivided into smaller pieces, and the extent and probable relevance of its "fixed sub-assemblies available for new recombinations." A system has learned *creatively* when it has "increased its ranges of possible intake of information from the outside world and its ranges of possible inner recombinations."[104] *Pathological* learning occurs when a system looses its capacity to process new information and control its future behavior.

The concept of goal-seeking *feedback* is central to Deutsch's discussion of societal learning for "feedback analysis permits us to identify and in principle measure a number of elements in either goal seeking or homeostatic processes. We can evaluate the efficiency of a feedback process in terms of the number and size of its mistakes, that is, the under- or over-correction it makes in reaching the goal."[105] Whether the system will make more and more mistakes, going into a series of oscillations and possible breakdown, or gradually approach the goal through a number of "diminishing mistakes" depends on four quantitative factors:

(a) *Load of information*—the amount and rate of change with which an institution or a government must cope.

(b) *Lag in response*—"How much time do policy makers require to become aware of a new situation, and how much additional time do they need to arrive at a decision? How much delay is imposed by broader consultation or participation?"[106]

(c) *Gain in response*—once a system has accepted new data, "How quickly do bureaucracies, interest groups, political organizations, and citizens respond with major recommitments of their resources?"[107]

(d) *Lead*—"What is . . . the capability of a government to predict and anticipate new problems effectively? . . . What is the effect of free public discussion, including freedom of unorthodox opinions, upon the predictive efficiency of a political decision system? What is the relationship of the institutions, organizations, or practices that produce forecasts to those that control their selection, evaluation, and acceptance for action?"[108]

According to Deutsch, political systems can fail to respond to change or crisis for six different reasons:[109]

(a) *Loss of power*—actions that dissipate or destroy vital material and social resources

(b) *Loss of intake*—"the overvaluation of memories over current ranges of intake, of internal over external messages, and of current ranges of intake over new data and new ranges of information"

(c) *Loss of steering capacity*—"the overvaluation of structure over function, increased delay and slowness of response to changing information"

(d) *Loss of depth of memory*—"the overvaluation of established routines for recalling and recombining data, and of established criteria of relevance and interest in the screening of new developments"

(e) *Loss of capacity for partial inner rearrangement*—rigidity of commitment to particular functions

(f) *Loss of capacity for comprehensive rearrangement* of inner structure—rigidity of commitment to basic values

All these modes of failure relate to "the overvaluation of the near over the far, the familiar over the new, the past over the present, and the present over the future. They involve overestimation or overvaluation of the organization compared to the environment, of its past methods and commitments over new ones, and of its current will and inner structure over all possibilities of fundamental change."[110] This is why, as Deutsch suggests (and Schon affirms), "very serious challenges to the functioning of a society or state . . . may only have those solutions that are fairly unlikely to be discovered by means of the standardized and accepted habits, preferences, and cultural patterns existing in the society."[111] They are often more likely to be found by deviant members of the community. But these groups are not likely to be able to form stable, cohesive, and influential social groups, and therefore their role in learning is to persuade others.

Schon[112] suggests the following sequences in such a process of adaptation to serious challenges to the functioning of a society:

(a) At any point in time social systems are "dynamically conservative"—they are characterized by a certain set of ideas in good currency.

(b) Disruptive events or a crisis occur producing a demand for new ideas.

(c) Ideas already present in "free or marginal areas of society begin to surface."

(d) They are mediated by "vanguard roles" who move ideas to public awareness (muckrakers, artists, utopians, critics, prophets). (Trist's "elites attuned to detecting areas of likely crisis?")

(e) These new ideas can be at different levels, from "inventions" to "root concepts."

(f) Diffusion depends on interpersonal networks and the media of communications.

(g) Ideas become powerful as centers of policy debate and political conflict, i.e., when organizations grow around it, when it is used to gain influence and money.

(h) Ideas gain widespread acceptance through the efforts of those who "push or ride them through the fields of force created by the interplay of interests and commitments."

Of course, there is no assurance that a given society, once confronted with a crisis situation—i.e., a fundamental dissynchronization of loads and capabilities—will succeed or even attempt an open search for new options that might eventually produce "creative learning" or a comprehensive reprogramming. Indeed, among our authors, only Hancock and Anderson foresee anything like such a response, with the majority anticipating one or another incremental and status-quo maintaining strategies. (See table 8.4.) It is also clear that none of our authors has made an extensive empirical analysis of any part of this stage of debate/search in conditions of mounting uncertainty. Nor have they tried to develop a full conceptualization of the complex interactions that are involved. Straussman's analysis of the growth and application of various technologies of societal guidance comes closest to the former, while La Porte and Abrams' model of unstable postindustria comes the closest to the latter. We have then sets of hypotheses, mostly unconnected, and some partial attempts at identifying critical variables and suggesting how operational definitions might be developed. To say this is not to fault them but to emphasize further the general weakness in the policy and policy process literature already noted above. The processes involved are clearly extremely complex in that they involve the interaction of ideas and power, complex organizations and individual initiatives, perceptions and misperceptions; the reevaluation of dominant paradigms and metaphors and basic issue preferences and coalition propensities; the invention and manipulation of resources, including new

Table 8.4.   Elites' Preferred Strategies of Debate/Search and Their
Presumed Consequences

Status Quo Maintaining	Open Search for New Options
Increase organizational complexity (La Porte)	Broaden dominant coalitions (Hancock)
Politics of psychic reassurance (La Porte, Tsurutani)	Adaptive specialization within policy paradigm (Anderson)
Politics of symbolic manipulation (Edelman)	Reevaluate basic policy paradigm (Steady-state Economy Theorists— Daly, Georgescu Roegen)
Cost-rationalization (Straussman)	
Increase planning, knowledge specialists, societal guidance, technocratic counsel (La Porte, Straussman, Gross)	
Increase repression (Gross, Marxists)	

information systems; and new criteria for policy choice, attempts to influence, educate, manipulate mass publics, etc. In seeking to bring into focus those processes of adaptation to crisis the outcome of which leads or is thought to lead a society down one or another distinctive developmental path, we are thus entering upon an ill-charted terrain dotted with contending metaphors, conceptualizations, technologies, and planning systems.

We will also confront a critical normative and epistemological problem that can be symbolized by contrasting concepts of societal "learning" or "adaptation" with the Marxian concept of "social reproduction."[113] The central issue raised here is the fundamental one of whether we can distinguish among the adaptive needs of "society as a whole" and those of the "dominant elite," or other groups in society, or of "the state" itself. If the focus of our research is upon societal adaptation to change, governmental learning, planning and political innovation, don't we run the risk of implicitly taking the role of the dominant elites in society, thus assuming that they govern on the basis of consensus and that no single group or coalition effectively dominates the capitalist state? Will we then not lose sight of the possibility or likelihood that adaptation to change is an inherently contradictory process in that different groups and interests have different stakes in continuity and in change, or that the kind of comprehensive reprogramming so many of the authors cited seem to think necessary, may imply basic transformations of existing national and international hierarchical and power relationships? In other words, an adequate *societal learning response* to problem sets postulated by a Heilbroner or La Porte and Abrams or others may be incompatible with an "adequate" governmental learning response. The following quotes from Schmitter make essentially the same point.

> The coherence of whole social systems and their subunits is not, as in the functionalist paradigm, assured by normative consensus and/or the automatic adjustment of interdependent functional imperatives, but by the deliberative acts of classes, groups or individuals who have power and, hence, are capable of elaborating and imposing upon others both the operative rules of the game and the substantive content of extractions and allocations made within these rules. . . .
>
> The next step is to recognize that the reproductive needs of a society and the social subunits are contradictory—incapable of simultaneous fulfillment. There exists, therefore, a hierarchy in the competition for scarce policy resources based on the structure of power in a given society. The Marxist prognosis is that the replicative and (especially) the growth imperatives of the system of private property distribution and productive resources will (in the first or last instance—depending on the version) set important and predictable parameters on how policy, public or private, will be used to "overcome" these contradictions.
>
> Public policy grows out of these contradictory but hierarchically-ordered reproductive imperatives.[114]

   2. "*Power-policy packages,*" *structural change, and alternative futures.* Our model offers two polar types as ends of a hypothetical continuum of possible development outcomes, from "status quo affirmation" leading either to social and/or ecological collapse or to authoritarian resynchronization, to "policy reprogramming" leading either to egalitarian democracy (on a Swedish model?) or to a renewal of "liberalism" (see figure 8.3). Many of our authors have clear views as to the kind of outcomes they consider most likely (see table 8.5), but would also agree that such views can have little empirical foundation. Tendencies in one

Table 8.5. Most Likely Development Outcomes

Status quo affirmation leading to further dissynchronization and eventually to breakdown and/or authoritarian resynchronization		New policy and coalition innovations leading to active relegitimation, adaptive generalization, and democratic resynchronization
	Heclo	
	Inglehart	Hancock (for Sweden)
	Anderson	Daly
Edelman	Tsurutani	Boulding
La Porte and Abrams		
Straussman		
Vickers		
Heilbroner		
Marxists		

direction or another are there, but we lack the analytical tools for engaging in the sort of "political assessment" or "political valuation" that such projections imply. Political assessment refers to efforts "to contemplate the total consequences for a society of any proposed set of policies,"[115] to trace the long-term consequences of small and discrete choices and the ways in which present choices may constrain those of the future. Political valuation introduces self-consciously "ethical" criteria[116] by means of which particular consequences of policy or the cumulation and aggregation of consequences into one or another societal type can be judged or evaluated.

Daunting as these tasks are, it is clear that they have long been on the agenda of political scientists, and not only of political philosophers, viz. empirical democratic theory, the theory of economic and political development, certain approaches to causal modeling. Both political assessment and political valuation are closely related to a consideration of the problems of learning and adaptation raised earlier, for an analytical concern for "learning" does seem to imply some kind of normative commitment to political order and stability, however it may be conceived. The fact is that political order is a prime political value and through time has been a central concern of political inquiry. It has connotations of social peace, harmony, integration, peaceful change, and social justice. While the ultimate vision of "the good society" remains diverse— some envision a Rousseauist "autonomous harmony," some technocratic efficiency, some an egalitarian service-centered society, some the dynamic and open equilibrium of perennial liberalism—the question of stability cum "right order" is at the normative center of political inquiry.

When political scientists become concerned with the impact of policies, with their distributive consequences, with their second, third, and fourth level consequences or externalities, they may thus appeal to a variety of normative criteria; but still lurking in the background is the overriding question of order—and with it, of adaptive capacity. Marxists would seem to be an exception, but only insofar as they look forward to the breakdown of an unjust order, not when they contemplate the design or governance of the "new order" that is to follow. Hence, the analytic and evaluative framework that seems central to political science is one which deals with the adaptive capacities of systems—and is concerned with the consequences of policies with regard not just to the "coping" capacities of extant or dominant elites, but the dynamic integration and conflict-resolving capacities of systems. In seeking to evaluate policies and sequences of policies, we are then concerned with the egalitarian or social justice or due process aspects as they are presumed to effect prospects for the value of political order itself.

Finding means for assessing long-range implications of choices, options that might be foreclosed, developmental paths, indicators of change, etc., is part of a concern for this overriding normative preoccupation. Adaptation in terms of established paradigms or the innovation and problem solving of nonroutine decisions, then, is the study of the *capacity* of elites to respond to change in order sustaining or enhancing ways. The need for improved models and measures of evaluation is to examine whether these adaptations will be successful for purposes of political order and ongoing adaptive capacity in long-range and distant contexts.

Whether issues of this complexity can be systematically addressed in the flux of ongoing events is another question, and presumes resolving at least two preliminary conceptual and theoretical problems, only the general nature of which can be indicated here. First, we require a much more searching consideration of the whole notion of development paths, of the presumed relationships between stages. Verba[117] finds three development path models potentially useful:

(a) *Many outcomes, one path to each outcome*, i.e., there are many types of political system outcomes, but a determined sequence by which one moves toward one or another.

(b) *Necessary condition or functional requisite*, i.e., in order to attain a particular stage other stages must be attained first.

(c) *Branching tree*, i.e., there is a sequence of choice points. At any point in development, there are alternative next steps. When one is chosen, options for others are closed, implying notions of irreversibility.

Verba concludes that "the study of . . . irreversibilities might be most useful for the development of sequential models."[118] It is interesting to note in this context that within the burgeoning forecasting literature, it is perhaps in the area of "decision-trees" and "scenario-construction" that some of the more suggestive work is being done.[119] Perhaps one area of future research will take the form of systematic efforts to employ such techniques in the assessment of specific policies adopted by governments in response to particular contemporary crisis circumstances. In this way we might improve upon the rather primitive and ideology-tinged notions of the secondary and tertiary consequences and political and social system consequences of particular policy choices presently implicit in the logical-deductive models of economists,[120] or in computer simulation models being used for policy purposes in government[121] or by such groups as the Club of Rome.[122]

The second problem is to seek to develop sets of operational indicators of political and structural change. Straussman raises this issue directly and offers some preliminary measures of "the incidence of technocratic counsel." He rightfully distinguishes between structural indicators and the predominant concern of the social indicator movement for "nonpolitical performances indicators." On the other hand, the "indicators of national development" movement sparked by Stein Rokkan[123] shows a greater potential of moving towards at least some political structural concepts as a basis of aggregate data collection. The development of an appropriate set of indicators itself presumes some theory or model of the polity, of the type attempted by Bertram Gross under the rubric of "social system accounting."[124] Some dimensions for measuring and evaluating political performance and structural change as suggested by our authors or in the literature we have cited might include:

The intensity of politically relevant cleavages

Structures of interest representation and styles of participation in decision making

Bureaucratization at the expense of individual liberty

Centralization of economic and political resources in "complexes" of state and private enterprise

Degrees of equality of condition (distribution of income, access to services, etc.)

Systems of social relations in production (bipartite, tripartite, enterprise-corporatist)

Extent of "shared policy space" among decision makers in different nation-states

Technocratic counsel

Organizational complexity

Social interdependence

Degrees of intraelite policy consensus

Policy and procedural consensus between elites and publics

Degrees of public alienation, cynicism, support, acquiescence

Particularly appropriate, in view of the emphasis placed by the literature on the increasing scope of political decisions as one of the distinctive features of the present and the foreseeable future would be concepts relating to the nature of the modern capitalist state itself. As Schmitter observes,

If policies can be structurally defined as acts and allocations of values designed to produce changes in society (or, conversely, as non-acts and non-allocations intended not to interfere with existing societal conditions), then some net or overall estimation of their effect will tell us what, functionally speaking, policies are . . . [and] more specifically what the nature or function of the modern State is.

From this perspective the State would not be analyzed, as previously, in terms of its formal structure (e.g., regime type) or its role occupants (e.g., social recruitment pattern or specific government). Rather, it would be studied and evaluated in terms of what it does or doesn't do—in terms of the substantive content of its extractions and allocations, and their net impact upon civil society.[125]

What is called for, then, is some set of summary concepts appropriate to the salient political structural characteristics of emergent "post-industrial" societies. One general model that might be emulated is Dahl's analysis of democratization or the historical emergence of polyarchies. Dahl identifies two principal theoretical dimensions: liberalization (public contestation) and inclusiveness (right to participate in elections and offices), and develops therefrom a typology of regimes and a logical set of development paths. He suggests that stability and democracy have historically emerged in a one- or two-stage sequence in which liberalization and inclusiveness must be ordered. The "best path" to polyarchy begins with liberalization of competition and veers toward inclusiveness only when the terms of political competition have been agreed to. Other paths are likely to lead to either "competitive oligarchies" or to "inclusive hegemonies."

Political assessment and political valuation of contemporary and future policy and coalition choices probably require something closer to a "branching tree" sequential model, and a more multidimensional set of structural characteristics, for only with the passage of time will we come to better understand the structural transformations which now appear as stones in the sand visible only now and then at low tide.

3. AGGREGATE TRENDS, THE LIBERAL (OR "BOURGEOIS-DEMOCRATIC") PARADIGM, AND ALTERNATIVE PATTERNS OF POLICY RESPONSE IN CAPITALIST NATIONS

In sketching the above model it was my goal to clarify the logical structure and epistemological dilemmas of statements about contemporary change and its presumed political consequences, to show where conceptual development is sorely needed, to indicate how macro and micro levels of analysis might be linked, to suggest where empirical research seems especially promising, and to demonstrate how a variety of different strategies (as represented by our authors) can be related to one another.

The research agenda that has been proposed centers upon comparative and longitudinal studies of governmental problem-solving behavior—upon *comparative policy dynamics*. But it is conceptualized in such a way as to link policy content and change in policy content to political processes, on the one hand, and to macro-level system change on the other.

The key concepts here are adaptation, learning, reprogramming, and reproduction. Politics, notes Heclo, supplies society "with the effective perceptions and substantive responses for adapting collective arrangements to meet problems" induced by economic growth or other patterns of economic and social change. "Apart from the policy process there [are] no 'problems,' only conditions."[126] Or in Karl Deutsch's words, politics is

> the method par excellence for securing preferential treatment for messages and commands and for the reallocation of human or material resources. Politics thus appears as a major instrument for either retarding or accelerating social learning and innovation. . . . Politics has been used to increase the rigidity of already semi-petrified social systems, and it has been used to accelerate ongoing processes of change.[127]

In my own research,[128] I have also tried to combine these different kinds of analysis, and in so doing I have wrestled with the epistemological, conceptual, and research design dilemmas discussed earlier. The choices I have made are described briefly here in order to underscore further certain critical points and by way of a concrete example of the kind of research suggested by this scheme.

In figure 8.4 I have indicated, in the *general form* of the model sketched above, the particular concepts and linkages with which I am primarily concerned. The focus of my research is on processes of elite problem perception and problem solving under contemporary conditions of rapid change and mounting uncertainty. I liken routine policy formulation to Thomas Kuhn's[129] concept of "normal science" in that both rest on a prevailing "paradigm," a distinctive set of appreciations, rules, standards, and models of reality. Policy response in a time of crisis or transition may thus resemble scientific thinking in a time when "anomalies" are less and less readily assimilated with the prevailing paradigm, and may similarly involve revisions in or discontinuities with that paradigm. Appropriate policy response in a time of societal transition may then be akin to Kuhn's notion of "scientific revolutions." In this context recall Heclo's distinction, cited earlier, between adaptive specialization and adaptive generalization. Adaptive generalization and dynamic policy change require a comprehensive reprogramming that involves "reinterpretations" not only of

> the internal system or external world but [of] the sense of unity between both sides of the dichotomy. Through dynamic changes in policy systems we reinterpret not just ourselves and/or the situation but ourselves-in-the-situation. . . . [It] emphasize[s], not replacement . . . but accumulation of prior forms and processes whose coexistence and interaction at later times can lead to novel, holistic qualities.[130]

I have tried to establish (following Anderson, Vickers, Shonfield, Kirschen, Marxists, and others) the extent to which such a dominant

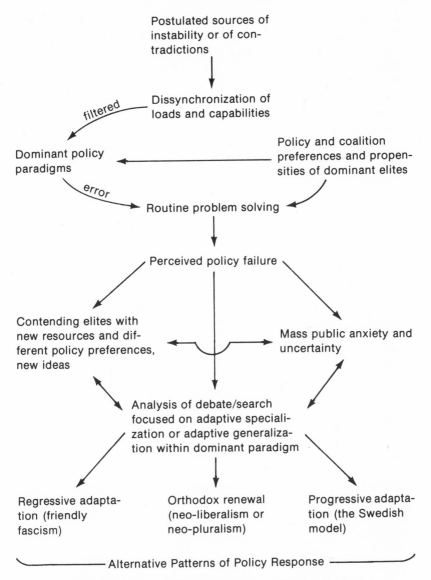

Figure 8.4. Elite Problem Perception and Problem Solving.

policy paradigm underlies policy formulation in capitalist societies, providing fundamental criteria for developing, debating, and selecting options for policy action. My concept of paradigm incorporates elements of cognitive psychology, political culture, "sound" or "orthodox" economic thinking, and "ideological hegemony." Policy paradigms reflect past and present policy and coalition preferences of the dominant elites in a society, hence they must also be viewed as products of class conflict, as elements of hegemonic domination, and therefore as inherently dynamic rather than static. National variations within what Marxists might term the "bourgeois-democratic" paradigm, as a consequence of the persistence of traditional or preindustrial value systems or of modifications induced by competing socialist paradigms are, however, important, both in helping to explain the differing policy experience of different countries, and in anticipating a range of variation in response to present and future problems that may call for or induce paradigm modifications or shifts.

My central concerns are with the ways in which these dominant paradigms may induce policy error when anomalous events occur reflecting system changes that call into question the adequacy of their constitutive elements, which I classify as reality models, norms, and decision-rules (La Porte and Abrams speak of cause-effect beliefs), and with the political and cognitive processes that ensue as (and if) dominant and contending elites (addressing each other and the general public) become aware of these strains and seek to resolve them. I have tried to develop a typology or classification scheme for comparing and evaluating public policy debates and actions in terms of alternative responses to the stress and uncertainty that ensues when assumptions about how the world is organized are disproved by events, when preferred policy strategies (and coalition partners) seem no longer viable because they do not produce desired results or are actually counterproductive or because they are no longer accepted by others, or when the normative standards or "rules of prudence" which define what is considered acceptable are widely called into question. This typology will be employed to analyze contemporary policy debates in several different countries and to develop a number of hypotheses about both the "appropriate" content of policy and the conditions and determinants of policy learning or adaptation.

This work is still in progress and only some of its main lines can be indicated here. This is organized around brief discussions of the decisions I have made relative to the following research design dilemmas discussed in part 2 of this chapter.

1. The problem of establishing or postulating those aspects of the contemporary flux that seem particularly likely to threaten the viability or stability of existing policy systems.

2. The problem of specifying the linkage whereby these trends, instabilities, or contradictions induce cycles of policy failure sufficient to dissynchronize established orders and to drive decision systems out of their normal, dynamically conservative mode of problem solving.

3. The problem of identifying the most salient issues, arenas, actors, interactions, institutions, and processes within the ensuing stage of crisis problem solving.

4. The problem of developing analytical tools appropriate to the twin tasks of political assessment and political valuation of policy and coalition choices.

It should be stressed that my "solutions" to these problems are in their nature not verifiable, that is, they cannot be proved or disproved, but must be judged according to their usefulness in research or their persuasiveness in "political argument."

Postulated Sources of Instability

I have argued that there are, strictly speaking, no scientific procedures whereby we can unambiguously establish what are the most salient dimensions of contemporary change. This is especially true in a period when we suspect that society is in a transitional phase or approaching a turning point of some kind, and when a great many contradictory trends are apparent. Not only are our theories partial and imperfect, but they are also themselves elements in the process of change. To paraphrase Vickers, the regularities we observe are not only "discovered" but "invented," and hence reality is in some sense the product of the competitive efforts of "human constituents" to impose "mutually inconsistent orders." Thus ideology, disciplinary persuasion, commitment or opposition to the political and social status quo, all play a role in generating judgments about contemporary change. These judgments are then hypotheses which can be logically examined, tested, and elaborated with the help of the model that has been outlined in this chapter.

Social scientists, humanists, policy makers, ruling and contending elites develop their own "theories" of what is going on, upon which they proceed to act. The method I used to generate a set of statements-judgments-hypotheses about the "heavy tendencies" in the contemporary flux of change was to make as systematic a survey as possible of such "theories," and to synthesize them into my own list of contemporary sources of instability. This involved, on the one hand, a wide reading across disciplines and ideological schools, and as seen from the perspective of observers in different societies and cultures, of the scholarly literature pertaining to the "contemporary problematique." On the other hand, it involved preliminary field research in four countries: the United States, Britain, France, and Sweden, in which I sought to monitor the "public policy debate" as carried on in political dialogue, in the media, in specialized party or interest-group publications. I also relied heavily on a series of in-depth interviews with elites in Britain, France, and Sweden—between thirty and forty in each country—selected primarily on the basis of position or reputation as responsible for "outlook" or medium to long-range planning, forecasting or strategy development for cabinets and prime ministers, government ministries, industrial associations, trade unions, and political parties.

This survey produced the following set of "primary sources of instability" that I argue serve to summarize or aggregate the change processes in advanced capitalist societies and to focus them upon the basic elements of processes of public choice in these societies.[131] They are then the hypothesized causes of a dissynchronization that could be observed in terms of changes in demands and allocations in issue distance, coalition preferences, relative political resources, patterns of conflict and mobilization, etc.

1. The extension of the scope of political authority, especially over the economy. There is a widely perceived extension and centralization of political power in general and of the discretionary authority of political executives—administrations—in particular. The economic market is in decline as an "automatic" and "depoliticized" regulator and allocator. More active and public state intervention highlights facts of dominance and hierarchy, increasing conflict and diminishing legitimacy and consensus on societal goals. Increased domestic conflicts (and international conflicts as well) may produce a growing use of the state's monopoly of coercion and violence, Michael Mann's "reawakening of the repressive side of Western society," or a reaffirmation that the Hobbesian model of politics may once again seem most descriptive of reality. But there is no assurance that the more complex, centralized bureaucratic machine of government can manage either its own internal organization, or the load of policy problems that have fed its growth.

2. The "symbiosis" of the state and the "planning system" or the "technocomplex." The phrase is Galbraith's and refers to the extent to which "the government, through its procurement and in providing for the various needs of the planning system [Marxists would say "monopoly capital"] plays a vital role in advancing the purposes of the planning system,"[132] and perceives its purposes as inseparable from it. As the power and scope of executive authority grows, so does the power and scope of what Gross calls bureaucratic-techno-industrial complexes. Self-contained "policy systems" are emerging in which specific sectors of the bureaucracy and the experts, technicians, and managers of highly organized vertically integrated corporations or conglomerates or their trade associations make public policy insulated from or bypassing electoral and legislative arenas. We are once again made aware of what "liberal, pluralist" political science has largely neglected, namely, the political power conferred by wealth and control over capital and investment, and of the extent to which the modern capitalist state itself contributes to imbalances of economic development, to the inequality of income distribution, and to the rigidities of class-based hierarchy in society.

3. Relative scarcities of resources and amenities. One of the main themes in the "postindustrial society" literature has been that advanced industrial societies have entered upon a period of affluence and an "end of scarcity." It is an important assumption for several of the authors represented in this book, notably Inglehart, Tsurutani, and La Porte and Abrams—although they seem to recognize its tenuousness without exploring the implications. But the events of 1973–1975 have confirmed that the newfound affluence of the working classes is very vulnerable to economic dislocation (as is the welfare state itself) in the twin forms of inflation and unemployment, and that industrial societies are operating within as yet poorly understood resource and amenity constraints. These constraints, as they affect energy, minerals, food, other raw materials, involve political as well as technological and "real scarcity" elements, and hold an unknown potential for disruption of the growth-dependent economies of industrial societies. Much the same is true if we consider complex tradeoff patterns among environmental, ecological, "quality of life" concerns, energy use and self-sufficiency, production and employment. Kenneth Boulding writes evocatively of how "the shadow of the stationary state falls upon our time," of the "imminent closure of the human environment," of the transition from "the infinite plane to the closed, limited round ball of spaceship earth."[133]

4. Persistent and systematic inequalities of income, wealth, access to public services, exposure to negative externalities and to cyclical fluctuations of economic life. One of the long-time secular trends in industrialized societies has been the mounting political salience of issues of equality, equity, and fairness. These seem likely to be intensified in conflict-inducing ways by the increase in the scope of overt and discretionary political power, by the growing public awareness of the principal beneficiaries of that exercise of power, by the renewed importance of scarcity, and by the employment-inflation-growth tradeoffs that seem characteristic of many—if not most—advanced capitalist societies. One can anticipate more demands for a policy switch from emphasis on "equality of opportunity" to "equality in actual life situations." And "if greater equality of actual situation rather than greater equality of opportunity is going to become a dominant line of future social policy, then solidarity rather than meritocracy will become a main organizational principle of modern society."[134]

5. Social interdependence and social exchange among organizations, institutions, and groups. As modern society becomes more complex, technologically sophisticated, and interdependent, the more it becomes vulnerable to disruption. Terrorism is the most spectacular example. But far more important are the impact of organizational complexities, the emergence of separate "policy systems" vertically joining bureaucratic groups and private associational groups resisting overall coordination and planning, advances in communications technology, and the diffusion of political and organizational skills via education and the media. The more political decisions prevail over the autonomous market, the greater the dependence upon overt regulation of activity and upon being able to manipulate incentives and preferences and to obtain the acquiescence of major groups in society. With this comes even greater capacities of groups to withhold consent and to undermine governmental policies and the greater importance of finding or creating appropriate "mutual appreciations." Yet the other "instabilities" suggest that such appreciations will be increasingly difficult to come by and might well require major changes in policy and structure or major resort to coercion.

6. *Internationalization, penetration, and the emergence of more symmetrical patterns of international interdependence.* International economic, political, and security systems are also changing—in some cases abruptly, in others as the result of the slow accretion of past changes—but as yet the shape of a future "international order" is obscure, and the chief implication for national policy making seems to be a high potential for surprise and uncertainty. Internationalization of markets (trade movements, capital mobility, flow of stocks), the increased importance of international externalities (viz. pollution), the growing system of multinational firms, all have had important implications for the efficient use by national policy makers of such policy instruments as monetary and fiscal policy, as well as exacerbating regional disequilibria, structural unemployment, and inflation. Because of the ever more complex web of international interdependence, "outside actors" (oil companies, foreign government, oil and commodity boycotts) have an increased capacity to intervene. National policy makers will be caught between the need for international cooperation and coordination in more and more policy areas, and the mounting domestic demands for more centralized national planning and control, and for action to deal with resource scarcities and internal distributional issues. What is distinctive is not that international dependency and interdependency effects exist, but that these are no longer exclusively asymmetrical in favor of the advanced industrial societies. We are witness to a time of real redistributions of power and resources (viz. oil revenues) at the international level, and such redistributions are always difficult for the losing party to assimilate.

Policy Paradigms as Sources of Error

My argument is that these six instabilities are especially likely to bring about system dissynchronization because, in addition to their direct impact on the load-capability balance (via increased variety of demands and diminished response resources), they also bring into dispute—make controversial—undermine—the policy utility of the fundamental reality models, norms, and decision rules of the policy paradigm that seems to characterize the modern capitalist state. At the level of the individual political actor or policy maker we may speak of "schema" or "pre-existing assumptions about the way the world is organized,"[135] that structure information, help make sense of complex environments, define what will be paid attention to, considered problematic, and what actions or responses are both available and appropriate. Normally, such "schema" are very stable and resistant to change, for individuals strongly resist the severe disruptive implications of abandoning such internalized and firmly cognitive guides to understanding and action. When environmental changes occur that in fact undermine basic elements of these schema, extended periods of error, surprise, doubt, uncertainty are likely to ensue before the schemas themselves are altered. La Porte describes the general problem as follows:

> A good fit between the present situation and those upon which current cause/effect notions were founded and refined, brings a perceived sense of order and reasonableness. If, however, the pattern of relationships in our environment changes, our connections to it vary in intensity, or multiply rapidly, cause/effect beliefs shaped in past and different times are due for a shock. Persons applying outdated categories to an altered present are likely to be increasingly surprised by what subsequently happens around them. Whether a person acts for himself or as a member of an organization, if his actions are based on ill-fitting categories the surprises can be personally or organizationally disastrous. This is the case in family decisions, policies of commercial firms, policy decisions, military actions, research projects, or radical movements.[136]

My literature survey and interviews led me to conclude that the present period could be described as one in which there prevails precisely such a situation of surprise, doubt, and uncertainty with regard to the appropriate grounds for public policy making, and in which there is a general perception that policies no longer produce anticipated results, that policy problems are distinctively intractable.

Besides their consequences at the individual decision-maker level, the postulated six sources of instability have important system-level consequences, in that these "schema" or policy paradigms derive not only from the historical experience of particular polities, but more importantly from the general forms of economic and political organization that are comprised by the notions of "liberalism," a market-based political economy, "contractual voluntarism," associational autonomy, etc., and that tend to provide normative justification and operational rules or codes of liberal capitalist society—or of what Marxists would call the "bourgeois-democratic form of the state." In this collective manifestation, then, such a policy paradigm in large part reflects and seeks to justify and perpetuate the power resources and relationships, and coalition preferences of the most dominant groups in the system. In the "bourgeois democratic" form, it is, however, important that these sets of world views, normative standards, and operational rules be generally accepted as ap-

Table 8.6. Destabilizing Trends and Corresponding Paradigm Elements

Aggregate Trends as Sources of Instability	Reality Models, Norms, and Decision Rules
1. Extensions of scope of political authority, especially over the economy	*The limited state*—housekeeping and offset functions —incrementalism in a self-equilibrating system —if planning, indicative only —antibureaucracy
2. Symbiosis of state and planning system or technocomplex	*The state as neutral umpire or arbiter* —or as assuring pluralist rules of game
3. Relative scarcities of resources and amenities	*Growth and income flow* —allocation as consequence of market forces of demand and supply plus technological innovation —decision-making autonomy of the firm
4. Persistent and systematic inequality	*Efficiency and productivity* —meritocratic and individualistic norms
5. Social interdependence	*A self-equilibrating system based on individual selfish actions and competition* —coordination via individual optimizing decision (possessive individualism) —system is "disenchanted"—not based on "conscious ethical postulates" (Weber)
6. Internationalization and penetration	*National growth and power as goal of system* —consolidation of nation-state —the liberal, sovereign state —nationalism as main source of legitimacy (authority norm) —Keynesianism is nation-state bound

propriate and legitimate by members of the dominant coalition itself, and by the population at large or by significant political contenders. Thus the strain on the system is great indeed when environmental changes occur that basically undermine such confidence and legitimacy. As in the case of individual "schema," it will only be after long sequences of policy failure that serious consideration of partial or wholesale alternatives will begin.

I have tried to develop this argument by linking each of the sources of instability to the element or elements of the schema or paradigm that I think it calls into question. Table 8.6 summarizes this argument. This entire formulation is, it should be noted, quite preliminary, as is the exploratory research I have carried out in applying it to certain selected areas of public policy. Clearly, further research on the impact of environmental changes at the level of individual "schema" and societal policy paradigms should be high on our future agenda.

Macro-Economic Policy and Growth Policy

So far we have six sources of instability and a matching set of elements of prevailing policy schema or paradigms which we wish to place at the center of research into the policy perceptions and strategies adopted by various elites and groups in contemporary policy-making sequences. What was needed next was some criterion for selecting particular issues or issue-areas upon which to focus the research. This is no small problem, since the tasks of identifying critical policy makers, of getting at their cognitions and changes therein, of identifying the institutions and other actors, groups and constituents within the policy system of that issue arena, and of aggregating perceptions and responses, are all quite complex.

My decision was to focus upon macro-economic policy (principally inflation) and energy policy. Not only were these issues both highly salient in the public debates of the period of my research, i.e., 1972 to the present, but each seemed to satisfy more general criteria in terms of the basic postulates of the study. Macro-economic policy seems particularly fundamental to an understanding of the modern capitalist polity, for these choices are distinctively decisive ones. Not only do they govern the overall distribution of benefits and burdens in society, by they also establish parameters for other specific areas of policy such as social and environmental policy. And, more broadly, macro-economic policy making is critical to the general capacity of these societies to successfully adapt to the rapidly changing economic and political circumstances that I have postulated above. Patterns of macro-economic "management" in particular countries may thus tell us a great deal about the relative resources of different organized groups, and about the preferences and powers of decisive dominant coalitions. Policy making in this field is also perhaps

Table 8.7. A Typology of Policy Response

Destabilizing Trend Model, Norm, or Rule Stressed	Foci of Policy Debate — Alternative Response Patterns		
	Progressive Adaptations	**Orthodox Renewal**	**Regressive Adaptations**
1. Extensions of scope of political authority, esp. over the economy / The limited state	*State as active determinant of social priorities* —as planner and participant in economic life —as coordinator (well beyond indicative planning) —bureaucracy a necessary price —socialized market economy	*Neo-laissez faire* (Lowi to Friedman) —regulatory law and regulatory commission	Planning by bureaucratic–techno-business complex. Professionalism and technocracy—improve and rationalize decision systems Efficiency in place of legitimacy
2. Symbiosis of state and planning system or techno-complex / The state as neutral umpire or arbiter	*"Emancipate the state"* (Galbraith) —adversary and participatory planning —neo-corporatist systems of interest representation	*Neo-liberalism and neo-pluralism*	Conceal and "mystify" via media manipulation, police, etc. "Friendly fascism," authoritarianism, corporate responsibility
3. Relative scarcities of resources and amenities / Growth and income flow	*Economy of stocks* (structure and quality) —regulation (rationing, priorities) of production (level and composition) and of consumption —public vs. private comsumption	*Internalize externalities* and restore the market as equilibrator	Growth as equivalent to *national interest* Consumerism and advertising Technological fix

Table 8.7 continued

4. Persistent and systematic inequality / Efficiency and productivity	Equality of condition —economic and social citizenship —solidarist-collectivist norms —human services, economy, public services economy, domination of the public sector	Equality of opportunity —economism —equity, fairness	Physical and psychological repression (Edelman on "language of helping professions") "Rationalize" public services Brave New Capitalists' Paradise (J. E. Meade)
5. Social interdependence / A self-equilibrating system based on individual selfish actions and competition	Social contract —a positive moral order —recognition of mutual interdependence —"spirit of sociality" —reciprocity, cooperation, solidarity —corporatist representation —error-embracing systems	Neo-medievalism (Anderson)	Weaken bargaining power and political power of obstructive groups, i.e., incomes policies and trade unions.
6. Internationalization and penetration / National growth and power as goal of system	International normative order—reciprocity, equity claims —international planning and coordination —international functionalism	—national self-sufficiency (Hymer and Keynes) —evolve order systems—quasi regimes	neo-mercantilism, neo-colonialism, economic nationalism

more readily amenable to the scheme I have proposed since there is less difficulty identifying the critical actors and accessing their policy explanations and justifications.

The second area that seemed relevant, especially in the longer term, was that of energy policy. For energy policy *is* growth policy and much more, implying social, environmental, and technology policy choices as well. It is also preeminently enmeshed in the system of international interdependency we described above. Energy policy choices thus relate closely to the rhythm of economic growth, to decisions as to the composition of production and the allocation of investment, to the distribution of resources between the public and private sectors, to the quality of the living and working environment, and to the forms that future international economic, political, and security orders are likely to take.

A Typology of Policy Response

As an analytical tool for ordering and evaluating the policy responses and policy debates in my group of countries I have developed a preliminary typology of possible policy responses to each of the six instabilities and the reality modes, norms, and decision rules they purportedly call into question. I have labeled these orthodox renewal, progressive response, and regressive response (see table 8.7). This typology can be seen both as a device for classifying and illuminating the structural implications of the ongoing policy debates in advanced capitalist societies, and as a basis for the development of a tentative theory of what pattern of policies will constitute a desirable and "truly adaptive" response, and what patterns are likely to intensify system instability or to lead to illiberal, authoritarian and socially unjust futures.

Progressive adaptation is defined broadly as policy or institutional innovations that are seen as following more or less directly from the logic of the analysis of the ways in which particular reality models, norms, or decision rules are stressed, called into question, or rendered ineffective as criteria or contexts for policy formulation. That is, such innovations implicitly or explicitly accept the reality and irreversibility of the postulated trends *and* assert the necessity for modifications or shifts in the paradigm itself, in order to secure and preserve democratic values.

Orthodox renewal refers to policies that although recognizing the reality of the postulated trends deny their irreversibility and argue that only such a reversal via a reassertion of the "pluralist," "liberal," or "bourgeois-democratic" paradigm will secure democratic (and liberal) values.

Regressive adaptation is so labeled (albeit invidiously) because it involves regression from democratic and liberal values in that the postulated trends continue unchecked, implying the possibility or likelihood of policy instability, output failure, public disaffection, and massive losses of legitimacy on the part of governmental and other political authorities and institutions. Governing and dominant elites seek to consolidate their positions by resort to improved means of control, repression, mystification, and media manipulation.

As we have seen, some theorists (Gross, Poulantzas) see this pattern of regressive adaptation as inherent in the logic of the evolving situation of advanced industrial societies, and hence as the most likely future. It seems more likely to me, however, that regressive adaptations will follow upon failures to devise or to legitimate appropriate progressive or orthodox renewal strategies. In any case this seems to be another important focus for comparative research, for historical and cross-national experience indicate that the capitalist system and its dominant schema or policy paradigms have shown far greater adaptive capacities than most Marxists have been willing to grant.

Finally, and very tentatively indeed, I hope to suggest some reasons for supposing that the typology might also be useful for policy evaluation purposes, that is, for suggesting that certain patterns of policy response might be more successful or more preferable than others. This would be based on an argument that the six sources of instability are not only the most decisive ones, but also that they form an interacting set that cannot be readily decomposed in responses to it. This is to say, it is likely to be counterproductive to seek to counteract or cope with the consequences of one sort of instability without considering the ways in which it is interdependent and interactive with the rest. This line of argument leads to proposals for what might be termed alternative overall development styles or strategies for advanced capitalist societies.

NOTES

1. Dankwart A. Rustow, *A World of Nations* (Washington, D.C.: Brookings Institution, 1967), p. 3.

2. Samuel P. Huntington, "The Change to Change," *Comparative Politics* 3, no. 3 (April 1971): 287.

3. For a general account see Andrew Shonfield, *Modern Capitalism: The Changing Balance of Public and Private Power* (London: Oxford University Press, 1965).

4. Dankwart A. Rustow and Robert E. Ward, eds., *Political Modernization in Japan and Turkey* (Princeton, N.J.: Princeton University Press, 1964), quoted in Huntington, "Change to Change," pp. 287–88.

5. The quotes are from Clark Kerr et al., *Industrialism and Industrial Man* (London: Heinemann, 1962), as cited in Goldthorpe, "Theories of Industrial Society: Reflections on the Recrudescence of Historicism and the Future of Futurology," *Archives Européenne de Sociologie* 12 (1971): 268–69.

6. Goldthorpe's characterization of Talcott Parsons, "Evolutionary Universals in Society," *American Sociological Review* 29 (1964), in Goldthorpe, ibid., p. 273.

7. For reviews of this pessimistic, antitechnology literature, see Roger Williams, *Politics and Technology* (London: Macmillan, 1971); Victor Ferkiss, *Technological Man: The Myth and The Reality* (London: Heinemann, 1969); and Herbert J. Muller, *The Children of Frankenstein* (Bloomington: Indiana University Press, 1970). See especially Hannah Arendt, *The Human Condition* (Chicago: University of Chicago Press, 1958); Herbert Marcuse, *One-Dimensional Man: Ideology of Industrial Society* (Boston: Beacon Press, 1964); Jacques Ellul, *The Technological Society* (London: Jonathan Cape, 1964); Lewis Mumford, *The Pentagon of Power* (New York: Harcourt Brace Jovanovich, 1964); and Norman Birnbaum, *The Crisis of Industrial Society* (New York: Oxford University Press, 1969).

8. Geoffrey Vickers, *Freedom in a Rocking Boat: Changing Values in an Unstable Society* (Harmondsworth, England: Penguin Books, 1972), p. 21.

9. Ibid., p. 27.

10. Ibid., p. 50.

11. Ibid., p. 183.

12. Ibid., p. 186.

13. Ibid., p. 189.

14. Ibid., p. 193.

15. Robert L. Heilbroner, *An Inquiry into the Human Prospect* (New York: Norton, 1974), chap. 2.

16. Ibid., p. 24.

17. Ibid.

18. Ibid., p. 92.

19. Ibid., p. 95.

20. Daniel Bell, *The Coming of Post-Industrial Society: A Venture in Social Forecasting* (London: Heinemann, 1974), p. 373.

21. Ibid.

22. Ibid., p. 483.

23. James O'Connor, *The Fiscal Crisis of the State* (New York: St. Martin's Press, 1973), p. 6.

24. Among Marxist interpretations see especially, Robin Blackburn, ed., *Ideology in Social Science* (London: Fontana/Collins, 1972); Lelio Basso, "Old Contradictions and New Problems," *International Socialist Journal* 15 (1966): 235–54; Louis Althusser, "Contradictions and Overdetermination," in *For Marx* (New York: Vintage Books, 1970); Ernest Mandel, "The Economics of Neo-Capitalism," *Socialist Register 1964*, pp. 56–67; Bill Warren, "Capitalist Planning and the State." *New Left Review* 72 (March–April 1972): 3–30; Paul Baran and Paul Sweezy, *Monopoly Capital* (New York: Monthly Review Press, 1966); Manuel Castells, *La Question Urbaine* (Paris: Maspero, 1973).

25. For a different and contrasting argument see Michael Mann, "The Ideology of Intellectuals and Other People in the Development of Capitalism," in Leon N. Lindberg et al., eds., *Stress and Contradiction in Modern Capitalism: Public Policy and the Theory of the State* (Lexington, Mass.: D. C. Heath, 1975).

26. Richard England and Barry Bluestone, "Ecology and Class Conflict," in David Mermelstein, *Economics: Mainstream Readings and Radical Critiques* (2nd ed.; New York: Random House, 1973), p. 395. See also O'Connor, *Fiscal Crisis of the State*, pp. 175–78.

27. Nicos Poulantzas, *Political Power and Social Classes* (New York: New Left Books and Sheed and Ward), at pp. 302 and 258.

28. Ralph Miliband, "Poulantzas and the Capitalist State," *New Left Review* 82 (November–December 1973): 91.

29. Ibid., p. 92.

30. Ibid.

31. Ralph Miliband, *The State in Capitalist Society: The Analysis of the Western System of Power* (London: Quartet Books, 1973) p. 247.

32. P. A. Allum, *Italy—Republic Without Government* (New York: Norton, 1973), p. 250.

33. Bertram M. Gross, "Planning in an Era of Social Revolution," *Public Administration Review*, May/June 1971, pp. 259–96.

34. Ibid., p. 282.

35. Ibid., p. 283.

36. Ibid., p. 286.

37. Ibid.

38. The literature is voluminous. See especially Assar Lindbeck, "The National State in an Internationalized World Economy," Institute for International Economic Studies, University of Stockholm, 1973; C. Fred Bergsten, *The Future of the International Economic Order: An Agenda for Research* (Lexington, Mass.: Lexington Books, 1973); Robert O. Keohane and Joseph S. Nye, Jr., *Transnational Relations and World Politics* (Cambridge, Mass.: Harvard University Press, 1972); Jagdish N. Bhagwati, *Economics and World Order: From the 1970's to the 1980's* (New York: Macmillan, 1972); Richard C. Cooper, *A Reordered World: Emerging International Economic Problems* (Washington, D.C.: Potomac Associates, 1973); Harold and Margaret Sprout, *Toward a Politics of the Planet Earth* (New York: Van Nostrand Reinhold, 1971); Harry Magdoff, *The Age of Imperialism* (New York: Monthly Review, 1969); United Nations, Department of Economics and Social Affairs, *Multinational Corporations in World Development* (New York: United Nations, 1973); Raymond Vernon, *Sovereignty at Bay: The Multinational Spread of U.S. Enterprises* (New York: Basic Books, 1971); Pierre Hassner, "The New Europe: From Cold War to Hot Peace," *International Journal* 27, no. 1 (Winter 1971–72): 1–17; Robert O. Keohane and Joseph S. Nye, "International Interdependence and Integration," in *The Handbook of Political Science*, ed. Fred Greenstein and Nelson Polsby (forthcoming); *The Multinational Corporation*, a special issue of *The Annals of the American Academy of Political and Social Science*, September 1972; Richard D. Wolff, "Economics of Imperialism—Modern Imperialism: The View from the Metropolis," *American Economic Review* 60, no. 2 (May 1970); Stephen Hymer, "The Internationalization of Capital," *Journal of Economic Issues* 6, no. 1 (1972); Michael Kidron, *Western Capitalism Since the War* (Harmondsworth, England: Penguin Books, 1970); Eugene B. Skolnikoff, *The International Imperatives of Technology* (Berkeley: Institute of International Studies, University of California).

39. Vickers, *Freedom in a Rocking Boat*, p. 122.

40. See, for example, John Maddox, *The Doomsday Syndrome* (London: Macmillan, 1972); Peter Passell and Leonard Ross, *The Retreat from Riches: Affluence and Its Enemies* (New York: Viking Press, 1972).

41. Huntington, "Change to Change," p. 290.

42. Harold D. Lasswell, "The Universal Peril: Perpetual Crisis and the Garrison State," as cited in Huntington, ibid., p. 291.

43. Shonfield, *Modern Capitalism*, p. 3.

44. Mann, "The Ideology of Intellectuals."

45. Ibid.

46. Ibid.

47. Claus Offe, "Advanced Capitalism and the Welfare State," *Politics and Society* 2, no. 4 (Summer 1972): 488.

48. Ibid., pp. 481–84.

49. Samuel P. Huntington, "Postindustrial Politics: How Benign Will It Be?," *Comparative Politics* 6 (January 1974): 190.

50. Ibid., p. 191.

51. Vickers, *Freedom in a Rocking Boat*, p. 112.

52. Sidney Verba, "Sequences and Development," in Leonard Binder et al., *Crises and Sequences in Political Development* (Princeton, N.J.: Princeton University Press, 1971), p. 302.

53. Ibid., p. 304.

54. Ibid., p. 306.

55. Ibid.

56. For a summary statement of this scheme see Leonard Binder, "Crises of Political Development," in Binder et al., *Crises and Sequences in Political Development*, pp. 3–72.

57. Huntington, "Postindustrial Politics," p. 168.

58. Ibid., pp. 167–69.

59. For a summary of the literature bearing on this argument see Martin O. Heisler, "The European Polity Model," in Heisler, *Politics in Europe* (New York: David McKay, 1974), pp. 27–89. See also Leonard Binder et al., *Crises and Sequences in Political Development* (Princeton, N.J.: Princeton University Press, 1971); Barrington Moore, Jr., *Social Origins of Dictatorship and Democracy* (Boston: Beacon Press, 1966); Seymour M. Lipset and Stein Rokkan, *Party Systems and Voter Alignments: Cross-National Perspectives* (New York: Free Press, 1967); Stein Rokkan, "The Structuring of Mass Politics in the Smaller European Democracies," *Comparative Studies in Society and History* 10, no. 2 (January 1968): 173–210; Arend Lijphart, *The Politics of Accomodation: Pluralism and Democracy in the Netherlands* (Berkeley and Los Angeles: University of California Press, 1968); Ralf Dahrendorf, *Society and Democracy in Germany* (Garden City, N.Y.: Doubleday, 1967).

60. Gabriel A. Almond, "Approaches to Development Causation," in Gabriel A. Almond, Scott C. Flanagan, and Robert J. Mundt, eds., *Crisis, Choice and Change: Historical Studies of Political Development* (Boston: Little Brown, 1973) p. 13.

61. Ibid., p. 27.

62. Scott C. Flanagan, "Models and Methods of Analysis," in ibid., p. 53.

63. Ibid., p. 51.

64. For an early development of this theme see Leon N. Lindberg, "Western Europe as a Laboratory for Studying Social Change and Policy Response," in *Political Science and Area Studies*, ed. Lucian Pye (Bloomington: University of Indiana Press, 1975).

65. Vickers, *Freedom in a Rocking Boat*, passim.

66. François Bourricaud, "Post-Industrial Society and the Paradoxes of Welfare," *Survey* 16, no. 1 (Winter 1971): 60.

67. See Todd La Porte, ed., *Organized Social Complexity: Challenge to Politics and Policy* (Princeton, N.J.: Princeton University Press, 1974).

68. Gross, "Planning in an Era of Social Revolution."

69. See in particular the three Appendixes by Scott C. Flanagan in Almond, Flanagan, and Mundt, *Crisis, Choice and Change*, pp. 651–95.

70. John McHale, *The Future of the Future* (New York: George Braziller, 1969).

71. Dennis Gabor, *Inventing the Future* (New York: Knopf, 1969).

72. For the notion of public policy as "quasi-experiments" see Donald T. Campbell and Julian C. Stanley, *Experimental and Quasi-Experimental Designs for Research* (Chicago: Rand-McNally, 1963); and Donald T. Campbell, "Reforms as Experiments," *American Psychologist* 24, no. 4 (1969): 409–29.

73. Gabriel A. Almond and Robert J. Mundt, "Crisis, Choice and Change: Some Tentative Conclusions," in Almond, Flanagan, and Mundt, *Crisis, Choice and Change*, p. 647.

74. For such a detailed treatment see my forthcoming *System Change and Policy Response in Advanced Capitalist Nations* (Cambridge, Mass.: Winthrop Publishers, 1976).

75. Donald A. Schon's phrase. "Taken at any given time, a social system is dynamically conservative in its structural, technological and conceptual dimensions." *Beyond the Stable State* (London: Temple Smith, 1971), p. 128.

76. Flanagan, "Models and Methods of Analysis," in Almond, Flanagan, and Mundt, *Crisis, Choice and Change*, p. 51.

77. See, for example, the work of Charles Tilly, Jerald Hage and Edward Gargan, Stein Rokkan, Wolfgang Zapf and Peter Flora.

78. Seymour Martin Lipset and Stein Rokkan, *Party Systems and Voter Alignments* (New York: Free Press, 1967), p. 47.

79. Stein Rokkan, *Citizens, Elections, Parties* (New York: David McKay, 1970).

80. Flanagan, "Models and Methods of Analysis," pp. 52–53.

81. See especially his chap. 3, "The Self-Exciting System," *Freedom in a Rocking Boat*, pp. 43–55.

82. For a variety of views on Sweden's likely future adaptability see Thomas Anton, ed., *Myths and the Politics of Change in Modern Sweden* (forthcoming). For critical views see Ingemar Dörfer, *System 37 Viggen: Arms, Technology and the Domestication of Glory* (Oslo: Universitetsforlaget, 1973); Roland Huntford, *The New Totalitarians*, (New York: Stein & Day, 1972); Marian Radetzki, *Den Ihåliga Välfärden* (Stockholm: Wahlström & Widstrand, 1972); and Rolf Millqvist and Sven H. Åsbrink, *Den Ofantliga* Sektorn (Stockholm: Seelig, 1973).

83. Flanagan, "Models and Methods of Analysis," p. 53.

84. See p. 255 below.

85. See Robert Dahl and Charles Lindblom, *Politics, Economics and Welfare* (New York: Harper & Row, 1953); Charles Lindblom and David Braybrooke, *A Strategy of Decision* (New York: Free Press, 1969); Charles Lindblom, "The Science of Muddling Through," *Public Administration Review* 19 (Spring 1959): 79–88.

86. Philippe C. Schmitter, "Notes Toward a Political Economic Conceptualization of Policy-Making in Latin America" (manuscript), p. 17.

87. Donald A. Schon, *Beyond the Stable State* (London: Temple Smith, 1971), p. 123.

88. Ibid.

89. Ibid.

90. "Policy Analysis," *British Review of Political Science*, January 1972, pp. 83–108.

91. Hugh Heclo, *Modern Social Politics in Britain and Sweden* (New Haven: Yale University Press, 1974), p. 305.

92. Ibid., pp. 308–12.

93. Ibid., pp. 313–15.

94. Ibid., pp. 316–19.

95. Ibid., pp. 313.

96. Ibid., pp. 315.

97. Ibid., pp. 317–18.

98. Ibid., pp. 312. The emphasis is mine.

99. See Miliband, *The State in Capitalist Society*, chap. 7; A. Gramsci, *The Modern Prince* (New York: International Publishers, 1957).

100. Heclo, *Modern Social Politics*, p. 1.

101. Herbert Simon, *Models of Man* (London: Wiley, 1967).

102. Hugh Heclo, "Conclusion: Policy Dynamics," p. 19. To appear in Richard Rose, ed., *Dynamics of Public Policy* (Beverly Hills and London: Sage Publications, 1976).

103. Ibid., p. 22.

104. Karl Deutsch, *The Nerves of Government: Models of Political Communication and Control* (New York: Free Press, 1966), p. 169.

105. Ibid., p. 187.

104. Ibid., p. 189.

107. Ibid., p. 190.

108. Ibid., p. 190–91.

109. Ibid., p. 221–28.

110. Ibid., p. 229–30.

111. Ibid., p. 173.

112. Schon, *End of the Stable State*, pp. 128–36.

113. See, for example, Pierre Bourdieu et Jean-Claude Passeron, *La Réproduction: Éléments pour une théorie du système d'enseignement* (Paris: Editions de Minuit, 1970); G. Balandier, *Sociologie des Mutations* (Paris: Anthropos, 1970); Yves Barel, "Prospective et Analyse de Systèmes," Travaux et Recherches de Prospective (Paris: D.A.T.A.R., 1971.)

114. Schmitter, "Notes Toward...", pp. 22–23.

115. David Easton, "The New Revolution in Political Science," *American Political Science Review* 63, no. 4 (December 1969): 1056.

116. Duncan MacRae, "Scientific Communication, Ethical Argument, and Public Policy," *American Political Science Review* 65, no. 1 (March 1971): 38–50.

117. Sidney Verba, in Binder et al., *Crises and Sequences in Political Development*, p. 308.

118. Ibid.

119. See, for example, Russell F. Rhyne, *Projecting Whole-Body Future Patterns— The Field Anomaly Relaxation (FAR) Method* (Stanford: Stanford Research Institute, Memorandum Report EPRC 6747-10, February 1971); Theodore Gordon, Richard Rochberg, and Selwyn Enzer, *Research on Cross-Impact Techniques with Applications to Selected Problems in Economics, Political Science and Technology Assessment* (Middletown, Conn.: Institute for the Future, Report R-12, August 1970); Richard Rochberg, "Information Theory, Cross-Impact Matrices and Pivotal Events," *Technological Forecasting and Social Change* 2, no. 1 (1970): 53–60.

120. For some pertinent critiques see Vickers, *Freedom in a Rocking Boat;* and Herman E. Daly, ed., *Toward a Steady-State Economy* (San Francisco: W. H. Freeman, 1973).

121. See Robert Boguslaw, *The New Utopians* (Englewood Cliffs, N.J.: Prentice-Hall, 1965); and Ida R. Hoos, *Systems Analysis in Public Policy* (Berkeley and Los Angeles: University of California Press, 1972).

122. For a trenchant critique of the models used by Meadows et al. in *The Limits to Growth*, see Christopher Freeman, ed., *Models of Doom* (New York: Universe Books, 1973); and H. S. D. Cole, "World Models, Their Progress and Applicability," *Futures* 6, no. 3 (June 1974); 201–18. The second study issued by the Club of Rome incorporates much more sophisticated models with political system elements. See M. Mesarovic and E. Pestel, *A Multilevel Computer Model of a Development System*, 6 vols. (Laxenburg: International Institute for Applied Systems Analysis, 1974).

123. See Wolfgang Zapf and Peter Flora, "Some Problems of Time-Series Analysis in Research on Modernization," *Social Science Information* 10, no. 3 (1971): 53–102; Stein Rokkan, "Data Resources for Comparative Research on National Development," *Social Science Information* 11 (1972): 287–302; Wolfgang Zapf, "Measuring the Quality of Life" (Paper prepared for the ISSC—Committee on Comparative Politics Conference, "The Comparative Analysis of Public Policy Formation," Princeton, 25–27 January 1972).

124. Bertram M. Gross, "The State of the Nation: Social Systems Accounting," in *Social Indicators*, ed. Raymond A. Bauer (Cambridge, Mass.: MIT Press, 1966), pp. 154–301.

125. Schmitter, "Notes Toward...", pp. 18–19.

126. Heclo, *Modern Social Politics in Britain and Sweden*, p. 288.

127. Deutsch, *The Nerves of Government*, p. 254.

128. To be reported more fully in my forthcoming *System Change and Policy Response in Advanced Capitalist Nations*.

129. Thomas S. Kuhn, *The Structure of Scientific Revolutions* (Chicago: University of Chicago Press, 1962).

130. Heclo, "Policy Dynamics," pp. 24–25.

131. Operational definitions, appropriate indicators, and aggregation procedures might be developed for each of these concepts and data on their change through time systematically gathered. The result might be dissynchronization profiles such as those suggested in Almond et al., *Crisis, Choice and Change.*

132. John Kenneth Galbraith, *Economics and the Public Purpose* (Boston: Houghton Mifflin, 1973), p. 241.

133. Kenneth Boulding, "The Shadow of the Stationary State," in *The No-Growth Society*, a special issue of *Daedalus*, Fall 1973, pp. 89–102.

134. Hans Günter, "Social Policy and the Post-Industrial Society," *International Institute of Labour Studies Bulletin*, no. 10 (1972): 126.

135. Robert Axelrod "Schema Theory: An Information Processing Model of Perception and Cognition," *American Political Science Review* 67, no. 4 (1973): 1248.

136. Todd La Porte, "Organizational Response to Complexity: Research and Development as Organized Inquiry and Action" (Working Paper No. 141, Center for Planning and Development Research, University of California, Berkeley, January 1971), p. 2.